ONE WATER

ONE WATER

dispatches from the streets and
backcountry of Interior Alaska

stories by

ROB MCCUE

Book design by Ann Basu

ISBN 978-1-59709-907-3 (tradepaper)

Library of Congress Control Number: 2018021962

The National Endowment for the Arts, the Los Angeles County Arts
Commission, the Ahmanson Foundation, the Dwight Stuart Youth Fund,
the Max Factor Family Foundation, the Pasadena Tournament of Roses
Foundation, the Pasadena Arts & Culture Commission and the City of
Pasadena Cultural Affairs Division, the City of Los Angeles Department
of Cultural Affairs, the Audrey & Sydney Irmas Charitable Foundation,
the Kinder Morgan Foundation, the Allergan Foundation, the Riordan
Foundation, and the Amazon Literary Partnership partially support Red Hen
Press.

First Edition
Published by Boreal Books
an imprint of Red Hen Press
www.borealbooks.org
www.redhen.org

Acknowledgments

Huge thanks to my friend and editor, Dawn Marano, without whom this thing would not have been possible. Thanks to Derrick Burleson for getting it to Peggy Shumaker and to Peggy for seeing the possibility in a rough piece of work. Thank you, Joeth Zucco, for your touch. Big thanks to Patty Burns and Nancy Bigelow for their invaluable insights into the geology and natural history of Interior Alaska. Hats off to Mike Knoche for his advice on biology and natural history. Thanks to Michele for her guidance and Cord for his patience. And thanks, Mom and Dad, for believing.

For Cord and Michele

Contents

ONE WATER

A Night on the Town, 2012

INTERIOR ALASKA IN WINTER is a dark ocean, and we live miles beneath the surface. The cold resents our presence, our warmth an impediment to its equilibrium. It's nothing personal, just a fact of our planet's orientation to its host star: the axis around which the Earth rotates is tilted slightly relative to the orbit it traces around the sun, probably knocked out of whack by a meteor impact way back, before history. Due to this perfect imperfection the north is angled away from the warmth and light for months each year.

Don't get me wrong, I'm thankful for these circumstances. If it were otherwise the hordes from the Lower 48 would've swarmed here long ago and obliterated this place with the same urban sprawl that's chewed through the natural world to the south. The cold here in January freezes your flesh in seconds, and during the few summer weeks mosquitoes rise from the swamps by the trillions and our streets are littered with the sucked dry bodies of their victims. All in all, these inconveniences are boons.

Another good thing about winter is that it generates its own economy, sustaining us when we begin to second-guess our memories of summer. Mechanics, septic steamers, snowplow operators, tow truck drivers, furnace repairmen, woodcutters, drug dealers, cab drivers—we're in it together up here, consuming food, booze, sex, money, diesel, sharing our mutual desperation until the sun returns.

I've driven a cab here in Fairbanks for twenty years. When the cold comes, people's cars quit working. They lose their will to walk. They need to leave the house before they hurt someone, or get hurt. They call me.

My wife, Michele, is a high school teacher, English and yoga. We first met some twenty years ago on a ferry traveling down the Inside Passage. It was December, cold and wind wracked. I was with a buddy, but Michele was alone. We slept in sleeping bags under heat lamps on the solarium, the glassed-in rear deck of the boat. The walkways around the ship were coated in slick ice, and we bucked into a strong headwind. We found that if you released the handrail near the bow of the boat, the wind would sweep you over the icy walkways to the stern in just a few seconds. We found that a buzz heightened the sensation.

My buddy was a guitar-playing, bear-biologist woman-wooer. Michele turned him down. She thought he carried his instrument as though he were displaying his penis. I never made my move, but on the last day of the trip she came and kissed me. She was waitressing on the Kenai Peninsula, just north of Homer. I was in school in Fairbanks, preparing to flunk out of college for the fifth time. We swapped phone numbers.

In the springtime I went to visit her under the pretense of watching Mount Spurr erupt, visible from the trailer she was living in. But before I left Fairbanks, I got together with another woman. I've never stepped out on a partner; despite my many flaws I've managed to hold onto that. Michele and I couldn't be together then, is what I mean—which was messed up too. She was lonely, and it probably would have done us both some good. She quit the restaurant and went to work for Fish and Game, counting salmon returns on an island in Prince William Sound. Eventually she came north and enrolled at the University of Alaska Fairbanks, but she never contacted me, and by the time we ran into each other again she was with another guy who she eventually married—and divorced.

We'd been leading separate adult lives until a few years ago— well, *adult* might be stretching it for me. She'd gotten her degree and a teaching certificate and a job at a local high school where she works to this day. Everywhere we go, people aged sixteen to thirty, smile and approach us and say, "Hello, Ms. Robinson." Her former students. A lot of people recognize me too, the cab driver, but usually they're not sure from where so they just stare a question at me to see if I respond. But regardless, there are a hundred thousand people in this town and six hundred thousand in this state, and we're part of that, part of something. And our son, Cord, he's almost three, he's a part of it now too.

He's upended my perspective on this world. He's how I take measure of myself, who I was, where I've been, who I am now. He's the reason for understanding the stories I've lived, the stories around me every day, so that from here on at least, I'm aware of trying to be the guy Michele saw something in a long time ago.

Driving a cab is essentially gambling, but it's a good enough bet and doesn't involve staring at a computer screen, working on a utility crew outside in the winter, or smelling like stale french fry grease. I don't show up at a certain time and leave at a certain time and get paid for the time in between. Instead, when I show up I owe the owner of the company ninety bucks for the twelve-hour lease. When I'm done with the car, I'll put around fifty bucks in the gas tank. I keep the balance, if any, and go home. Nobody much cares if I show up in the first place. Most of my fellow drivers would prefer I do something other than take food out of the mouths of their children.

There are usually enough drivers to keep the owner relatively rich and pay the dispatchers, insurers, managers, and mechanics. There are usually even enough to get the customers picked up in a somewhat timely manner. In fact, there are often more drivers than good fares on a given night, and we battle each other like dogs for the scraps that cover our expenses.

The company doesn't really care how an individual driver makes his money. We get to do it how we want, as long as we pay the lease and don't get caught by the police doing anything illegal. Some choose to make their living by providing transportation to the people who call the company for a ride. Some like to sit around the airport or cater to personal calls. Others might choose to sell drugs, arrange for prostitutes, or steal trips from other drivers.

However one decides to approach the job, it starts with the dispatcher, usually an underpaid over-caffeinated guy with enough attitude to take the shit from drivers, management, and customers and throw it right back. He spends his eight hours seated at a desk equipped with five phone lines, a two-way radio, a clipboard full of trip logs, and an upright steel board, sixteen inches tall and thirty inches wide.

The board displays a grid of three rows by seven columns. Each column represents a different zone in the city. Cabs in the top row are red and are available for a trip; cabs in the middle row are green and have customers; cabs in the bottom row are picking up. They don't get a color. The drivers are represented by numbered magnetic buttons stuck to the board, each button corresponding to a particular cab.

You radio the dispatcher telling him where you're going, or where you're clear, or when you change zones, and he moves your button around the board as you try to pick up the most trips and win the big money. We're little free-willed markers on the board game of Fairbanks.

It's 4:30 when I show up. The sun's been down more than an hour, early January, forty-five degrees below zero. The yard is layered in ice fog churned from the rumbling V-8 motors of the cabs waiting for night drivers. The warm water vapor from a car's exhaust is cooled nearly three hundred degrees within ten seconds of leaving the tailpipe. The super cold air is too dense to absorb any of the vapor, so it turns into tiny hovering ice crystals. Add in the warm water discharged from the power plant; the emissions of all the woodstoves, furnaces, and boilers; and the exhalations of every living thing and our town is swaddled in a toxic gauze.

From negative forty on down, the taxis are left running to avoid the risk of freeze-up and lost revenue. Can't see fifty feet.

I walk into the smoke-filmed walls of the dispatch office that smells of stale cigarettes, fresh cigarettes, coffee, old dog, and microwave. Smurf is dispatching, talking on the phone. All lines are lit up. There are thirty-eight buttons on the board.

"I can't send ya a cab if you won't give me the apartment number. So last chance, what's the number? Ten or less, belookin'," he slams down the phone, picks it right back up. "United! . . . Which door ya at? . . . What's your name? . . . Okay, Randy, I'll send one."

Slams down the phone, picks it back up, "United Cab! . . . Is who
workin'? . . . No, he went home already, ya need a cab?" Slams
down the phone, picks it back up. "United! . . . At the parking lot
door? . . . Five minutes." He slams down the phone, hits the foot
pedal microphone key while writing in his personal hieroglyph-
ics on the trip log. "United 17!" he says.

"United 17," a surly nasal male voice croons back.

"Get Tanana Chiefs at the parking lot door!" Smurf replies,
depressing and releasing the foot pedal in rhythm, moves 17's
button.

"Check," says United 17.

"Cab 72."

"Cab 72," answers a guarded female voice.

"Take it south, get the Rescue Mission for Duano."

"Cab 72 check."

"United 46 . . . United 46!"

"United 46."

"You called me, 46!" yells Smurf.

"Oh, um, I'm green to um (squawk) . . . Fred Meyers."

"Oh, um, geez, which one!"

"Oh, um, in the west."

"Oh, um, golly, why don't you get Tristan at the B door?" bel-
lows Smurf. But there's no answer. "United 46!"

"Um, United 46."

"Listen to your radio and get Tristan at the B door when you
clear."

"Uh, United 46, check?"

"Now who's next?"

A wall of static erupts from the radio as several drivers key
their microphones at the same time. Smurf stretches back and
sighs, lights a Marlboro.

I throw five dollars on the trip log in front of him. Part gratu-
ity, part protection money.

He turns to me. He has a big drinker's nose, a thinning mane of golden hair, and a wolfish Irish grin. I've watched him battle his personal demons for close to twenty years now. A trail of broken bottles, used hypodermics, meth memories stretching behind him, out of sight. Now, all that's left are the medications, the battered liver, the clogged arteries. The doctors told him he can have a new liver if he stays clean for a year. I hope he makes it. The man's got the love in his heart, and that's all that matters to me.

"What d'you want?" he asks.

"I don't know. I thought I'd try drivin' a little taxi cab."

"I don't know. You think you can handle it?"

"I'm not sure. I heard it requires great mental agility."

"Fuckin' A right."

"But they let you do it?"

"'Cause I'm fun to watch. What are you drivin'?"

"I'll take twenty-nine."

"Go get the Fred Meyer liquor for Regina."

"Thanks."

"You still here? . . . United Cab! . . . That was number twenty-eight? All right, right away." Slams down the phone. "Cab 100 get Wedgewood M like your mama 28." Slides one hundred's button from the top row to the bottom row in the north column.

A voice with a Tajikistan accent says check.

"Okay, drivers, red cars only, one at a time please." I close the door as another wave of static breaks from the radio.

I feel like a pinball that Smurf has shot into the night. Like some intricacies of spin, velocity, and position have cast me to the inevitable.

-:::-

Town sneaks up on you in the ice fog. Stoplights and other cars appear out of nothing, and then they're gone. Ghost lights. A hundred years ago the roads were just trails from the river, through the spruce, to the cabins of the pioneers and prostitutes. In 1938 residents approved a measure to pave the roads. It had been a hot-button issue for many years. Incoming pilots had been able to identify the dust cloud of Fairbanks from eighty miles away.

It takes five minutes to get to Fred Meyer. When I enter the parking lot, I catch a glimpse of an old Athabaskan man in a Carhartt suit with the hood up. He holds a sign with big military surplus mittens. The sign says, "homeles veitnam vet plese help." No sooner than I see him he's gone in the fog and steaming train of headlights.

At the liquor door Regina comes striding out pushing a load-ed cart with three kids under ten behind her, respectful. I pop the trunk of the Ford Crown Victoria and help load her bags.

As we leave the lot she sees the man with the sign. "Jesus Christ, is that Uncle Melvin, kids? Could you stop for a second?"

"Sure."

"Uncle, is that you? Jesus Christ, what you doin'? It's too cold to be stannin' around like that."

A big beauty of a broken-tooth smile breaks across the old man's weathered face like sunrise. He steps toward the cab and raises his hand.

"Uncle, get in the car with us, huh, we got moose stew at home. You can stay there."

The old man seems hesitant.

"We got beer there too, c'mon and get in with us." The smile gets bigger, and he climbs in. Cars behind us start to honk.

I take them to a house in the Hamilton Acres subdivision, a middle-class neighborhood north of the river. They give me $8 for a $6.20 meter. I thank the lady and help get the groceries to the door.

Back in the car I call on the radio, "United 29."

After a pause the dispatcher comes back, "United 29."

I say, "Red North, Glacier Street."

"You're six North."

Yikes. This means I'll get the sixth call out of this zone. I decide to move, gun the car sideways on the ice back up Farewell, catch the yellow light on the Steese Expressway, and make a left. I have the mike in my hand and call as I go through the intersection. The dispatcher calls back, and I tell him I'm red City as I cross the bridge over the Chena River.

"Get Smith Apartments, number nine."

"Check."

A young Athabaskan man is outside the drab building. This place has an unfavorable reputation, a home for low-income tenants and their no-income friends. When I get a call here, I go in with the doors locked, ready to check for money, which is kind of an awkward thing to do. But this guy's holding some, and I unlock the doors.

He gets in, midthirties, weathered, smelling of vodka. The rigidity pickled out of his bones, a rumpled ten in his hands.

"Where to?"

"Twenty-First and Gillam, I guess."

"Okay."

"Time to quit drinkin', I guess. Just gotta get someplace where I can rest."

"All right."

After a couple minutes he says, "You ever feel alone?"

"Yeah, sometimes."

"What you do?"

"I try and remember it doesn't last forever. Like the good times, I guess."

"Yeah, I guess. . . . Hey I'll pay you extra, can you turn this song up?" It's the Red Hot Chili Peppers.

"Sure," I say twisting the knob to the right until the bass is vibrating my solar plexus. "How's that?"

"That's good. Gotta like the Chili's, huh?"

"Yeah." I remember when the song came out. How cool it all was. Now hearing it on classic rock radio, I smile.

My passenger says, "Hey, can you just go around the block a little bit? I'll pay you."

"Sure." We're both singing when we go around the corner. "When I find my peace of mind . . ."

"Hey, it's okay I have a shot?"

"If no cops see you, then I don't care."

"Okay, all right." He pulls a half-full fifth of Rich and Rare from deep within his coat and takes a long pull. A few minutes later we're back in the parking lot, $8.60 on the meter. He hands me $10 and tells me to keep it. "Wanted Dead or Alive" comes on the radio. "Oh, man, I love this song. I lost my uncle listenin' to this song."

"Sorry."

"Can you hang out till this song's over?"

But I've already called Smurf, and he's sending me to the Twenty-Third Laundry, where I pick up a large African American woman with dozens of thin and perfectly twined braids falling to the middle of her back. There are four children under the age of ten skating around her like waterbugs on the ice. "Montrel, quit torturin' your sister and get the rest of these kids in the car. And you better all have your seatbelts on by the time I get in there, or you will know my pain." The kids become very serious and do as they are told. I get out and help her load mesh bags containing more than a hundred pounds of freshly laundered clothes. The warm clothes steam into the cold. I take them three blocks. The woman gives me $3 for the $2.20 meter, and I put the laundry by her door.

This brings me to $22, around 15 percent of my expenses, an hour into this. I call in and Smurf puts me one South. I tell myself to remain calm, go and park by the Dollar Store, try to flag. Listen to the radio. There are two City and three North. Ten minutes. Smurf sends a couple cars from the west into the University zone. He chews out a driver for stealing a trip that he had dispatched to a different driver. Says, "Listen to your radio, seventeen. If it happens again, you can gas it up and get it in here. You won't get another trip outta me." Fifteen minutes. Sometimes I feel like a shark, like if I quit moving for too long I'll die. Eighteen minutes. Smurf sends a City car to the Westmark Hotel, sends me to 1227 Twenty-Third Avenue.

When I graduated from high school, my parents bought me a Ford Tempo, which I drove all over Kansas and then all over America, taking odd jobs to keep it gassed up. In order to *get* my diploma, I had to break into the school, steal the answer key for an economics project, copy it, and sneak back in to return it. From these two details of my formative years you can correctly conclude that I was a delinquent little upper-middle-class shit with a peripatetic itch, even though I was raised better than that.

My father was from Eureka, Kansas. He brought us back there from Kansas City when I was six because my grandfather was retiring from the helm of Eureka Federal Savings and Loan, which he built himself in the aftermath of the Great Depression. He and my grandmother still lived in the little pink house on Myrtle Street that my dad had grown up in. My grandpa held stockholder meetings with us during which he divvied out change that my two sisters and I subsequently spent on candy. He smoked unfiltered cigs through a black plastic cig holder, filling the little pink house with blue smoke. Grandma smoked too. I mean, why not. In the backyard were apple and cherry trees. She picked the fruit and made pies, which she served warm after endless portions of fried chicken, mashed potatoes, gravy, bread, and green beans.

We must have seemed fantastically rich to the many working poor families in town. Some people despised us for it; most didn't care. But we were a little different and I was kind of oblivious to the hardships some of my friends endured. Sports, cars, girls, beer made that a little less obvious to my peers. We'd have parties way out on farm roads, at the low-water bridge, at the old quarter-mile drag race strip. We'd stand by a fire on the side of the road in the wind with the outlines of cows and silos close in the darkness.

In my early teens my folks sent me to a camp in Colorado for five weeks every summer. We climbed mountains, rafted rivers, hiked through forests and canyons. I loved to sleep outside and ponder the immensity of the Milky Way and my own insignificance as I drifted off. Back in camp, at dances, I was awkward and clumsy next to smooth city kids from Des Moines, Indianapolis, and New York, but alone under the stars I was free. I was nothing. The world could proceed.

Eureka was surrounded by hundreds of miles of dirt farm roads, and I'd spend hours driving them, listening to music, thinking. I loved the sensation of movement through space.

One night, a few years later, I was driving home to Kansas from Morristown, New Jersey, where I had a job at the Bell Labs loading dock. I was smoking a joint and thinking about the contrast between my life and the lives of just about everyone else I knew. I thought that this was largely due to the fact that I had the resources to live this vagabond lifestyle, that more people would choose to live similarly if the choice was available. I began to feel that it was important, somehow, that some people did live in this manner, that surrendering to the winds that blow us through our lives was as valuable a perspective on the human condition as any other.

Along the way I realized that I thought in the second person, that I used the pronoun *you* to talk to myself in my thoughts. *You should do this. You shouldn't have done that.* I realized that this was causing me to think of myself as two entities. Sometimes it felt as if my personality were splitting to accommodate both perspectives. One that allowed me control of my life versus a more rigid ideology foisted on me by some mysterious other, a blunt instrument to hammer a niche in the malleable substance of the world. I chose to let go. I spent the rest of that long drive ridding myself of the habit of thinking in the you. *I should try this; or I really fucked up there.* I stopped arguing with myself. A few years later I woke up on a beach in Alaska.

The thing is, most of the riders in my cab come from places, from circumstances that I'll never know about. I've spent a little time in remote Alaska villages, but I could never know what it's like to be from one, where there are few jobs because there is little economic activity. Traditional work like hunting, fishing, berry picking, woodcutting, sure, but the price of a can of gas gets in the way of even these practices.

The influenza epidemic of the early twentieth century decimated the Alaska Native population and claimed wide swaths of traditional knowledge that had been passed on orally for thousands of years, a void that can't be filled with well meaning, sometimes racist, attempts to change them into people more eager to compete in a capitalist economy.

In his book *Yuuyaraq: The Way of the Human Being*, Harold Napoleon argues that the trauma of losing up to 60 percent of the population in a generation left many of the survivors with acute post-traumatic stress syndrome. This condition has been passed on to subsequent generations, he explains, through the scourges of domestic violence, alcoholism, and drug abuse.

I can't help but wonder how much more of this generational trauma is woven into the fabric of our culture from all the wars of the last century, slavery, Jim Crow, poverty.

That's why if I'm behind the wheel, nobody in the car is in the second person. Anything they might be is more complicated than what's merely apparent—larger than *you* and than me.

Clutching a bag of customized Magic Markers, an old Inupiaq woman with mussed bed hair is waiting in the parking lot. I don't understand what she says through her blue lips, but it doesn't matter. She's one of our bingo babes, and they'll be opening the halls any minute, so I know where we're going. After I let her off at Downtown Bingo, Smurf sends me to 401 on Seventh Avenue, a retirement complex. Sara, an Athabaskan woman in her eighties, winces at the cold as she gets in.

"Youth Sport," she says, agitated, not looking at me. She means Youth Sports Bingo, next to Downtown Bingo. It takes me thirty-eight seconds to get her there. She pays the $1.60 in quarters and a dime and gets out without looking back. Most bingo babes live within blocks of their favorite bingo enclave. They're mostly elderly Alaska Natives. And while the thrill of winning the big money is the primary motivation for playing, the social scene is also important.

These elders come from villages strung along sixteen hundred miles of the Yukon River, up its tributaries, over the Brooks Range, and across the North Slope to the Arctic Ocean. People who survived the epidemics of influenza, typhus, and diphtheria that came with the first white men. People who remember hunting nomadically and whaling in skin boats. They've seen world wars, statehood, big oil, the division of their land, and the Internet. They've seen more change in their lifetimes than a hundred generations before them.

Now they're in Fairbanks, the big village. They visit relatives, shop, see the doctor, go to funerals, take taxis, party. The bingo halls and the pan houses, where a form of rummy is played, are places to see people, visit, and hear stories from home as much as they're places to gamble.

I call in and Smurf says, "You're one City. I'm holdin' one South, you want it?"

I say, "Check."

"Get F.M.H. in the lobby for Richard."

"Check." I get on Airport and drive west and then south to the hospital.

"United 57."

"United 57, how many times I gotta tell you we don't serve Mexicans on this channel," Smurf says.

"It's a good thing I come from Texas then. Red South."

"I thought Texas was in Mexico. Oh well, uh, can you fit five passengers in that thing?"

"Five Asians, maybe, no way five Americans."

"All right then, get two packs of Newports and a three-pack of magnum-sized condoms, and take 'em to 1111 Nenana Street. He'll pay you for 'em when you get there."

"57 check."

Richard doesn't look well. He shuffles to the cab pulling an oxygen tank on wheels. He seems prematurely old. He's tall, and you can tell that he had once been a strong man but now he is shriveled and bloodlessly pale, his hair and lips the color of dried bone.

He tells me he's going to Yak Estates but wants to stop at a pharmacy on the way. I say no problem.

He's out of breath after the walk to the car and doesn't say anything for a couple minutes. Then, "Sorry, man. I move slow. I'm all fucked up."

"That's all right. You didn't take too long."

"No, but I will though, at the pharmacy. You're probably gonna charge me for that, huh?"

"Yeah, sorry."

"That's all right. You've gotta make a living. How old are you?"

"Forty-six."

He laughs fatalistically. "I'm only three years older than you. Found out a couple years ago I had hepatitis C. Now I'm dying. I got sclerosis of the liver and my knees are shot. I was hopin' they could fix my knees so I could take one more walk before my liver gives out, but it doesn't look good."

"Damn, man. Sorry about that."

"Yeah, they're just figuring out this stuff can live outside the body for years. I could've snorted a line of coke with a contaminated twenty back in the day, and it could've hung out in my nostril until I got a cut in my nose and that was that."

I swing into Fred Meyer west and up to the pharmacy door. He gets out and pulls his oxygen tank inside the mechanized whir of sliding glass and sits in an electric shopping cart and hums in to the din of the store. I turn the meter from mileage to time and let it tick, fifty cents a minute, thirty dollars an hour.

Cab 74 tells the dispatcher he's getting no response at Alaska Motel, room fifteen. The dispatcher tells him to pick up the Ranch, room 208, for his dud. He tells cab 93 that he has a personal at the Golden North, room 107, for Stormin' Norman.

"I ain't pickin' him up. He ain't never got no money."

"He says he's got some now. Wants to pay you off."

"Well, in that case I'll check him out after I take Ruth home from work."

"He's ready to go, 93, go get him or he'll call you back later."

"Well, shoot, I guess I better go get him then."

"Well, shoot, check. Waste a little more air time why don't ya. Who's next?" A car crash of static from the radio.

Ten minutes, the meter a bit over fifteen dollars. A guy on a mountain bike swoops out of the ice fog, hops onto the sidewalk, and coasts to a stop at the bike rack. His head, chest, and shoulders are covered with frost, and ice fog pours from his clothes and mouth. He has an empty backpack on over a down coat, snow pants, balaclava, mittens the size of beavers. There's a plastic five-gallon water jug strapped on a reinforced rear rack. A freakish strobe flashes from the back of the seat, and he forgets to turn it off when he goes inside.

Twenty-one minutes, the meter almost to twenty bucks, I see Richard roll back into the entryway with a couple bags of groceries. I hop out and carry them to the car while he wheels his oxygen. We're off. It takes him a few minutes to catch his breath.

"Man, it's like I'm invisible to people. Like I'm a ghost. I have to bump into people with the cart before they acknowledge my existence. I just want to shout, 'I'm still here,' sometimes."

I think about when I first saw him and felt a moment of dread knowing that he was my passenger. Like that made him real when I didn't want him to be. Didn't want this specter of death fucking with my perspective.

"Well, you seem real to me, man. A lot of people have it, right? I mean a friend of mine has it. He's doin' okay, gets tired easy. But you don't hear much about it."

"Yeah, more people have hep than AIDS in this country. They're calling it the silent epidemic 'cause, you know, who gives a shit about a bunch of old junkies and hippies with blood poisoning? I guess it's the price I gotta pay for all those years stayin' up all night dancin', drinkin', whateverin'. Man I used to love to dance. Loved the ladies. And you know what? If I had it to do all over again, I wouldn't change anything.

"There're some new meds coming out too. I'll just try and hang on till they get here."

We get to his condo, and I carry in his groceries. I wish him good luck and shake his hand. He manages a weak smile and something sparks in his eye. For just a second I can see him dancin' and makin' moves on the ladies in some bar with a band, and I kinda believe him.

Smurf sends me to the Holiday House Apartments, and I pick up three young engineering students from India and take them to Safeway. They speak in Hindi. I listen to the cadence and bubbling tones, and they soothe me. I like hearing languages I can't understand, all that yearning stripped of meaning and removed from me, an instrumental, a symphony.

They pay seven dollars and Smurf sends me to the Klondike, room 238. The Klondike is a bunch of Atco trailers laid out end to end. They were brought to Alaska in the seventies to house workers building the pipeline. Cheapest rooms in town.

I knock on 238 and a six-year-old Athabaskan boy answers. He looks at me with big dark eyes. I ask him if he needs a taxi and he shrugs and steps out, closes the door behind him. It doesn't latch but hangs limp and gray in the frame. He follows me to the cab and gets in. "Where to?" I say.

He says, "Ninety-Nine Bentley Drive," real fast, like he'd been rehearsing his big line for a school play. Well, Ninety-Nine Bentley Drive is a sketchy address, so I ask him if he's got any money. He kind of shifts around like he's trying to screw himself down into the seat. "My mom's there. She's got the money."

"You promise?"

"Yeah, I promise, she's there." He wears a "Kiss Me I'm Irish" T-shirt beneath an unzipped red coat, no hat, no gloves.

"All right, man." And I put it on Airport Way to Peger to the Johanssen Expressway to College Road to Island Homes. I slide around most of the turns because I like the way it feels.

It takes twelve minutes to get to Bentley Drive. We walk to the front door of the buried-in-snow ranch home. Reaching no higher than the knob, he knocks on the door. I barely hear it over the noise of the TV inside. Feeling the cold, I knock again, higher and louder. A big man, of mixed race, with a shaved head and a beer gut alive with distended blue tattoos swings open the door. He has little fidgety eyes, looks at me hard. "What you want?" The can of Natural Ice in his right hand is slightly crushed, like he squeezes the beer out.

"Uh, hi, yeah. I'm a cab driver. I just brought this guy over from the Klondike. He said his mom was here and was gonna pay for the cab."

The guy looks down at the kid for the first time. Turns around and walks back in. "Desiree!" he shouts ahead of him. "Elliot's here. Come pay the cab."

I stand there as the warmth bleeds out the open door and the moisture supercools and hangs in the air. I smell the Hot Pockets in the oven, the kitty litter, smoked fish, dirty socks.

The woman appears in the entryway. "Jesus Christ, Norris, you born in a fuckin' barn!" she shouts over her shoulder.

"Sorry, honey," the voice yells back from the room with the TV. He has a downriver accent, chopped with German and Russian. The show sounds like *Cops*, one of those where police chase minorities through the ghetto.

"Well, come in and shut the door," she says. "Hi."

"Hi." She's a knockout. Early twenties, wearing a short white dress with pink and blue polka dots and a frilled hem that shows off her brown thighs. Past the thin waist where the fabric draws tight across her tummy, the subtle roll of her breasts, low neckline. When I get to her face she's smiling coquettishly, her head tilted just to the right so that the long wave of black hair falls behind her shoulder.

"So . . . how much is the cab fare?" She raises her eyebrows playfully.

"Um, sixteen dollars'll do it."

She steps toward me and reaches between her breasts. She pulls out some bills and counts two fives and six ones, puts two more ones back between her breasts and comes to a stop a few inches away. She hands me the money. "Keep it," she says and smiles again. "You want to come back and give us a ride later?"

"Sure. I'm number 29."

"All right, number 29, I'll call you."

"Jesus Christ, Des, you gonna blow the guy or finish cookin'?" The voice from the TV room. "Me and Elliot's hungry."

Her eyes linger a moment before she turns back in the house.

I let myself out.

The older I get, the less stuff surprises me. One thing that does is how Cord has caused the love in my heart to grow beyond all proportion. Before Cord I hardly knew it was there. It scares me sometimes when I think about what would be left of me if this were removed, scares me to be so vested in a fragile boy in an uncertain world.

I had a tough time accepting the wisdom of my parents, but not their love. That was always pure and abundant. I was the oldest with two sisters two and four years behind. I tormented them mercilessly. I viewed them not so much as individuals but as a part of my existence, there to be manipulated. I hid their dolls. I threw balls at them when they weren't looking. I probed weak spots like weight and popularity. Somehow we have a good relationship these days, though we're strung out from Amsterdam to Alaska. Maybe all we needed was a little space and time.

My family ate dinner at a round barrel table in the kitchen; a small black and white TV was usually on. My mistake was thinking it provided a distraction, that I could continue to shovel my canned green beans into the hole in the barrel supporting the tabletop indefinitely. My mom had been noticing a smell of decay but waited to pounce until she caught me in the act. I was immediately grounded and sent to my room to await a spanking. But she couldn't do it. We stood there, me with my pants around my ankles and her with the belt dangling limp from her hand for a long time. It was pretty traumatic for us both.

When I was fourteen my folks decided to remodel the house. I moved into the apartment above the garage. My youngest sister moved out of the room she shared with my middle sister into my old room. My sisters' and parents' bedrooms now opened onto a communal landing at the top of the main stairs. I had my first taste of autonomy. I covered the walls of my new digs with collages of my favorite sports stars and *Sports Illustrated* swimsuit models. Using rappelling skills I'd learned at summer camp, I was able to lower myself out of a window into the cover of night. At first I'd meet other friends, and we'd ride bikes around town and let the air out of the tires of our least favorite teachers' cars.

Stuff like that. Soon enough, though, we were riding in cars, drinking beer, chasing girls. It makes me worry about what's to come. I feel like I was lucky to survive those years. Lucky I didn't hurt anyone. I'm hoping Cord got healthy doses of Michele's DNA regarding this behavior, but I don't know. I can already see the mischievousness sparkling in his eyes.

After the remodel we ate in the new family room with the big TV on, though Mom would insist on a couple dinners a week where we just talked about Dad's day at the savings and loan, our classes at school, Mom's volunteer work at the local Red Cross.

But TV was terribly important. Next day the previous evening's programming would constitute much schoolkid discussion, and too bad if you were the kid unlucky enough to have had to go to bed at ten. Michele and I were talking the other night about how, when there were only three or four channels, the whole country was essentially tuning in to the same message, the same projection of who we were as Americans: white heterosexuals with jobs and money. People who didn't have drug habits or drink until they puked, or beat the shit out of each other because their fathers beat the shit out of them. What in the world would a young boy like Elliot have made of *Happy Days*?

I once saw my dad weep at the end of an episode of *Little House on the Prairie*. This was when we were still eating in the kitchen and watching the black-and-white. I think he was moved by the transience of their experience. How their sod-roofed homestead simply turned back in to the land when they left. How this acted as a metaphor for our own existence, barely a ripple to mark our passage. He's a sentimental man; I got it from him. But this wasn't an easy characteristic in the savings and loan business in Eureka, Kansas, during the farm loan crisis. The nightly nightcaps multiplied as the years wore on and the farm foreclosures gave way to the S and L crisis. Cocktail hour stretched past bedtime and often occupied the whole day on the weekends.

The first time I got drunk was one summer when my folks were away at a savings and loan convention and my sisters were at camp. I was fifteen, staying with my grandparents, and security there was decidedly more lax than at home. I met up with my evil friend Hank, and we went to my house and did serious damage to my parents' liquor cabinet. When my folks came home from Shangri La (seriously, that's the name of the resort in Oklahoma where they'd been), I told them that I'd fallen while looking for food and wiped out five or six bottles of booze. Right. Wanting me to fess up, they probed me with open suspicion.

Not long after, Dad and I were in the kitchen. He was slicing salami, making us sandwiches, and I noticed that he was crying. His tears were splatting on the cutting board. I asked him what was the matter, and he told me that it was a sin to lie. I saw it differently. Lying seemed a part of the skillset of secret agents, undercover cops, and wise criminals. I wanted to be an actor at this point and lying seemed central to that mission. Plus, I was pretty sure that God was bullshit too, so the whole sin thing held little sway.

But honesty was important to my dad. He made sure I knew that. Now it's important to me. I always sensed there was some truth beyond the holographic walls of our upper-middle-class projection, just as I knew there was sheetrock and studs and wires beneath the slick veneer of African animal wallpaper in my bedroom. I craved access to that truth. Still do. Though it exists everywhere, it can be hard to see. But the cab is a piece of that truth, driving one is like diving into a sea of humanity.

I can't get through on the radio. Smurf's in a rage because a cab ran the stoplight at Geist and Johanssen. "It's busy as hell in here, Cab 16, and now I've got to tie up the phone lines takin' complaints, and not for the first time either, about your crappy driving." While he's talking we can hear phones ringing off hooks. It's his way of punishing everybody for the sins of one. Letting us hear all that unanswered business hanging up and trying another company. "So remember, you guys are driving billboards out there. Got my phone number written all over 'em. Surest way to shut these phones down I know of. Now, sixteen, you need to call Don before I give you another trip. Who was next?"

Sibilant static leaps from the radio and explodes in my inner ear. From it emerges a panicked beep. I clamp my hands over my ears and stifle a whimper. It's Morse code. A few years back the Federal Communications Commission decided that in the interest of national security and personal freedom, all registered radio frequencies need to beep out their call letters and frequency at a tympanic tissue-piercing pitch every fifteen minutes. We're all thankful.

Smurf says, "That's too many of yuh, try again." Just the crash of static. "Goddammit, that's too much! One at a time! Ah, fuck it, I'm on the phone, and I don't wanna hear anybody callin' their number till I get back! Oops, forgot I'm not supposed to say *fuck* on the radio."

Eventually I get through. Get sent to 15 Farewell. There's an elderly lady in the entryway. She steps into the night and asks if this is for Opal. I tell her it is, and she asks if I could help with her things, pointing to a brown paper sack filled with hot food in aluminum foil. I put this in the backseat, and she gets in the front. "Where to?" I ask.

"I'm going to the Elks. Do you know where the Elks is?"

"Yes, ma'am."

"You just go down this road. I guess it's Farewell or something and go past the first few stoplights and then turn left and then right and go in that way."

"Okay. How are you doin' today?"

"Oh, all right I guess. I'm just going to meet my friend. We always get together on our birthday and have some drinks and talk about the good old days."

"Well, happy birthday."

"Thank you, young man. It is my birthday. I'm eighty-four."

"Congratulations."

"I don't know that congratulations are in order, but if you help me get my stuff inside that'd be appreciated. Eighty-four's a bitch, young man."

"I'll carry the stuff."

"I came up here with my World War II hero in 1947. After the war he was having a hard time, and he asked me if I wouldn't mind giving it a try up here. So that's what we did. I met the lady I'm going to meet now not too long after we got here, and we found out we had the same birthday. We've been friends ever since."

"Wow, you've seen some change, huh."

"Oh, yes. This town's about ten times bigger now than it was then. All that Bentley land, my husband used to look for moose there. Now, I won't even go."

"I liked it better when it was woods, myself," I say, referring to the several square miles on the northeast end of town that in the span of the last decade has been leveled, buried in gravel, paved, and developed into Walmart, Home Depot, Sportsman's Warehouse, Sports Authority, Barnes and Noble, a new Fred Meyer, Old Navy, Chili's, Carl's Jr., Boston's, the Holiday Inn, the Hampton Inn, and a host of other chains.

"It's like aliens came and dropped the Walmart from space.
I'll just stay with Safeway."

"I go to the old Fred Meyer," I say as we pull up to the Elks.

"All right, I like that one. How much do I owe?"

"Five's fine." She gives me six and gets out. I carry her bag in,
let her hold my arm on the ice. Smurf puts me four North. I gun
it past the Big International Bar, the oldest joint in town, dating
to the forties. There was recently an effort to have the building
removed to make room for a new bridge over the Chena River.
The outcry was loud enough that the city decided to remove
every building but the Big I and build the bridge around it—
proving that you can rip down any historic Fairbanks building
you want, as long as it's not one that serves alcohol.

I cross the old Chena River bridge not far from where E. T.
Barnette ran into shallow water in the steamship *Lavelle Young*
in 1901. Barnette's intention had been to establish a trading post
near Eagle, where gold had already been found, but the deal he'd
made with the boat owner stated his provisions would be un-
loaded when the boat could go no farther upriver. So, a long way
from Eagle on a river that doesn't go there, brush was cleared,
supplies offloaded. The boat left. There was nothing else here.

Barnette established his trading post at the site his provisions
were thrown off the ship. He sent word throughout the territory
of large gold strikes in the region. It was a good thing that the
Italian miner Felix Pedro actually did discover gold the following year; otherwise, the thousand or so folks who responded to
Barnette's promotions might have made good on their threats
to string him up. But between Pedro's hard work and Barnette's
bullshit, a town was born.

I call City and get a two position. I drive down Second Avenue
and park in front of the Mecca Bar, the last bar on Two Street. In
the seventies, when they were building the pipeline, there were

close to thirty bars along these two blocks. Those were the days when you laid your gun on the bar to hold your money down while you did lines on the pinball machines in back, when a fight or a prostitute were equally available to everyone, when Vietnam vets were the ones trying to get away from it all.

There's a wildness to this town that goes beyond the tens of thousands of square miles of wilderness that surrounds it. It's a town of misfits. People who weren't making it other places somehow find a home here. Nobody tells you how to build your house. Men are bushy and long haired. Women shoot moose and operate heavy equipment. People do what they want. But it goes beyond that. It's like when a rock is formed there's a unique magnetic signature derived from that stony matter's orientation to the constantly shifting magnetic poles of the planet, but the signature on this town feels unfinished. So there's this sense of newness, of our actions continuing to form the kind of place this will be.

I flag an Inupiaq man in his fifties out of the bar. He's too drunk to remember which hotel he's staying at. I ask to see his room key, and he digs it out. The key ring says Golden Nugget Hotel. We pass the sign for the Elbow Room bar jutting sideways from the abandoned concrete monolith that was once the Polaris Hotel. I remember nights in that bar crowded with Alaska Native people, a band with guitars and fiddles and drums, marijuana pipes passed between strangers disappearing into the night. It's a meditation center now.

The man pays the three-dollar fare with a hundred, takes his change, and stumbles in.

I call red City and Smurf puts me one after sending another car to Big Daddy's Barbecue. I count my money: ninety-six dollars, 8:05 p.m. So, after three-plus hours of work I only need to hustle up another fifty bucks before I make money. I've got the cab for another eight hours, if I can hang. Remain calm. Breathe in for four counts, hold it for four more, release it for four, hold this for four, and repeat the process.

I open my eyes when I hear a rapping on the window. There's an older Athabaskan man smiling at me. He's wearing a royal blue cap with a white bow in front. Dark eager eyes shimmer behind tinted glasses. He's just a spruce needle taller than the cab. I smile and release the power locks. "Jeremiah!" I say as he ducks into the car. "How are you, my friend?"

"I'm good, good. Good to see you, my friend."

"Good to see you too." His lips are a shade gray from the cold. I am, as always, impressed by the size of his hands relative to the rest of him. Big meaty mitts always open and ready to begin some undiscovered chore his eyes are constantly seeking. "You have that baby, yet?"

"Yeah, man. But he's not much of a baby anymore."

"Same one I meet that time, huh, Michele?"

"That's her."

"Oh, that's good. Good for you. You guys bring that baby up Venetie, huh? We go around that country. I got new boat this year."

"Jeremiah, we'd be honored. That sounds great."

"Hey, can you give us a ride? I got some lynx skins I want take to the buyer. You know where, huh?"

"Alaska Fur?"

"Yeah, that place. Can you take us?"

"Yeah, sure."

He hops out of the cab and waves to a younger man standing by the door of the hotel with a large black trash bag. The man jogs over, and they both get in. We take Tenth to the expressway and head north to Farewell.

"How many lynx you got?"

"Only six right now. I only go out for couple weeks, though. I got sick really bad this winter. Had to go to Anchorage for operation. No good. No good."

"Geez, that's too bad. How're you feeling now? You look great."

"Oh, I feel good now. Ready to go back trapping. The price is good. He say maybe thousand dollar for six skins."

"That *is* good."

"He was really sick, though," the man with the bag says.

"Oh, yeah?" I look at him.

"Yeah, he make us all nervous, didn't you?" He slaps Jeremiah's shoulder with his leather gloves.

"Oh, I guess. I make myself nervous. No good at all. But I'm better now."

"How're you, man?" I say to the friend.

"I'm good. I've been in town waiting for job out of Carpenters Union but nothing yet. Maybe I go back to the village soon if nothing come up. Try again later."

"Not much happenin' this winter, though, huh?"

"Economy's no good I guess. I been okay, though." He smiles.

We're pulling into the driveway of a small house on a residential street. Nothing marks the house as a business other than a small, neon OPEN sign in the window of the garage door. Jeremiah and I agree to have coffee tomorrow. I wish them well.

A car clears North as I'm grabbing my mike. Smurf puts him six. I don't bother calling until I'm in the city.

Smurf says, "Eagle 29 get the Comet Club for Leroy."

I go in the squat block building on the airport access and shout, "CAB! UNITED TAXICAB!"

A row of regulars looks over their shoulders from the horse-shoe bar and then turns back to their drinks and smokes. "That'd be me, partner," a short, wiry guy in a cowboy hat and bolo tie says, his blond hair and beard half gray.

In the cab I say, "Where to, my friend?"

He says, "Man, why don't you take me to the Mecca. See if I can't find me an Indian gal to keep me warm tonight. What'd'ya think about that?"

"Sounds like a winner, man. You'll never know if you don't put your boat in the water."

"Ain't that the truth. Hey, where you takin' me? The Mecca's over that way. You got to go right here."

"All right, but it's over this way, too. Remember 'cause it's a one-way street I have to go up to . . ."

"Hell no, man. I've been up in this town thirty years. I know how to get to the Mecca. Don't go runnin' me around, jackin' up the meter."

"I wasn't runnin' you around. I told you I have to go to Cush-man before I can get there."

"Bullshit, I know which way the Mecca is. Don't be tryin' to fuck with me, 'cause I know better."

"You don't know shit, and I don't like people accusing me of cheating them."

"You know, I think I'll just get out here. I don't need this crap."

"Fuckin' A right you will." I said pulling the cab to the curb.

"How much I owe you?" he says pulling some bills from his chest pocket.

"Nothin'. I don't want your money. If you leave any in here I'll throw it out. Just get out."

When he's standing outside with the door open he says, "What's your name, man. I call this company all the time."

"Fuck you, man." And I gun the car and the door shuts itself and the guy disappears in the ice fog. *Remain calm*, I keep saying, restarting my breathing. I call in a minute later and get sent to Chena Courts, another pipeline Atco ensemble. I say *check*, but there's no one in number nine so I return to the car, fight through the radio, tell Smurf it's a dud. He says, "You're back one City."

Then he asks if I want one on Post, and I say check and drive to the visitor's center at the main gate of Fort Wainwright and park and go in to get a pass. This is a U.S. Army installation. The MP examines my paperwork and licenses behind bulletproof glass. Scrutinizes my face even though he's issued me at least fifty passes since he's been stationed here.

The base was established as a landing strip known as Ladd Field in the early forties. The nation was gearing up for war and the strategic location of Alaska was recognized by the U.S. military. One of the first uses of the base occurred after the German army invaded the Soviet Union in 1941. American flyers brought fighters and bombers from the Lower 48 to Ladd Field where their Russian counterparts took over and delivered them to the eastern front. The program was top secret. Unless you lived here.

I put the yellow pass on the dash and roll through the gate where the private security contractor examines my licenses and pass again. Then I call in on the radio and say, "Eagle Cab number 29, advise."

And Smurf says, "29 take it to 3206 room 231 bravo for Menendez."

And I say, "Check," and drive to the barracks. It's a sprawling three-story concrete cavity that houses close to a thousand soldiers. Most of them returned home from Iraq a couple months ago. Since then they've consumed enough alcohol to make up for the year they were gone.

The Stryker Brigade has only been here a few years. Before that the fort was a sleepy base where guys who liked the woods ended up. I remember the euphoria that swept the town those first couple years as a few hundred million dollars were spent building new housing and infrastructure. All the businesses in town were rocking and people couldn't cut down trees fast enough to build more big stores.

Now, a couple deployments later, the economic lift the brigade gives is no longer a bonus but a necessary slice of the pie if the town is to sustain the enlarged commercial base. A bunch of local stores have closed. Crime is up. And there's gonna be a spike in the number of single mothers in a few months.

The war economy. It's changed the town.

But this is nothing new. The paranoid Cold War climate that followed World War II military spending here and at Eielson Air Force Base, southeast of town, quadrupled Fairbanks's population in less than ten years. It's continued to be one of the primary economic engines driving us ever since.

I roll in front of the barracks and three shadowy forms holding the collars of jackets over faces dart from the glass entry to the cab.

"Holy shit, man, it's cold out there. You mind if I smoke?" the guy who grabbed the front says.

"Go for it. Where you headed?"

"How about San Diego?" the Hispanic guy in back says. The other two laugh.

"Sounds good to me, man. But I'm gonna need some money up front."

"Yeah, no shit, huh. No seriously, dog, take us to Kodiak Jack's."

"All right, man."

"So how long you been up here?" the Hispanic guy asks me.

"Twenty-five years, now."

"No shit?" There are exclamations of amazement from around the car. "How can you stand it? What do you do here?"

"Well, I like the country, like the woods, you know. This is as good as it gets."

"Shit, man, I like that country down in Texas. I can go outside and barbecue in it anytime I want. Plus there's like a hundred times more women down there."

"Yeah and there's way more hot chicks, too," the skinny, sharp-faced kid sitting behind me says. "Up here it's all fat chicks. And the ones who aren't fat are like the queens of the fuckin' universe, you know. Even the fat ones act like porn stars. Hell, I wouldn't even be lookin' at 'em back in Chicago. Here you gotta fight through like ten guys just to talk to 'em. I hate this fuckin' place." Everyone nods in agreement.

"It is beautiful in the summertime, though. I've seen some truly beautiful shit here in the summertime," the Hispanic guy says.

"Yeah, whenever it's not all fuckin' smoky from forest fires or raining, it's fabulous," the guy from Chicago says.

"Where you from?" I ask the guy in front.

"West Virginia."

"You like it there?"

"Yeah, I'm from the western part, in the Smoky Mountains. It's nice country, kinda like the mountains north of town. Not many jobs, though."

"You got deer there, huh?"

"Yeah dude, tons. Whitetails. My family eats a lot of venison. Wild turkey too."

"How's that?"

"Like anything, it's good if you do it right. If somebody knows what they're doing."

We're pulling into the lumpy parking lot of the bar.

"I'd eat some whitetail tonight," the Hispanic guy says.

"Fuck, I'll eat any kinda tail I can get my hands on," the Chicago guy says.

"Fifteen dollars," I say. They give me seventeen and shout *fuck* when they open the doors and run to the building.

Part of the reason I chose this place as my home was because of the women I met. Many live here because of a desire to be close to the natural world. They chose this place because, here, nature is not the exclusive domain of men. Western civilization arrived scarcely a century ago. Its presence must often sublimate itself to the demands of survival in the subarctic.

When I was younger I was drawn to the wildness of the women I'd meet here. To women who could shoot and butcher a moose or row class-four whitewater and then spend the rest of the evening drinking whiskey and getting down to some rock band while wearing dirty Carhartts and Xtratufs. But as the years have gone by, this has evolved. I still appreciate the bawdier aspects of femininity, but I also appreciate the vast reservoir of love in a woman's heart from which she can draw the patience necessary to compromise and co-evolve as circumstances require. And I need her toughness. Not tough like going out and getting in bar fights or anything. But tough in her ability to not just endure unpleasant circumstances but to work through them.

Maybe the kind of woman I'm drawn to is largely a reflection of myself, with the belief in herself to stand up to me when I'm wrong, or stand up for herself when she knows she's more right. But I also like it when she puts on a short dress and looks sexy and reinvigorates us both. My wife grew up on a working cattle ranch. She herded cattle on horseback, mended fence, and cut firewood in the winter. Yet her smile and the way her motion comes from her hips continues to turn me on.

My friend Ruth, from Venetie, is in her seventies. She tans moose hides by hand. She helps fill the smokehouse and keeps a smudge fire going while chopping wood for the house, which always has kids running through it. She feeds them, gives them a place to sleep whether they're descended from her or not. Maybe their parents are in Fairbanks for meetings or in jail or out hunting or drinking somewhere. Raised on the river between Arctic Village and Venetie, she knows that hunting and fishing and gathering—that living off the land—isn't a lifestyle choice. It's life.

The old ways are hard, but she seems happy breaking down the fibers in a moose hide using the same type of caribou leg-bone scraper her ancestors used a thousand years ago. She travels to other villages in the area, teaching tanning, skin-sewing, and the Gwich'in language. She worries about the future of her people and their gradual estrangement from the land but not for the illusion of the romance of the past. The occasional hunger and lack of access to medical care—not romantic.

When I see Ruth, working and smiling, I see transcendence. Not that it's not painful for her to work a hide with those fingers that have already worked so many, but I see an acceptance that her actions are resonating, joining some greater narrative. And I see her making a choice to enjoy it.

Ruth and her husband, Garry, often call when they're in town. Sometimes I pick them up in the cab, take them to bingo. Garry still likes to party a little, though. Ruth quit drinking years ago. She takes care of herself, and all those village kids, and in town she takes care of Garry too.

When we found out my wife was pregnant, there was never a question of going to the hospital. She wanted to be with the midwives at the natural birth center. Part of the reason was that she didn't want Cord to be born in a sterile delivery room and then taken away from her. She didn't want the drugs either. This might be her only birth, and she wanted to be conscious of this act that so many women throughout human history have expe-rienced. She wanted this communion with womanness as a way of better understanding who she was, what this life is.

At first I didn't really consider this much of a factor in our decision. I wanted Cord to be left with us, and I was inspired by the devotion of the midwives. These factors along with Michele's desire were all I needed to support this choice. But as I watched her body swell, as I massaged her hips that felt like they were about to burst from the pressure, I came to want her to have this experience she sought.

But in the delivery room with the fecund smell of amniotic fluid like a pink mist that clogged pores and slicked hair, with the spray of blood soaking through one absorbent cloth after an-other, I had to wonder. It took a long time for full dilation, and Cord was in the chute for a while. Michele was screaming from the effort of trying to push him out and was exhausting herself. Dana, the midwife, said we'd give it another twenty minutes, but then we'd have to go to the emergency room. She sent her assis-tant to start the van, but to Michele she said, "You can have your baby!" And I was shouting out these countdowns between her pushing, and her focus was narrowed to this fine point like the rest of us weren't even there.

Dana shone a large Maglite into Michele's birth canal. She pushed away a lock of sweaty hair and motioned for me to look inside my wife. At the top of her vagina was the slime-streaked dome of my son's head, punctuated with a few bolts of slicked dark hair. It was the first time I saw him. He slowly slid toward us over the course of the next hour. It was excruciating.

It was four in the morning. The thought that something could go wrong seeped into my consciousness for the first time since her water had broken that morning. For the first time, I realized that Michele was actually risking her life to bring this

child into the world. For the first time, I understood what a badass my wife truly was.

Then Dana was reaching inside her and pulling Cord free. He
was pissed, screaming nonstop. His soft skull was tube shaped
after being in the birth canal for so long. He was hungry but
unable to nurse because his little neck was jammed from being stuck. I was scared there was something wrong with him,
but eventually we got him to have some milk Michele squeezed
from her breasts by hand and I spoon-fed into his eager lips.
We slept a little, smeared with blood, amniotic fluid, and breast
milk. I didn't feel much of anything. I mean, I guess I loved him
then, but we were all too exhausted to think about that.

In the next few days his head assumed a normal shape. We
saw a chiropractor who gently manipulated the tiny vertebrae so
he could turn his head and nurse. I began to relax. Dana told us
that it had been a difficult birth in her experience; though from
her behavior in the delivery room, I would not have guessed.
She's been delivering babies in this town for thirty years, and
she was nothing but calm and solid.

And it's a wild world, full of passion and uncertainty. It's just
as well that his birth was an introduction to this. It's just as well
that it shocked us all into a posture of never having seen any of
this before.

Michele was back at work in two months' time.

I'm amazed by how much energy she devotes to her students.
How much time she spends grading their papers. She needs
them to take something from her that they can use. She's driven
by empathy and ferocity. It was her will that put the garden in
this year, even though we were working long hours finishing the
new house and repairing and cleaning the old one to ready it for
the rental market. Even though she's teaching summer school
and raising Cord. She's an inspiration to me, and I have to work
to be the same to her.

-:::-

On the radio Smurf is telling Cab 93 that he has a personal call, or PC, at the Bentley Mall.

"Well, I'm on another trip right now. Why don't you send another cab and let her know I'm sorry."

"She's your personal, 93; she already knows you're sorry. Next."

I get through after a couple others and let him know I'm red City. He sends me to 653 Eighth Avenue. I double-park beside a row of buried-in-snow cars in front of a gray split-level across from the state office building. I honk the horn, hop out, knock on the door, get back in, hit the meter. The woman comes out four minutes later. She's in her late twenties with thin brown hair and baby fat in her cheeks. She's wearing gray sweats a shade lighter than her eyes. "Take me to the Golden Nugget, please." She's crying.

"Okay."

"I'm sorry."

"It's okay, don't worry about it." I hand her a McDonald's napkin my relief driver left in the door well.

"Thank you. I'm just, I was supposed to go out with my boyfriend tonight, but he turned off his phone, and he's probably out having sex with another girl right now and . . ." She dabs at her eyes. "And I'm just gonna get a room for the night. Figure out what I'm gonna do."

I pull up to the door. "You seem like a good person. It'll be okay."

"Thanks. What do I owe you?"

"Two bucks."

"I'm sorry I can't afford to give you a tip. I know it's a short trip."

"Don't worry about it. Have a good night."

"Yeah. Good night."

"Cab 62 could you repeat that address for me again, please?" a whiny voice asks.

"Uh, I don't know 62. What'd you write down?" Smurf replies.

"I didn't write it down."

"Yeah, well, maybe you should've, huh? Next."

A mass of mutilated static detonates inside the car. I find a seam in the noise and get sent to the downtown parking garage. "And by the way 62, you're going to 169 on Four, number three. Write that down! I don't have time to be repeating myself every time I give you a trip."

I pull into a parking space behind a red-and-gray bus in a slot on the Lacey Street side of the garage. There are people getting off the bus with duffel bags and backpacks. One of them walks to my cab. "Hey there, you here to pick up Stick?" the man drawls.

"Yep, I am. You need the trunk?"

"Nah, I can just throw it in back here. I'm goin' out to the airport?"

"All right, no problem." A terrible noise blurts from the radio followed by the shrieking beep. We slap our hands over our ears.

"Goddamn, what the hell was that?" Stick asks.

I explain to him about the FCC.

"That sounds like our government, all right. I'm a gold miner and you should see the hoops they make us jump through. You can't even fire up a piece of equipment without gettin' an environmental 'impasse' statement. I'm from Montana, and that's completely shut down. I have to come up here to work."

"Is that where you're headin' now?"

"Yeah, back to the family for a couple weeks and then back to the mine for a month."

"That's a hell of a commute."

"Yeah. Well, at least I'm workin'. Price of gold stays where it is, this job'll last awhile too. Got a family to support."

I drop him at the departures door, and he tells me to keep the twenty, and Smurf tells me to pick up at Pike's, a bar-restaurant-hotel on the way back to town.

I pull into the parking lot on the Chena River, just upriver from the confluence with the Tanana. An ice bridge leads from the lot across the river to the University West subdivision. Snow machine tracks arc off the ice road to head up and down the river and into the woods on either side. Like wormholes to the wilderness that rolls away in all directions from this pinprick island of the twenty-first century.

I pull up to the door and a guy in his late twenties walks from the log bar to the cab. He throws a duffel in the back, and the car sags to the side it lands on with a clanking of steel tools. He gets in the front. He's wearing an Arctic Cat snow machine jacket. Pulls off a sweatshirt hood and runs his fingers through combed back brown hair, rubs the few days' stubble on his chin. "Hey, take me home, Twenty-Seventh. I've been up north for six weeks." *Up north* means Prudhoe Bay, the oil fields on the shore of the Arctic Ocean. He's been at work.

"All right, welcome home," I say.

"Thanks. Hey, uh, I don't suppose you know where to get anything, do you?"

I look at him. See a beat guy after a long shift. "I don't know. What're you looking for?"

"Oh, something from South America, powder."

I don't really like the cocaine economy. There's too much blood and too many feet on the product by the time it makes its way to Alaska. It feels dirty. But gasoline and alcohol are pretty dirty too. And this guy'll probably find some whether I help him or not. And if they'd make it legal and tax it, this guy's money could be helping people overcome addictions rather than funding drug cartels. And it's his money. And I do know where to get some.

I say, "I know a guy who's got fifties and hundreds. You'd have to give me the money then wait someplace. That's all I know about." The guy is opening his wallet, the crisp edges of new hundreds. "And the cab'll be about fifty bucks in addition to this."

"So about $270 altogether. That'd get me two and pay your fare."

"Yeah, that'd do it."

"You're not gonna fuck me, are ya' bro?"

"No. Trust me or don't." I look at him and smile and return my eyes to the road.

"Okay, here you go." He hands me the money. I take it and put it in the inside pocket of my canvas coat.

"So where you wanna go?"

"Just take me home. What'll you be like fifteen minutes?"

"Maybe twenty."

"All right." He tells me he's got two weeks off. He's going down to the Alaska Range to ride snow machines. He's going to drink and chase women and sleep.

I let him out and take Cushman north, across Airport, over the bridge to the Miner's Home Saloon, just down the road from the Big I. The door is at the northern end of a long low concrete building. Home to a pizza joint, a barber shop, a liquor store. The neon glows miasmic through the fog from wide, short windows on either side of the door. I can hear "Freebird" on the jukebox. The volume doubles as I go through the first door, into the entryway, and quadruples when I enter the bar.

The fog rolls in behind me and washes over the old plank floor. There're two guys wearing Hell's Angels jackets in back

shooting pool. A thin couple in black jeans and canvas mukluks throws darts at the far wall. The horseshoe bar is half full
of heavy, unshaven men and skinny women shouting over the
music. I catch a shred concerning some sheet rock that had been
hung poorly. "Had to twist in every screw by hand." Hear a guy
ask, "Why does a pussy have hair?" and then, "To hide the hook."
Insulted shrieks of laughter and the sound of a small fist hitting
leather.

I head to the end of the bar where a short, muscular guy
with long, curly black hair sits next to the free phone. He has
prominent facial bones, like Native Americans of the northern
plains, and the flesh hangs from them loosely beneath artificial-
ly tanned skin. It gives him a look of relaxed incredulity. He's
watching me with dark eyes and his high forehead is tilted back.
I take the stool next to him and put my boots on the heated brass
foot rail. "How's business?"

"The colder, the better." He smiles. He's wearing a pound of
gold. Raw gobs of nuggets with ivory beads and bear claws on
gold chains around his neck and welded onto the rings on his
thick, short fingers and all over the watch and band and hanging from his ears. He has two Corvettes and a half dozen snow
machines. He sleeps with a different woman every night.

"I know the feeling." Show him the two bills folded in my
palm. "Can I get a couple reds off you?"

He takes a pack of Marlboros from the right breast pocket of
his denim vest, which he wears unbuttoned over his bare bronze
chest. He opens it and shakes out two folded pieces of glossy paper cut from a porno hot rod mag. I hand him the money with
my right and take the pieces of paper with my left, place them in
the inside pocket. He keeps Marlboro lights on the other side. In
case somebody wants a half.

"You need anything?" the bartender asks from over my shoulder. I hand her my coffee cup and ask for a refill, which she gives me for free. I thank her and the guy and return to the cab.

The guy is waiting when I get back to his house. He hops in the cab, and I hand him the pieces of paper. "Wow, thanks man, that's awesome. You, uh, you want any of this?"

I think about it but say no.

"All right, man. Have a good one."

"You too." He disappears in fog. I go back City. Smurf puts me three. I take out a sandwich and do the numbers. It's ten thirty and I've got $175 booked. So I'm up $30 after five and a half hours.

My phone rings and I answer it. It's Michele, home with Cord after the handoff at the school where she works. "Hey, hon, you got a minute?"

"Uhh, yeah, what's up?"

"Oh, not much. I talked to Tim today and it sounds like the district isn't going to approve our contract."

Even though she's been working without one for over six months. Before Michele and I got together, I didn't understand what a politicized job teaching is. But every time the budget gets tight, people clamor for the blood of educators. It's only gotten worse since the recession. Our legislature is packed with right-wingers who seem to think that teachers should work for food swaps and love of the job. Meanwhile, the ranks of the district administration swell with high-paying jobs in human resources and the curriculum department.

"Yeah, damn, that sucks. Maybe you guys should open up a hot dog stand or something." I swerve around a section of broken exhaust pipe in the road.

"Yeah, thanks, I'll bring that up. I mean it's bad enough the legislature cut our funding again and we're going to have to teach bigger classes next year. Then they say patronizing crap in the paper like it shouldn't matter to really good teachers how many kids they have to teach."

She currently has thirty students or more in each of her classes.

"Maybe Senator Kelly could come in and give you a hand with those freshmen in fifth hour."

"Right. But get this: The kids, without any prompting from anybody, are organizing a protest in support of us. They've been making signs at home so they don't get accused of using public resources. And they're going to stand on Airport Way after school tomorrow."

"Wow, that's pretty awesome."

"I know. Honestly, I got a little teary when I heard about it. But there was an article about it in the paper."

"Uh-oh."

"So, of course, I had to go online and read the comments."

"Pretty ugly?"

"It's hard to believe some of the people in this town. They're calling the kids 'brainwashed stooges.' They're accusing teachers of doing the brainwashing. Honestly, with class sizes as big as they are, I don't know how anybody could find the time to do any brainwashing. It's such bullshit."

"Maybe we just have to become a community of dumb asses in order for people to appreciate the value of public education."

"Yeah, but by then we might be too ignorant to know the difference."

Smurf sends the first two City cabs to Youth Sports Bingo, and after a short pause sends me there too, tells me to pick up Mary.

I'm reaching for the mike, sandwich in the free hand, turning onto Noble, steering with my knees, and the phone tucked between head and neck when a black pickup careens out of the fog on a collision course with my door. I scream and drop the phone and the sandwich and punch the cab. The truck honks and swerves and misses me by a foot.

I grab the mike and check the trip, rescue the sandwich and the phone.

"Are you okay? What happened?" Michele asks.

"Oh, traffic. I should probably go. I'll be home soon."

"Okay, well, be safe, hon. We love you."

As my heart rate returns to normal I think about being a part of a family, about the bachelorhood I left behind. Primarily, what I feel is an urgent need to not fuck this up. I mean it would've been one thing to be a bad dad when I was twenty. Honestly, I don't see how it could've gone any other way. But if that happens at my age, I don't know if I'll be able to live with myself.

There are people waving in the street in front of the bingo hall. I recognize them. They're the local bingo babes, and none of them are going farther than five dollars, but Mary goes to Sandvik Road, twelve dollars away. She's the queen of the bingo babes. Plus she's cool.

She's between the two sets of doors, an eighty-year-old five-foot-tall Athabaskan woman with stylishly coifed silver hair. She walks to the cab making efficient use of a cane with a spiked fitting over the end for sticking in the ice. I get out and open the door for her.

"So how'd the bingo go?" I ask.

"Oh, I make enough for my cab ride that's all. But I won twice this month, already. Maybe I'll try again tomorrow. I just like to go and see people, really."

"See anybody interesting?"

"Some people from Fort Yukon. That's where I'm from. But I haven't been there in twenty years. Everybody from Fort Yukon comes to bingo sooner or later, though. Really, though, I was from Chalkytsik."

"On the Black River?"

"Yes, but we were nomadic too. We moved around all over that country.

"I remember when I was a girl. My mother marry her third husband, and he was not a good man. He try to abuse us, me and my sister, you know. He try to touch me and one time he raped my sister, and he held a knife up against her face and tell her that he cut her all up if she ever tell anybody.

"One time I was with him in camp, and he came and got into my bed. I jumped up real fast and said 'Oh I have to go to the bathroom.' And I got the gun and put it on him, and we sat like that all night.

"He tell me I don't need the gun anymore, that I can put it away 'cause he's better now. But I said, 'No, I don't believe you.' And I tell him to get the dogs ready. We were traveling by dog sled then. I held that gun at him all the way back home.

"When we got there my grandmother ask me what was the matter. So I tell her and she told me, 'You go to bed now 'cause you gonna wake up early.' And she get me up real early the next day and tell me get dressed. And she put her hands on my shoulders and said 'You remember those three long lakes you pass yesterday?' I said, yeah.

"'You going to go past those and go this way.' She was doing with her arm like this 'cause she was speaking our native language, and we don't have word for right. She said, 'You're going to follow that trail to Black River where your auntie stay.' The whole time she talking to me I feel power coming into me from her hands. She was a shaman, you know. Then she tell me get going.

"I walked all day, but you know I don't remember any of that walking. I only remember seeing my auntie and she ask me 'How was your trip?'

"I say 'I don't know. I don't remember any of it.' We looked at my boots. I was wearing those canvas mukluks and they were completely dry and this was in April when everything was wet. My auntie say that my grandma had made me a wolf for that trip, and I believe her 'cause I walk all that way and I don't remember any of it and my boots were dry when I got there."

We were coasting into the handicapped space in front of the door to her building. "That's a great story."

"I been thinking I'd like to tell that one to somebody. That one and I got some others, too. Maybe somebody could write them down while I still remember. Is twelve dollars okay?"

"Yeah, that's good, thanks." And soon, Mary too is gone in the fog.

Author's note: Although many of the events recounted in this story occurred in 2012, many of them also occurred in the 21 years that preceded 2012.

Mulligan, 2006

WILL AND I FLEW from Fairbanks to the south slope of the far-thest north mountain range. We wore earplugs to dull the roar of the twin props. Half a mile below, tundra sprawled toward the horizon, a fractal flood of crimson, sage, gold, and bone. Lichen, blueberry, willow, and spruce rooted in the abandoned pathways of ancient rivers, the depressions of reclaimed lake-beds, the rubble of mountains laid low by time. The land at altitude, sinuous, like a current in a nascent universe, drawn by dark energy.

Will sat in the seat across the aisle. The cabin was too short for us to stand up. The bald pate of the pilot's head shone like a ghost in the glass that gazed out into the cloud-whisked blue sky. We were going to Arctic Village, a small Athabaskan communi-ty in the eastern Brooks Range. Will's friend Sara was a teacher there. Will had helped her move there several years earlier, and he'd been strongly drawn to the country and became friends with some of the locals. He'd been returning annually to hunt and explore. This year he invited me.

I had met Will in the eighties. We were bussing tables at Dante's Den, an upscale food court atop Purgatory Ski Resort in Colorado. We earned minimum wage and a lift pass. We skied to and from work, figured we'd go to Alaska and become commercial fishermen at the end of the season.

Sam, a wiry gray-haired local, and I mixed fuel on the gravel boat launch beside the East Fork of the Chandalar River near Arctic Village. From this point near the Canadian border the mountains fold westward more than seven hundred miles to the Chukchi Sea. It was late August; the nearest road a hundred miles away.

Five-gallon gas cans and two-cycle oil containers lay on the black rocks. Sam, bush chemist, measured gas and mix using cut-off cans as beakers. "This one just need little bit more, I think. How 'bout that one?"

"I don't think we've done that one yet."

We ran out of mix. Sam walked to the shade of some willows and spoke in Gwich'in with a stooped elder. The gas cost seven bucks a gallon, more than twice the price in Fairbanks. David Lee, Sam's nephew, brought more two-cycle oil on a borrowed four-wheeler and then set out on other errands.

Sam and I finished mixing the gas and stored it in the stern of Johnny James's eighteen-foot riverboat. David returned with a bag of fry bread and a plate of boiled meat—a moose he'd shot on the Junjik River two days earlier. "I give it all to some women. They make sure everybody get some, huh." David was twenty-five.

The moose was good. Some of it got stuck in my broken molar.

We poured gas into a cavity of the fifty-horse Evinrude where the carburetor was thought to be. David hooked the negative terminal to the battery and the motor caught on the eleventh try. "We got to remember to unhook the battery, huh. Otherwise it go dead," he said.

I'd known these guys less than twenty-four hours. Will knew Sam from past excursions in this country. We'd run into him that morning. When he heard we were going for sheep above Timber Lake he told us he'd be ready in an hour. "I'm packed already, man. I keep a backpack with a week of food for three men. I haven't been there for over twenty year."

Johnny James was Will's main contact in the village. He was Sara's new boyfriend. She was thin, strong, and puckish. She had long brown hair, a dog team, a 30.06. She'd told me a little about her work. "Yeah, there's a lot of absences. I mean it's cool if they're going out hunting or fishing with their families. I support that. But sometimes they'll go to Fairbanks for like a month and not even tell me and then just show back up out of the blue. Sometimes they just hang out playing video games. But I like it here. We finally got a third teacher. And there's a woman that teaches Gwich'in, now. I've taken some killer trips. Caught some caribou."

We'd been staying with Sara and Johnny for two days in a small cabin fronting the dirt four-wheeler trail that comprised the village's road system. Johnny had recruited David Lee to drive his boat as far up the Junjik River as it could go. From there, we'd hike the rest of the way to Timber Lake, where Will and Johnny awaited, having flown there earlier in the day.

We headed upriver, north, in high water. The air was fat with sun and freshly washed by a month of rain. The east fork was slate blue, swollen to the tops of the banks. Probing fingers of boreal forest grew sparsely from the flow's alluvium. Due north, Nichenthraw Mountain was dusted with snow from the storm.

David sat before a steering station midship starboard. Sam and I sat on folding chairs on a gray sheet of three-quarter-inch plywood, laid across the aluminum ribs of the hull. The green paint on the gunwales was faded and cracked. It was an older boat, long and narrow. Open air and the wind was cool.

"You see that?" Sam said. "'Cause all that rain, rivers full, too deep for that jet. Move too slow." He spoke to no one in particular. "You got to stay in the channel. No! No, you never slow down once you get speed."

"I am driving here, huh," David said.

"Okay, you be the captain," and then to me, laughing through the hole where his lower incisors had once been, "I'm just tired of being a private."

David directed us to reorganize gear in an attempt to trim the boat. He shouted over the drone of the outboard as we tossed around fuel tanks, backpacks, guns, and a black lab named Otter.

The rusty chairs weren't exactly accommodating, but occasionally Sam and I sat next to each other. "I like moose few time a year, caribou few time a year, but for me sheep is the best, man. I been hunting sheep twenty-seven years, now, only one time I get skunked."

I tried to imagine him at thirty. Smoothed the murder of crow's feet stamped around his eyes from a lifetime of squinting against the sun and wind. Added a layer of supple muscle and subcutaneous fat beneath his hide. I saw a strong handsome young guy returning from military service in the early seventies, his eyes quick and alert, eager to return to his mountains. "That's pretty good." I said.

"Oh yeah, you watch, I see sheep five hundred yards that one is mine, huh. Don't you worry, we gonna be eatin' us some sheep ribs real soon." He grinned big.

We turned west, up the Junjik River. Dun mountains rose two to three thousand feet on both sides of us like fists punched through from below.

The limestone they're composed of precipitated, grain by grain, from a warm sea 360 to 300 million years ago, settling into beds that grew more than two thousand feet thick at the bottom of this sea. Amphibians ruled the world, and the south coast of Alaska lay roughly where the north one is now. Shale was deposited atop the limestone. The land to the north was thrust up and hundreds of feet of sand and gravel were dumped on top.

In the age of reptiles, 180 million years ago, heavy oceanic crust to the northwest was being consumed in a subduction zone, becoming a magmatic arc that was obducted, or pushed over, the lighter continental crust. For the next 60 million years it shoved the layered beds up into mountains.

The land to the north ripped 120 million years ago. Maybe this was northern Alaska breaking away from the Canadian Arctic. No one knows for sure. Nobody was there. Nobody was anywhere. The mountains eroded into gaping amphitheaters and plunging gullies studded with spires.

The language of geology, or of poetry, seemed inadequate. "Wow, nice country," I said.

"Oh you ain't seen nothin' yet, dude. Wait till you get farther up here. There's mountains like, BOOM, comin' up right next to the boat," David said. He grimaced slightly, as if he were about to strike something with a hammer. He drove standing up, with 50 Cent rapping from the headphones of his Discman. He held a camcorder and narrated as we cut a thin wake through the gorge.

Soon he pulled over on the north bank. "You guys gotta get out," he said. "The boat's too heavy with you."

We stepped from the camo bow into the brush.

"I'll meet you at that camp below glacier," David said to Sam before zooming up the shallow river unencumbered. Sam shrugged, shouldered his rifle, and smiled. "Let's go. I know the way," he said before knifing into the snarl of willow.

I lunged after him. It was all I could do to keep up as we trudged through deep moss and tussock-riven muskeg. His .223

hung on his shoulders. Hazy sunbeams shifted between white spruce.

We stopped to examine some fresh grizzly shit. "Looks like he's been eating some roots or something," I said.

"Yeah, roots. Here, I show you. But stay farther behind me, okay? Sometime I might have to jump back really far, okay." He carried his rifle in his hands.

"Okay." I chambered a round, clicked the safety back on.

"Oh, here this one," he said, dropping to his knees in the moss, pointing to two thin yellow stalks. He dug into the bryophytes and pulled out a fat knuckle-sized root. "See, this the one the bear eating, it's good, pull off that brown and eat it." It was good. Indian potato, harvested in spring and fall. Roast, fry, or eat it raw.

"When we get to camp," Sam said, "I'm going to grab David, and then you punch him in the stomach, okay?"

"Uh, I guess, why?"

"'Cause we got to walk all that way, and you hear him he just drive the boat around, take him maybe thirty minutes."

"Okay, then it sounds good, unless he's got a fire and some food for us."

"Okay then, amigo, we give him that chance."

Three hours later we walked into camp. There was a fire and two moose ribs two feet long were propped beside it on sticks. Sam whipped up some mac and cheese. We laughed at a story about Bobby Charley. He'd stayed at this camp alone the year before and shot a small caribou and then ate the entire animal before the rest of the hunting party returned from upriver. It was an act that could have caused some tension if the others had returned empty-handed or if Bobby was known more for his hunting ability than his appetite. But as it happened it was just a good story, a thing as essential as anything else to a trip.

The sun set in a gory northwestern haze after being up for seventeen hours and fifteen minutes, a nine-minute loss from the day before. We slept on the ground.

The next day, we attached a fifteen-gallon gas barrel to the outboard and left a small cache of food tied high up in a tree so the bears couldn't get it.

David fired the motor, but when he gave it gas it died. Sam noticed that the lower unit was loose, so we disassembled it. One of the bolts was stripped. "See how this one got two washer on it? That mean he know it stripped, and he just had it rebuilt in Fairbanks, too. Fuckin' lazy mechanic," David said.

Reassembled, the motor still sputtered, died. We blew out fuel lines and removed spark plugs, cleaned them furiously, burned them on the fire, put them back in. No go. We considered beginning our hike from there.

"If we weren't using that fuel barrel when we drove here last night, maybe we're not drawing fuel properly," I said. "Maybe we should try one of those cans we were using yesterday."

David seemed to ignore me, messed with the carb, reexamined the fuel line. We got ready to go backpacking. Then: "Hey, Sam, hand me one of those other cans, I wanna try one more thing." David transferred gas into the smaller can, primed it, fired the motor. He gave it gas, and the boat jumped at its moorings. "That seem little better."

Underway at last, Sam and I lay on our stomachs in the bow. I stared up the unwinding river, lulled by the smooth hum of the outboard. David made the navigation seem effortless, but soon he was pulling over again, telling us to get out. Otter, the black lab, watched us curiously from the stern of the boat as he pulled away.

Sam and I headed across a gravel bar. David called on the radio asking how long before we caught up. Sam said, "Tell him just wait, we'll be there when we get there. Turn that thing off."

The smooth gray stones under our feet were the size of grizzly skulls. Undulations of black sand covering the rocks marked shallows in dry channels. Tufts of juniper and wild grass sprouted from drifts of dirt.

"That David Lee, sometime I think he not all there. He listen to that headphone, take those pictures. Yesterday, he hit rock while he take those pictures, I don't know."

We moved over low benches, passed a jumbled rock outwash where a receding tongue of ice had left a pile of moraine ten thousand years ago.

David met us below the confluence with Water Creek. "Fuck man, I left my radio back on that hill where I waited for you. I was tryin' to get ahold of Johnny and them."

"Well, we've got another radio, but if you wanna go back and get it . . ."

"I don't think we got enough gas . . ."

"You talk to Johnny?"

"No. Nothin'."

We rode for a while, hopped out, walked another hour. David returned, having shuttled our gear to a dry slough below Spring Creek where we'd camp.

Dinner was basic, protein and carbs: moose ribs and Spam, noodles and pilot crackers. I had to cut my meat into tiny pieces; my broken molar was infected. Sam and David noticed the swelling and led me to a fat spruce tree, amber pitch seeping from every pore. "Here, this one the right color," Sam said, handing me a malleable piece of the pitch. "Like this," he said, showing me how to mold it with his hands. "You put it in that broken tooth. It keep the food and air out. Kill that infection."

"Yeah, I have to do that one time," David Lee added. "I leave it there one month not have no problem. It just kill the nerve, you know."

"Kill the tooth," Sam said. "But it make it stop hurting."

That sounded good to me.

The next morning the swelling was gone, the pain a fraction of what it had been.

The boat was out of gas and far up a river still heavy with rain. The sun had burned the stratosphere clear of vapor by ten o'clock as we crossed the delta of Spring Creek. Its braided channels cut down from the mountains to the north where its headwaters gathered on the continental divide, ten miles away as the raven soars. From that point one could walk through Carter Pass and down the north buttress of the range onto a treeless plain rolling 120 miles to the Arctic Ocean.

Seventy million years ago, when the earth's climate was warmer and an interior seaway reached from the Arctic Ocean to the Gulf of Mexico, the plain was covered in dense forests. Metasequoia trees towered above the steaming canopy. Peat bogs stretched between the rivers. Dinosaurs foraged and hunted: a three-ton, forty-foot-long plant eater known as Edmontosaurus was the most common. Its main predator was a three-ton, thirty-foot-long cousin of *T. rex* known as *Albertosaurus*. Over that pass these days, the flora and fauna were very similar to ten thousand years ago: wolves, bears, caribou, endless tundra, bowhead whales bending in the Beaufort Sea.

Eight thousand feet beneath the surface is a porous bed of sandstone called the Sadlerochit Formation, the stratum of sand and gravel dumped onto the Lisburne Limestone 245 million years ago. It was buried beneath a thousand feet of mud rich in organic matter, presumably marine life from a Triassic sea, which was compressed into shale by the matter deposited atop it. The shale was further compressed and heated by the action of the planet's core, two thousand miles below. Overlain by nonporous siltstone, it slow cooked, like a buried pig at a summer solstice party, for millions of years. By the time the Brooks Range rose to the south, it was crude oil that was injected into the Sadlerochit Reservoir by the crushing force of the orogeny.

Just to the west is Prudhoe Bay, largest oil field in the history of North America. There was probably oil over Carter Pass, too, under the coastal plain of the Arctic National Wildlife Refuge. My friends, the Gwich'in Athabaskans, were opposed to its development. They were often cited by opponents of drilling in their efforts to keep big oil out. The Gwich'in were worried about the effects development could have on the caribou migrations, which they have depended on for thousands of years. The extraction of oil is a messy, toxic process. The epicenter of any ANWR activity could take place in an area where the caribou come to have their calves in the spring.

The Gwich'in see the sharp contrast between the wealth their Inupiaq neighbors have reaped from Prudhoe and their own daily lives. They realize if they are again excluded from the proceeds of development and the caribou don't come, then Arctic Village might cease to exist. There's little economic activity, no sewage and no fire or police protection. It's not the place to be if you want a steady job. However, if what you want is to live upon the country where the bones of thousands of years of your ancestors still lie just below the frozen ground; if you wish to live in a manner more in tune with those ancestors and the land, then there's no other place.

-:::-

I was hustling to keep up again. They traveled fast and light. On a knoll below Spring Creek we ate more Spam and pilot bread. Sam and David were going up Spring Creek to hunt sheep and said I should go with them. They were apprehensive about me continuing to Timber Lake alone.

"I have a canoe at Timber Lake, plans, a bro who'll freak the fuck out if I don't show up," I said. They had reduced the equation to a beautiful simplicity. Either do it the way we planned or do it differently. Do not be distracted by the preparations that have been made, or the expectations of others. It was a form of freedom that I could fully appreciate, if not participate in.

Sam's eyes danced. He licked his lips, the lower incisor gap a small piece of a big smile. "The finest meat in the world," he said. "And when I see one, that night we gonna be eatin' better than the president. I can taste those ribs already."

We tried the radio a final time before taking our separate trips. "Hey, goddammit, Johnny, you gotta copy?" Sam said.

"Yeah, I hear you."

"Oh, good! Good to hear you guys. Where are you?"

"I'm on a mountain with this white guy. We're looking at some sheep."

We exchanged fist bumps and high fives. Plans were reorganized. We decided to go to Timber Lake together.

Maroon and olive lichens crawled up the southern flanks of Little Njoo Mountain to top fins of dolomite. Talus cliffs swept three thousand feet from the tundra's edge, reaching with broken fingers for the flung gravity of space. Below in the valley, creeks drew the mountains into the curves of the Junjik River, everything moving down and away.

We passed a thin lake between the base of a hill and Little Njoo. It reflected the mountain and the sky. A lone white swan skated motionlessly across its surface. "Sure is pretty," Sam said. I agreed.

"We got to keep goin', though, huh," Robert said. "We still got a long way to go."

We dropped into spruce and camped on a bluff above the Junjik. Fire. Mac and moose.

A boreal owl cut soundlessly through the twilit penumbra and grabbed a branch above camp.

"Ninja," David hissed respectfully.

"Ah, ninja," Sam whispered.

He watched us silently.

Sam wiped down his semiautomatic rifle, smiling. It was an old blue steel gun with a wood stock. It bore little resemblance to the AR-15s used in so many mass shootings. Except for that thirty-round clip sticking out of it. And the outline of a second clip in the cargo pocket of his camo pants.

"You like that rifle, Sam?" I asked.

"Oh yes. I have this one for over twenty year, now. I'm real accurate with it up to about three hundred yards. After that, you know, you just look where the last one went and adjust for your next. This is my number one gun, man."

"What's up with all those bullets, though. You really need, what, sixty bullets."

"Eighty bullets, I got a twenty clip in my pack. You never know, man. You could run into thirty wolves out here. We could get stuck out here for a while. Like if that boat give us trouble. I can shoot a duck or ptarmigan with this one, too. Or if a bear come I might have to shoot it a bunch of times. One time I even shoot a fish with this one. This gun will keep you alive out here, man. And ammo's real cheap." He grinned sagely.

We smoked the last of the bud brought for this leg of the journey. Not to worry, though, because my friends had saved every
roach, scraped every smidgeon of resin. I was impressed.

The next morning I got the fire going and had coffee and oats
ready by the time Sam and David rolled out of the moss. David's
military surplus pants were in shreds. They were purchased too
big in the waist and worn gangsta style, hanging low off his bare
ass. I'd been impressed with his ability to climb over rocks and
fallen trees with the pants restricting the movement of his legs,
but his efforts had taken a toll on the pants. He had on a T-shirt
and an old flannel. It was below freezing. He squeezed closer to
the fire, got too close, and the flames raced up his pants. He suf-
focated them with his Sponge Bob blanket. He was okay.

We hiked for several hours and radioed Will and Johnny
when their base camp was in sight; they headed down to meet us.

I made bacon, eggs, and fried potatoes with the food that
had been flown in. Afterward, we cut slices of pot butter and ate
them on pilot crackers.

We laid prostrate to the sun on the tundra, cupped within
the headwaters of the Junjik watershed. The various strands of
the river poured from the mountains around us, following paths
carved by Pleistocene glaciers.

I closed my eyes and felt the flow of space and time through
the valley. Saw the glaciers building, ebbing, surging. Saw them
vanish and knew that mammoths had walked here after the ice
peeled away. Realized that relatives of my companions hunted
for them here. I looked around, not completely convinced that I
wouldn't see one trudging off to its extinction.

Otter, the black lab, had stolen a wayward piece of pot butter, and she was completely fucked up. She staggered and wove

and then crashed in the hot sun. We moved her into the shade of spruce trees as shadows came and went, put a bowl of water near her mouth. She put her nose into the water, forgot to drink, inhaled, and lazily snorted out a stream. She laid her head back and stared curiously into the pure blue sky. We laughed, unable to hold it; her expression seemed wounded, as though each guffaw was a psychic dagger.

When Will and Johnny James made it to camp I was making cowboy coffee on the stove. Johnny stood about five feet two; black hair fell to his waist from a worn black bandanna. Black accusatory eyes glared under an edificial brow, vicious cheekbones jutted wide. He wore a torn sweatshirt emblazoned with SKATE PUNKS. Will liked to tease him: "Johnny James, I think you missed your calling. You should've gone to Hollywood and made cowboy and Indian movies."

Johnny stared into me, said, "The fuck's that?" and tilted his head at the stove.

"Makin' some coffee," I smiled.

"Fuck's the matter with fire?" He grinned wryly, gestured to the flames licking the pit.

"Nothing, I started it. I guess the stove seemed a little easier."

"Hmmmph," he said. "Why don't you go get some water. I'll make us dinner." He was pushing from the start. I decided not to play.

"Sure, soon as I make this coffee."

When I returned with the water, Johnny was pulling potatoes, carrots, noodles, and Spam from a locking white plastic box the size of a large aquarium. I set the water down beside him and asked what was for dinner.

"Mulligan," said Johnny, glaring at me as I smoked one of his Marlboros.

The food I'd packed for this leg of the journey had been shoved in the box along with Will's contributions. When it came out of the box it was mulligan—everyone's food, together with what Sam had brought, feeding five now.

The sun eased behind the mountains to the southwest, bruising the sky a salmon hue. Otter ran away from camp, overcome by paranoia. David went to get her, and she tried to bite him then disappeared into the night. A wolf howled down the valley.

I was thinking how, when we had left Arctic Village, I was more interested in seeing the country than getting a sheep, but now, given the paucity of our food supplies, we kind of needed to get one. Will didn't seem bothered by this. In fact I'd say that the prospect exhilarated him. This situation is the kind of thing he lives for. Grocery stores piss him off after a while. He resents the security they seemingly offer as a façade obscuring our true animal nature.

"I almost went after them," Will said of the thirteen sheep he and Johnny had seen. "But Johnny said wait. He was right, I didn't even have a sleeping bag, and they were on this massive mountain behind the one we were on."

"In 1975 I bring boat up here. We shoot four ram," Sam said. "I never come back since. Sure is beautiful." He said it without a trace of self-consciousness, his voice ranging between a smooth tenor and squeaky alto. He was looking at the fading blue shadow of dusk cloaking the mountains. I liked that he wasn't afraid to appreciate beauty in the world. Didn't give a shit whether anyone thought he was tough enough or not.

We slept in and woke with limbs still heavy from the butter. Johnny divvied out food from the box and handed me the butt of a Marlboro.

"So you didn't bring no cigs, huh?"

"Smoked 'em on the way up."

"We'll have to ration, huh." He pulled a Ziploc from a pocket half full of butts.

David went to the creek to look for his dog. He found her crouched, suspicious in some willow. She slunk back into camp eyeing us warily. I felt bad for Otter. She hadn't asked to come along, and there was not much food for her. When I think of black lab country, I see lakes with ducks surrounded by deciduous trees. Not this brutal mountain range far north of the Arctic Circle. David seemed to expect her to fend for herself, go wolf or something.

Around the breakfast fire I asked if anyone wanted to help me carry my tent and stove and was met with silence.

"The ground is good enough," David said.

The day's heat built as we hiked north, up the valley of a nameless tributary that we crossed and recrossed on slick, shifting rocks, pausing to empty boots and wring out socks. We drank from shallow pools in the tundra and carried empty water bottles.

The valley widened, and the stream broke apart and vanished into its sources. The Labrador tea and willow grew shorter and sparser until the vista was only broken stone and lichen, a thousand shades of red, yellow, and green ladled over the valley floor.

I recalled that back in the fifties when atmospheric testing of nuclear weapons was conducted in Alaska and across the Bering Sea in the former Soviet Union radioactive fallout contaminated lichens all over the Arctic. The lichens were eaten by caribou, which were consumed by humans—a disastrous poisoning of the food chain. Cancer rates for this generation of Athabaskans were closer to what you'd expect to find in a uranium mining town in Utah.

This coming after the great epidemics of the early part of the twentieth century. And the forced separation of many children from their parents to attend racist boarding schools. Not to mention the disproportionate numbers of young Native men who've died in this country's wars over the last hundred years.

A breeze coursed through the valley bearing a blizzard of cotton grass tufts that, as in an impressionist painting, lent the sunlight a sense of motion. Just beyond the mountain vantage where Will and Johnny had spied the sheep, we stopped at the last stand of spruce, the northern timberline.

We had a fire. Johnny made more mulligan. I noted that you could land an airplane in the valley. "Yeah, a 747 with tundra tires," David added.

After coffee and a cigarette butt, we cached some gear and began hiking around a small mountain seemingly dropped into the middle of a pass leading north to a narrow high valley. "We go this way to get back behind the mountain," Sam whispered. "Those sheep, they got the finest eye in the world."

We stopped occasionally to glass the earth rising sheer around us. Someone remarked that it looked like we'd stumbled into Afghanistan. "Maybe Bin Laden hiding round here someplace," David added.

Silence rushed into the wake of his words.

In golden willow and orange dwarf birch, we came upon a massive blueberry patch, fell to our knees onto the blood-colored leaves, and fed till lips, tongues, and fingers were dyed deep purple. Although blueberry plants were everywhere, they hadn't produced much fruit that summer; this was the only patch we'd come across that we could truly dive into. "It make it hard for the bears when it like that," Sam explained. "Make them want to come into the village." And indeed a griz had been shot in Arctic a few days before Will and I arrived.

We paused on the northwest slope of a six-square-mile pile of marine microorganism bits, two thousand feet above the floor of the valley.

"This stuff here, it burn real good," Sam told me. "One time, friend of mine run dogs down to Venetie, and he sleep in that canyon there. I ask him, 'There's no wood there, what you do for fire?' He tell me he use this stuff." He fingered a dwarf birch. "But you sure gonna need a lot of it!"

We shared almonds, banana chips, and sharp cheddar for dinner and wedged our beds into folds in the slope to prevent a slow surrender to gravity during the night. Will spotted six white dots on the talus slope ascending to the black summit of a mountain to the north, four miles across the valley. He was getting out of his bag, tying his long blond hair into a ponytail.

"No," Johnny said.

We focused scopes and binos on the sheep as they reached the summit ridge and disappeared, one by one, into whatever lay on the other side. "Do you think they seen us, Sam?" David asked.

"I don't think so. Only one way find out, huh."

Hushed speculation ensued.

Twilight yielded to Orion, Ursa Major, the Pleiades. A solar wind traveling 250 miles per second blew into the earth's magnetic field. Its protons and neutrons reacted with charged particles in the ionosphere, fifty-five miles above, producing pale phosphorescence in the north sky, a haze of motion between us and the cold mystery of the cosmos.

We burned dwarf birch to prepare coffee and oatmeal in the morning. Three of us cut boughs of it as fast as we could to keep the fire going long enough to boil water. The leaves burned hot and fast, giving off whiffs of turpentine, and the strategizing began. Will and David would climb the mountain. Sam, Johnny, and I would circle around its western extent to a narrow drainage that spilled from its center. There was a small pass at the top of that creek. We'd meet there.

On the hike Sam spotted two sheep, a ewe and her lamb, eating lichen high up the fluted black slopes of a lopsided mountain. We crouched and watched them, but they saw us and clambered higher.

Being the world's only wild white sheep didn't seem like much of an advantage. Then again, to get close enough to take a long shot would have required hours of mountaineering with gear we didn't have.

But why would natural selection choose for them a white coat that a human can see from miles away? It works well in winter. Or during the Pleistocene, when these mountains were glaciated.

And Dall sheep were here in the Pleistocene. They arrived during the Wisconsin Glaciation, which began a hundred thousand years ago and lasted ninety thousand years. Much of the earth's water was frozen in continental ice sheets then, lowering sea levels by three hundred feet. A rocky land between western Alaska and Siberia was re-exposed. Foot travel between Asia and North America was possible.

The interior of Alaska was part of an arid, ice-free grassland—or steppe—that stretched to the north Atlantic. Cut off from North America by ice, Alaska was part of Eurasia. Sheep made their way across Beringia and fed on the succulent sedges and grasses of the mammoth steppe. They liked the high country, but most of the good stuff was under ice. So they did what they could, got preyed on by lions, saber-toothed tigers, short-faced bears, and possibly cheetahs. And, of course, wolves. Wolves have been here licking their chops at the tasty succession of Beringian fauna for a million years.

Ten thousand years went by. The sheep ate willow and bunch-grass alongside some bison in a subalpine valley. It got warmer and a bunch of ice melted. The sheep expanded into the newly exposed habitat. Some of them moved down the Canadian Rockies into the area we now call the United States of America.

Another ten thousand years went by. It got cold. Water froze into thick sheets of ice that blocked the migration. The groups of sheep were separated for thirty thousand years. When it got warm again and the ice receded, there were four kinds of sheep: Dall, stone, desert, and bighorn.

The sun circled low above the horizon, poured atmosphere-altered light through cut spires, lopped off chunks of mountains, and obliterated canyons with shadow and silence. We reached the stream descending from within the mountain just past midday. We climbed in a crouch.

Soon the only thing above us was a sweep of cliffs reaching to the summit ridge. We tried to make radio contact but got only static and decided to return to the creek and hike up from there. But Johnny lost his radio, and we had to look for it.

Johnny grumbled something I couldn't make out.

Then the shooting began. Reports singed the air, a dozen rounds from up the drainage. We saw sheep charging up the mountain opposite us. One of them, hit, fell behind the others. He lay down on a ledge high up the jumbled talus as the rest of them disappeared through a notch in the ridge. Will and David were running up the side of the mountain. Without a radio, we could only watch as they approached the ram. I think we tried to yell at them from two miles away. When the ram heard them, he was up and through the notch. They never knew he was there.

-:::-

We hiked up the creek and met Will and David in the pass to walk down together as the sun bled out in the northwest.

They'd seen them from the summit, thirteen sheep, five of them full curl rams. Will and David had spent hours picking their way down the loose rocks to a depression in the slope they crouched within. David had told Will not to kick any rocks, and Will—as he told me privately when we were back in camp—had wanted to say, *No shit, huh?* but didn't.

The sheep lay four hundred yards below by a small pool of water. Tufts of scrubby willow grew close to the ground around them. They were positioned so that each member of the group faced a different direction. Not in a circle like musk ox, more casual. Heads up. Watching. Chewing their cud. Watching.

Will and David had spent an hour glassing the quarry. They nicknamed the largest one Marco, after the endangered Marco Polo species living in the Pamir Mountains border region of Afghanistan, Pakistan, Tajikistan, and China. They have the longest horns of any sheep in the world. Seventy-five inches is the record.

They weren't sure what they should do. They couldn't get closer without being seen. Then something spooked the sheep.

In camp by the creek we ate meager portions of meatless mulligan. David had a threadbare tarp, a Sponge Bob blanket, and a ghillie suit to sleep in—120 miles north of the Arctic Circle in September. His warm sleeping companion, Otter, had refused to climb over the summit of the mountain, so he'd left her. When he returned for her, wearing his ghillie suit, the dog thought he was a terrible monster and took off.

Instead of letting David shiver through the night, the rest of us unzipped our sleeping bags and laid them out to form one blanket, which we covered with two overlapping tarps. We huddled for warmth.

-:::-

By morning it was raining. Over the course of the night the tarps had ceased to overlap. I was wet; my bag, soaked. I glanced at David, dry, beside me and recalled his words, The ground is good enough, and I bolted from the tarp. I knew the anger I struggled with was bad, unhealthy, uncool. I gathered dead willow twigs to make a fire.

Sam was soon up and was as soggy as I was. We silently waged a battle of wills over control of the fledgling flames. I cleared a spot for water as he returned with a load of wood. "That fire not ready yet," he scowled. "You gonna put it out."

"No, I'm not. And don't be grumpy with me. I can't even count the number of times someone's taken over the fire from me."

Everyone was tense and hungry. We had instant oatmeal.

I said something, jovially.

Then Johnny barked, "No more yelling, okay. No more yelling at this camp." About ten minutes later he banged a metal pot against a rock to knock coffee grounds out of it.

"Hey, no yelling," Will said.

Johnny divided us up. Will and I would track the sheep over the mountain. David would circle around its eastern face, below us. Meanwhile, Sam and Johnny would walk around the west end of the mountain to a small pass below its north wall. They would look for the rest of the band.

Will, David, and I walked up the valley. Black clouds hung low and obscured the mountain two hundred feet above the creek bed. About halfway up, the drainage narrowed to a small canyon and then into a defile that we scrambled through by bracing ourselves between the rock walls, a dozen feet above the running water, an intimate gorge.

When the drainage opened back up, we separated. Will and I climbed through the gauze of cumulus to the notch the sheep had chosen. Visibility was around ten feet, and we decided it was too dangerous to walk the ridge. We sat, smoked a bowl.

Will, veteran of several trips with the people of Arctic, grinned at me. "So how you been?" he asked.

"I've been good. These guys know the country. They tell me how to build a fire, how to put wood on the fire, what to pack."

Will was laughing. "How to use the willow twig for a toothpick."

I was laughing. "How to use the moss for cleaning out your bowl."

"Oh, Rob, I'm glad you've experienced it. I could tell that I wasn't doing a good enough job explaining it. I needed somebody to understand what I was talking about."

"Yeah, it's weird. It's like they want me to acknowledge that they're my guides; that I'm dependent on them out here, and I'm resistant to that. So there's this tension, this constant balancing between wanting to learn from them but also wanting us to be part of something together."

"It's a trip, man. Sometimes I think they just want to impress the city slickers. I mean for some of them going to town is like coming up here for you and me. Like remember when Martin stayed with me last summer? He called 'cause he was broke and didn't have anyplace to stay and he needed a ride to the E.R. He stayed with me for two weeks. And I'm happy to help, it's just that sometimes I think that out here they kinda want to compensate for not knowing town as well."

"I take it for granted all the time," I said. "I mean part of it, for me anyway, is that I don't see myself as being that good in town. I mean I'm a cab driver. I'm constantly late with the bills. I drink too much. And I've kind of come to define myself a little by my abilities in the backcountry. And it seems like our perspectives are kind of . . . running into each other a little, you know?"

"Totally. They do have mad skills out here, though, huh?"

"Yeah, it's pretty impressive. Sam's like part of this place. Like it's his living room or something. I've learned at least one thing from him every day. And David already knows more about this country than I ever will. Johnny's a bit of a hard guy but he's kind of earned it, too. I mean it's a great adventure. Thanks for bringing me along."

"I'm glad you're here, man."

Many folks from remote villages still enjoy this lifestyle. This relationship with the land. Though the future of the relationship becomes more tenuous with every elder who passes on, every bump in the price of gas, every new Xbox or satellite dish. Village life occupies a precarious niche.

I remembered coming into town on the back of Johnny's four wheeler, the air heavy with dust churned from the loess trails. People gathered around the post office and visited. There was a laundromat with corrugated metal siding where you could fill jugs with purified water, though most people seemed to fill them in the river. There were some tribal offices and a clinic and a school.

Many of the cabins were constructed of old gray logs or faded sheets of plywood. I noted single-pane windows, gaps between logs, doors that didn't close all the way. These things were more a reflection of the cost of getting building materials flown to this far corner of the Brooks Range, hundreds of roadless miles from the nearest Home Depot, than anything else.

People fought forest fires, worked stints at construction, cut firewood, or ran traplines. Some took jobs in town or up north and commuted via small plane. There just weren't that many other jobs.

But this was their home and they welcomed us into it. They looked after each other. They're proud of their hard life among the big mountains and wild rivers and all the space a restless soul could wander. They should be.

An hour passed atop the mountain, within the cloud, before David's voice crackled over the radio. "Hey, you guys there?"

"Yeah, what's up?" I said.

"Hey, I found that ram."

To get to where David was, we descended a steep scree chute between serrated blades of limestone. David was at the bottom, and we could see him between our boots for the last hour of the descent. He had the sheep mostly quartered by the time we arrived.

"He was just up there, huh," David gestured to a ledge of solid rock jutting from the slide. "I walk right up to him. He try to get up but he too stiff. He just look at me when I shoot him."

He was a big full curl ram, probably 250 pounds, not Marco, but the tightly curled horns and head must have weighed 50 by themselves. We finished the butchering, tied everything but the hide and the lungs to our frame packs, and walked around the scree chute and up a steep swell of tundra to the pass. From there we went down into the creek and through the mini gorge to camp, about four hours of hiking.

An hour later Johnny and Sam returned with part of a second ram that Sam had killed. We laid the meat on the moss and lichen. Johnny cut off a side of ribs and hung them from a sharpened willow stick propped up by a forked willow stick so that the concave side of the ribs faced the fire.

For the next three hours we brought back armloads of willow and heaped them on the flames. At intervals we turned and flipped the ribs so that both sides and ends were seared by the pungent blaze. Just before they were done the rain started. Johnny braided some willows together and spread a tarp over the resulting frame. It was a tarpitectural masterpiece.

We ate the ribs in a steady drizzle, felt our bodies soak up the fat, nutrients, protein like the taiga sucking up a shower during a dry summer. They were good.

Happy and smeared in grease, we crawled under the tarp where our unzipped bags were laid out so that all of us would be covered. If there had been any space between us, the guys on the ends would have been in the downpour.

The next day we woke and toked in the queer blue-tarp-tinted light. It was overcast. Energy levels were low. We laid around the fire, cooked meat, and ate it. Johnny James spread gossamer sheets of stomach fat onto the coals. Will cut pieces of intestine and placed them on the ends of sticks suspended above the fire. David set a chunk of liver on the hot rocks surrounding the pit. I cut fatty chunks of meat and fried them in a pan. We ate and ate and smoked pot and slept and then ate more. Sam put the hooves into the embers and when they'd turned to charcoal, showed me how to break open the lower forelegs to access the marrow. From inside the hoof structure he cut a tiny brown membranous sac that he squeezed to deliver one or two drops of fluid on his tongue. "This one here is good for going on long hike, it make you not hungry for your hiking."

The warm juice was rich, earthy, salty; the way my body absorbed it, I felt like I'd just had a bowl of stew.

I moved away from the rest of the group and sat against a boulder, started writing in my journal. A shadow came over the page. I looked up and Johnny was standing above me, smirking, which is to say, almost smiling. "Hey Cab Cloud 9," he said, calling me by my trip name, "anybody ever gonna read all that scribbling."

"I don't know, probably not. But who knows."

"Well, if they do, you got to tell them we don't want no drilling for oil on the coastal plain. They say it not going to change the caribou migration, but they don't know that. Nobody know that. We always depend on the caribou to live, you know.

"Even just the tourists floating the rivers changes the caribou. The really big ones don't come here much anymore. We have to catch more of them, and they don't have as much fat as the big ones.

"So if you ever write your book, you got to tell the people that, otherwise don't even write about this, okay?"

"Okay."

"Now, me and Sam's going to get the rest of that sheep. You wanna come?"

"Yeah, give me a minute."

Late in the afternoon Sam, Johnny, and I left to retrieve the rest of Sam's sheep from the other side of the mountain. David climbed up the other side of the drainage in an attempt to rescue his dog, lost on the summit ridge for two days.

We hiked from camp, along the base of the eastern side of the fifty-eight-hundred-foot peak, to a small pass below its north flank. The autumnally lit tundra was a naked skin upon rolling slopes that rose to mountains laced with wispy tendrils of vapor.

We continued over the pass to a narrow ravine between ridges descending from the summit. I could see where Will and I had sat in the fog the day before.

The sheep was a speck of white high up the black rock of the ravine. Sam was pointing to the ridge describing how he had crept up the other side of it, taking hours, while Johnny stayed below in full view of the sheep. "Fuck, I was just decoy," Johnny interjected. "Them sheep, fuck, they just look at me the whole time, huh, then I see Sam," he giggled, "way up there aiming his gun."

"That first shot was kill shot. But I shoot it two more times just to make sure. 'What'd I tell you, amigo, I going to kill you and eat your heart out!'"

Sam had a litany of lines, like this one, always at the ready, from spaghetti westerns. He'd seen *Fistful of Dollars* more than a hundred times. He was grinning like . . . well, probably grinning the same way he had when he'd caught his first sheep as a boy.

We climbed up to the animal and finished butchering it, almost within sight of where we'd butchered the ram the day before. As we worked we gazed north, up the valley of another Junjik tributary, to the seven-thousand-foot peaks of the continental divide. From the east, light poured through the demolished ocean floor the way the sea floods a hole in a ship on the rocks. Each mountain a distinct mass separated from the others by broad valleys flowing together, gathering the land. Not a tree in sight. Not another human in the world.

We got back after David returned from rescuing Otter from the summit ridge. He had to carry her down the more treacherous sections. At one point, exhausted, he'd contemplated shooting her. I slept outside. David had his heater back.

The next day Sam cut the smooth disc of fat from the back of the sheeps' necks. He handed me a piece. "What's this, Sam?"

"*Divii vach'a helho.*"

"Oh, all right." I popped it into my mouth. "What's that?"

"*Divii* mean 'sheep.' *Vach'a helho* mean 'neck fat.' Chew it like gum. It give you energy for your hiking."

We tied slabs of meat onto our pack frames and walked back the way we'd come. From the camp where we burned the dwarf birch we looked down on a long lake from which the dirge of a lone loon ululated. If you looked close you could have just made out the V of its wake on the lake's still surface, a mirror of sky, in the folds of tundra.

We didn't circumnavigate the mountain within the pass but cut directly south to the last stand of timber where we'd cached gear.

It took about one minute to get a fire going from the spruce. "Hey Sam," I said. "This fire was too easy, maybe you could run back up there and get us some dwarf birch, huh?"

"Okay, just as soon as you go wrestle some willow from by that creek." He chuckled, laying back in the thick moss. We boiled sheep and ate it with pilot crackers.

Our attention was drawn back into the vacuum of the high valley, the windborne cotton grass and lichen-hued mountains.

"I saw two little brown frogs by that long lake below sheep mountain," Will said.

The Gwich'in were surprised. "I never hear about no frog up here. They got frog down Venetie, but I never seen one up here," David said.

"I know they live here, but I not see one for long time," Sam said.

They must have been wood frogs, which ranged from these mountains to northern Georgia. In the fall their livers converted glycogen into glucose, which flooded the cells of the vital tissues and acted like an antifreeze that prevented the cells from bursting. Extra cellular fluids froze solid; they became hard as rocks.

Beneath two feet of snow and at temperatures of thirty below zero, they maintained a body temperature of twenty degrees. Which was good because all data from the Lower 48 suggested they were history if it got any colder than that. But in a recent study outside Fairbanks a group of them survived after their temperatures plunged to ten degrees. We have tough frogs up here.

There was a debate over whether to camp, hang the meat and smoke it, or push on to base camp. We voted for the latter and walked strung out over a quarter mile. At base camp we recovered Johnny's last pack of cigs and smoked and told stories and ate. Johnny, a sardonic glint in his black eyes, said, "Isn't it bee-yoo-tee-ful, Will, all these mountains?" looking sideways at me.

"To tell you the truth it isn't so much the beauty of this place as it is the wildness that gets me," Will said. A wolf howled up the valley. "Although I can appreciate that it is a beautiful place."

It took two trips to haul gear, meat, and folding canoes to the Junjik the following morning. Sam helped Will and me set up the Ally boats while Johnny cooked sheep soup. Evening set in before we had the boats in the water and loaded.

The water was shallow and swift. The boat was heavy with three people, sheep meat, and gear, making it difficult to steer. Sam and Johnny James were nervous about my paddling: "Stay in the channel," "Stay right behind Will," "Do everything that Will does." I wanted to hit the mute button, wanted to appreciate the sublime mountains sliding by. Low-angle sun ebbed between peaks and cast the earth in a fuzzy glow.

I pulled out before a rocky stretch that Will had gone through and walked to where he waited below. "I'm not going any farther today," I said. He agreed it was too dark. Johnny directed everyone to carry everything from Will's canoe, including the canoe, a hundred yards back up the river.

We woke up to a blue-sky Arctic morning, had noodles and sheep meat for breakfast, and then spent an hour scouting the shallow rapids. David and Otter opted to walk ahead and catch up with us later, so Jimmy rode with Will. Sam and I shoved off. We coasted through the mountains and sunshine. He whooped it up at times. "I never even know you can go through ones like that!" He grinned, gesturing at the foamy water.

It was early evening when we came to a rapid that bent right before dumping down a narrow rocky chute. I didn't notice Will pulled out on the side of the rapid until we were almost upon him. He was gesturing to us. We shot past him and pulled over. Sam ran back to them while I tied up the boat.

Gear was in the water, and we waded to retrieve it and stacked it on the bank. Their canoe was smashed up good. It had hung on a rock midship and turned perpendicular to the current. Johnny had jumped out the upriver side, flipping the canoe so the open end faced the flow. Water flooded the boat, but the canoe was stuck and the river kept gushing in until the aluminum frame collapsed around the rock. When all was ashore Will walked away muttering, "Dammit—I was looking at a fucking duck!"

I began taking his boat apart, organizing the pieces on the ground. I bent the keel into shape and started on the chine rods, thinking we might get back on the river that day. The rods, similar to tent poles, can be broken down along a series of sleeve joints that are shock corded together. I was working slowly, bending it over a smooth rock, when I snapped an inner sleeve. "FUCK!"

"What happened? Did you break one?" Will shouted from the fire. We agreed not to work on it anymore that night, but the conversation continued to revolve around the broken rod. Johnny came up with the idea of sliding something inside the tubes. Sam suggested fitting some kind of sleeve over the joint. We pulled objects from our stuff that might serve one of these options. Will, meanwhile, recounted the debacle that now had us all laughing: "The canoe is completely full of water, and Johnny's sitting there in it up to his knees like nothing's going on. Finally I was like, 'Johnny, you gotta get out of the boat.' But he tried to carry so much stuff, and it was all stuff that floats, so when he got in the water it buoyed him up and he fell over, all the stuff just floatin' there."

The handle of Sam's knife sharpener almost fit inside the broken sleeve inside the tube. We cut away the shock cord and shaved away aluminum. The brass threads of the handle screwed into the widened tube. We wrapped the other end in electrical tape until it was the appropriate diameter to beat into the other tube. And then we wrapped the whole thing with more electrical tape.

The next morning we bent the rest of the rods and put the canoe back together, and it was good, except for a hole in the hypalon shell of the boat. So we patched that. But the instructions on the glue called for it to set up for twenty-four hours. So there we were—on a hot, dry, dusty day, with nothing to do but build a cache to hang and smoke the meat. David decided to walk to Johnny's boat as we were going to be tight on weight in the canoes. He and Otter departed, and we climbed a hill to some standing dead trees. Johnny opened fire with an axe, demonstrating his felling method. "See, first you hit up, then down." He sliced angles that cut a wedge that he worked around the trunk. Wood chips flew as he worked.

Will nudged me. "Almost everybody in Arctic heats with wood. And most of them still cut their wood with an axe." He grinned.

"Wow."

We took turns at the tree until it looked like something a beaver had sharpened his teeth on and then pushed it over and went to work on two other trunks while Sam cut firewood nearby. After hauling the wood to camp, we tied three poles together to form a tripod. Another pole was run from the tripod to a spruce tree. We hung the meat so the smoke from the fire wafted over it, preserving it. We cooked sheep on sticks until we fell asleep, dreaming of carbohydrates.

The next morning we floated past the south face of Little Njoo and the mouth of Spring Creek to the dry slough where we'd abandoned Johnny's boat ten days before. It was out of the water and the stern was propped on the motor, wedged in the muddy shallow. Johnny tilted it up; the bolts we'd tightened were loose again and had to be fixed. Meanwhile I started a fire, and Sam busted out a package of Mexican rice he'd cached there to go with some sheep. David and Otter arrived, wading through the river in time for lunch, then we sat in dry grass and smoked. Johnny sharpened his impeller blade with a file; Sam sharpened his pocketknife on a flat rock.

A plan took shape: Sam and Johnny would drift the boat down to glacier camp where we'd cached five gallons of fuel. Will would stick with them. David and I would head out first in the canoe and hunt moose on the way down.

He and I had been moving for half an hour when Sam's voice came over the radio. "U.S. Carrier Junjik we are underway. We

have one destroyer accompanying us. Do you copy there, battle-
ship?" Ham radio.

The ride down was calm with enough water to cover the rocks.
The wide valley was hugged by mountains. We were floating by a
gravel bar when David said, "You see that griz?" He pointed to a
four-hundred-pound boar sleek and fat cruising through golden
willows turning brown.

We were twenty-five yards away. "Yeah," I said.

"Here, give me your 30.06 I'm gonna kill 'im."

"Oh, man, really?"

"Yeah, it's what we do. They kill the moose calves, man, they
come into our village." I unclipped the rifle. The bear was loping across an open stretch of gravel, thirty yards from cover. I
hesitated a second before I handed it to him. I turned the canoe.
Slow.

David raised the rifle and tried to follow the animal, ten feet
from cover, for a half second before it crashed into the brush. He
lowered the gun.

"Yeah, man, there's lots of bears round here. I just kill 'em
man."

We floated on, silently. David put his headphones on.

When we came to the top of the glacial outwash, the channel split in two. "Go that way," David said, pointing right, but
there was less water going that way, and it was rocky. We would
have had to drag the boat to get in the channel. I went left and
spent the next hour in the water pulling the boat through shallow braids that broke apart and came together in a labyrinth of
aimlessness.

"I don't see how they can get the boat through here," I said.

"I told 'em go right at the top. I hope they do."

We got to camp and I hauled our gear while David got a fire
going. He hiked up a hill to climb a tree from which he radioed

Arctic and arranged for someone to bring us gas the following day. "I talk to those guys too," he said. "I told 'em turn right, but Jimmy say he turn left. I told 'em good luck."

We put on dry clothes, made a dinner of fry meat and pasta, and smoked cigarettes from a pack David had cached. We waited.

They showed up two hours after us.

Will had gone first to scope the channel, he told me later. Sam was in the bow of the boat with a long stick. Johnny was driving. "Johnny wasn't able to drive his boat very well, and Sam knows how to drive one real well, and I know he was getting frustrated. The boat kept getting stuck, spinning around, going the wrong way. At one point Sam and I were standing knee-deep in the water for like five minutes, and Johnny's switching gas cans around tryin' to start the boat. Sam's starting to talk under his tongue and finally he's like, fuck it, and grabs the bowline and started jerking the boat so Johnny couldn't fuck around anymore. I helped him and we got the boat moving again. So Sam jumped back in the bow, and I got in my canoe, and we're cruising, and they hit a rock. Sam's stick breaks, and he does a full somersault into the water. I think Johnny might have hit him when *he* fell, knocked him in. Anyway, Sam pops up out of the water and he's singing. I was fuckin' freakin', jumped in after him, and he comes up singing, ya know, like nothin' else is going to bother him after that. And it didn't."

David and I had hot food and a fire ready. They'd all put on dry clothes and began regaling us with the details of their predicament with Sam demonstrating how he flipped out of the boat.

The mood shifted. We clustered around the fire as dusk fell away to reveal our ridiculous insignificance within the immensity of the galaxy. Pale aurora borealis flickered above the northern horizon. I sensed Johnny's gaze and looked up to meet his eyes.

"You should have let him shoot that bear." He smirked. I sensed he was more into provocation than making a point.

I shrugged, said, "I turned the boat."

Sam said, "It's okay not to shoot them. I like to watch them, too. Till they come in the village, anyway."

The next morning a man named Gregory brought us fifteen gallons of fuel from Arctic Village. He was a fit guy wearing freshly laundered Carhartts. His long black hair was tied in a ponytail. When he smiled he revealed teeth that each came out of his gums at slightly different angles, the gaps between them almost as big as the teeth themselves. He handed us sandwiches in plastic baggies, along with some bad news. Two local women were in the hospital in Fairbanks. "No brain wave," he said.

"Alcohol?" David asked.

"Alcohol. They say her liver too bad to operate on."

Nobody said anything for a long time.

"Well that's too bad," Sam said. "My own cousin. Dammit. I guess it's disease, and I'm glad she not suffer from it anymore."

Other events included the return of the wildland firefighters from blazes battled in Idaho and Montana.

"Everybody have money, whiskey. Fighting all night, I guess," Gregory said.

"Oh boy," said David, rubbing his palms against each other. "There gonna be big card game tonight. "Sometime, maybe, $10,000 on table."

"Jesus," Will laughed. "Arctic Village, huh?" He had told me once that he thought the village had adopted economic rhythms modeled upon their relationship with the caribou. "They spend most of the year waiting for them to return, catching the occasional moose or ptarmigan. Then suddenly tens of thousands of caribou come through the mountains, and they kill as many of them as they can and gorge and stack them up for winter. I mean it's really not that different with money. By the end of every month people are just scraping by, waiting. And then all of a sudden the checks come in the mail. Or the firefighters go to work. Or something."

After Gregory and Sam departed, David took off on foot to a place near the confluence with the East Fork to hunt moose.

Will, Johnny, and I sat around the fire. From a tripod beside it, a skinned and de-horned sheep's head hung from some twine tied to a ring of green willow tied around the base of its skull. Anyone walking by spun the head on the string so that as it unwound it roasted evenly. Johnny had caught some fat grayling from a clear pool below camp using monofilament wrapped around a tin can. They lay on the coals roasting.

"I used to fight fires," Johnny was saying. "We work in Alaska in the summer, and then in the fall they send us all over the place—California, Idaho, Montana—if it was good season. I make some pretty good money doing that.

"Pretty hard work?" I asked.

"Pretty hard work when you're on the fire. I usually run chainsaw. When you do that you work with one other person. One person cutting and the other one moving the brush and logs out of the way. But a lot of the time we just waiting around. Waiting for the wind to change, or waiting to get dispatched or something. If there's no fires, then they looking for stuff for us to do.

"After that space shuttle crashed, they send us to Texas to pick up pieces. You have all these Alaska Natives walking around that desert, in that heat. And they have fire ants there too. They crawling up my legs, up my walking stick." Johnny grimaced, shook his head deliberately.

"Did you find any space shuttle pieces?" I asked.

"I find one piece of melted metal, not even as big as my fist. I couldn't tell what it was, but they tell me it was from that shuttle.

"It was good to come back with that money. Everybody in the village probably touch that money before springtime." He grinned. "Like the caribou, we use it all, huh. There hardly anything left of it when it leave Arctic."

Hunks of red meat hung from a log over the fire in the sun, smoke, and wind. Willow and blueberry leaves stuck to their sides. In the week that had passed since we caught the sheep, the five of us had eaten close to a full ram.

"We used to trade with the Eskimo on the coast," Johnny said. "I'm talking about long time ago, before I was born. Before we ever trade with the whiteys." He looked up mischievously, gauging our reaction. "They got no arrowhead, man. We trade with them for that. What they got is good harpoon, spear you know. But we have to be careful. Sometime they trick us, attack us, you know, take our stuff for nothing."

He looked at the world fiercely. Broad face, widest at the eyes, that squinted at the corners and pulled against the flat nose. Fu Manchu mustache, lips and chin jutted defiantly whenever he spoke his native tongue, which he did 5 to 10 percent of the time, when he couldn't find the words in English.

We heard Sam's voice on the radio. He was sitting on the small hill called Tai Chok waiting for David. I wondered how many years their people had sat there, looking for moose, sheep, or caribou.

Many archaeologists estimate that the ancestors of present-day Athabaskans began to traverse Beringia twelve to fourteen thousand years ago. The Far North was in transition. Sediment cores containing pollen show the abundance of birch, dwarf birch, and willow increasing, indicating a moister climate that would have produced more snow. And because glaciers were rapidly receding, the winds that rushed off them and scoured snow from the steppe would have been waning. Most of the extinct Pleistocene species were adapted to grazing on a wind-swept plain. Snow depths of five feet would have hampered their ability to take nutrition from the land. The size and range of these species began to decrease.

And then this two-legged predator with thousands of years of experience hunting the animals of the great grasslands arrived. Their history exists in strands of physical evidence and DNA strewn over thousands of years and square miles. Micro blades of chipped stone that can be mounted as spear tips in bone or antler extend from central Asia into archaeological sites in the Interior only hundreds of years old.

Dental anthropology establishes Athabaskans as one of three distinct groups that crossed the land bridge in the last thirty thousand years. They came after the first group, which went on to settle most of the Americas, and before the third group, commonly known as the Eskimos, who settled the northern coastlines as far away as Greenland. The Athabaskan, or Na Dene, language shows a migration up the Yukon into northwestern Canada. The language is distinct from the Eskimo languages and the broad linguistic family that includes most of the other Native American languages spoken at the time of contact with Europeans. Interestingly, the Navajo language is also a member of the Na Dene family, indicating that they are also descendants of an ancestral group of Athabaskans.

Unfortunately these people didn't leave many clues behind. They were constantly on the move, living in seasonal hunting and fishing camps, one step ahead of starvation and oblivion. Their possessions amounted to a few stone, antler, and bone tools that have not stood up well to the acidic soils of the Interior.

The land that connects Asia and North America is underwater, rendering that crucial link inaccessible to archaeologists.

Perhaps the arrival of these people hastened the demise of the doomed species. No fossils of mammoth, saber-toothed cat, short-faced bear, antelope, lion, horse, giant ground sloth, or camel less than eleven thousand years old have been found.

The earliest Athabaskans had some adapting to do. The climate continued to change. Blueberry and cranberry began to appear. Lichens and bryophytes arrived with the migration of spruce. By eighty-five hundred years ago the Interior was covered in mature spruce forests. The first modern moose came on the scene, drawn to the corridors of willow along rivers and the emerging deciduous forests. Smaller herds of caribou exploited the expanding tundra.

The ancestors of the Gwich'in probably subsisted on birds and fish, supplemented by the occasional moose or mammoth. On the brink of extinction themselves, they depended upon finely honed skills, traditions, and intellects. My envy of their relationship with the natural world is misguided; they weren't part of a relationship. They were part of this place. And if I were able to meet them and tell them of my admiration, they'd probably tell me to go back to my time and bring them some food.

"Henry, he two bends below us. He got engine trouble, but he shoot one moose, and Jimmy Evans he shoot one moose, but Charley, he with Edward James. Got trouble with motor. He is on Medicine Man Mountain. And that's your news update," Sam concluded his radio report.

We were up before sunrise in time to watch the full moon sink below a spruce-stubbled hill to the north. Everything covered in frost. We packed our gear and hauled the meat down from the drying racks. Then we were on the river. Johnny's boat wouldn't start. He ran the battery low trying.

"Jesus Christ, Johnny, what the fuck you doin'?" David said. They pushed off and floated down. Will and I quickly left them behind. When we came to the hill called Tai Chok we paddled into a slough that wrapped behind it.

We climbed a small rise, laid down, and hid when they passed. Then we hopped in our canoes and caught them: river games. We rafted up and smoked, spinning round and round. Scattered clouds scudded across the taut blue sky. Willow burned gold along the banks and rushed up the mountains. A pair of ravens speaking in croaks flew up the valley.

An hour after we separated, we heard an outboard rip to life. David and Johnny caught us quickly, mentioned hunting moose. David was in a hurry. "Maybe got two holes to dig, one for my auntie," he said.

"They gonna have big potlatch, though. Gonna need a lot of meat," Johnny said.

"Yeah, but maybe I have to go and check on Charley. Or maybe we just go up to Old John Lake and shoot some caribou."

"Hmphh," Johnny said. Then they were gone.

Will and I pulled out on a gravel beach and had noodles with sheep. We said nothing. After coffee we pushed back onto the river and soon arrived at the confluence with the east fork of the Chandalar. It moved swiftly and dark within mud banks topped by tussock-riddled taiga. Hawk owls and northern harriers hunting voles and shrews cut through the spruce and willows. A pair of tundra swans flew over, bleating reedy calls back and forth. Red-eyed ducks disappeared beneath the black water, exploded from clusters of brush against the bank. We camped just past sunset as the moon rose in the east and cast a silver reflection across the surface tension of the current.

The float to Arctic took three hours the following day. We tracked our progress by the river's meanders against the east flanks of Undercloud Mountain, then Paddle Mountain, and finally away from and back to the long ridge of Shark Edge Mountain. I called Johnny on the radio when we came within sight of the galvanized roof of the school. He met us at the landing, and we threw our gear on his four-wheeler. David showed up and gave us a bag of his mom's fry bread, still warm.

Everett from Venetie was there too and offered me one of the last smokes from his crumpled pack. He was in his forties, and I could see his ribs through his brown T-shirt when it blew against his torso. His hair had been buzz-cut ten days previously and the bones seemed fluid beneath his skin. He and another man had recently run a boat up river from Venetie. The two villages were woven together like families. The water level of the river had dropped since they'd arrived, and now it seemed unlikely they'd be able to take the boat back down.

Everett laughed as he told us he didn't have any money to fly home, "That's all right, these two villages help each other out, you know. I got lots of places I can stay." I recognized him from a few taxi cab rides. He didn't seem to be the same person here. He was sober and carefree. We talked about how good it was to be in the woods at that time of year, the crisp texture of the air and motion of color. He seemed to recognize me without knowing from where. Like that part of him was elsewhere.

Four planes from Fairbanks would land that day, bringing mourners, moose for the potlatch, and the body of a young woman. The people of Arctic had already dug the grave in the permafrost.

A few days later, Will and I would hear that Everett had been hunting from the bow of a boat, had a seizure, and fell in the river. By the time he was pulled out, it was too late. I'd remember him smiling beside the river in the autumn sun. Knowing that he'd surely started his journey home.

Goldstream Valley, 2012

DAYS IN THE LIFE of Cord and Rob tend to be seasonally affected. During the school year, Michele's teaching, and I'm the domestic warrior. I wake at five, have coffee and a smoke, and write until Cord and Michele get up an hour or two later. I make breakfast, Michele gets ready for school, and Cord catches *Sesame Street* or *Daniel Tiger* or *Dinosaur Train*. When Michele leaves, Cord and I do the dishes. He's very helpful, whether it's the cooking, laundry, or sweeping. He has a toy Dirt Devil vacuum cleaner that lights up and makes a revving sound. We work on going on the potty. It's coming along. Still, there is a lot of poop in my life, under my fingernails, ground into the furniture. I cheer, hug, and carry on after success and am more somber and reflective after failures.

In the winter we ski. Cord goes in a sled-stroller we got on Craigslist. We can walk from the house a hundred yards to a trail that winds around to other trails through the original homesteader's fields. Before Cord could walk, I was stuffing him into down snowsuits and under heavy blankets to go for a ski. When it's below zero, I boil two quarts of water and fill Nalgene bottles that I tuck into old wool socks and place under the blankets, between his legs and feet. Negative thirty-five is the coldest

temp we've braved. He got out and ran around in the fields near
the abandoned hay rakes and brush cutters, our breath-streams
neutrally buoyant in the cold, dense air, so tactile, like the two
of us underwater.

When we get back to the house, we have lunch. He can watch
Curious George or *Caillou*, if he's inclined. After, we go upstairs
and read some books and take a nap. I haven't thought much
about naps in the last forty years, but I've decided I like them.

I've always been an advocate of talking normally to kids. I
mean, sure, I speak to him a bit more slowly and loudly, take
time to enunciate, but you know, we have conversations. Even
if it's about stuff like blankies, buhs (pacifiers), or stuffed animals—or real animals and trees and wind. We spend a lot of
time outdoors. I want him to grow up with at least one foot in
the natural world. He and I haven't gone on a trip yet, but I'm
hoping we can float the river I call the Skoog this summer.

Michele and I have only been camping once. We hiked the
Pinnell Mountain Trail together a few years ago. It's possible
that's where Cord was conceived, on a bed of lichen under a clear
blue sky. I want him to feel comfortable under the sky always,
in nature, in his bones and tissue, even if he grows up to be a
Republican Drill-baby or a computer geek in some godforsaken
city. I will love him. I know this already. It's a new feeling for me.
It has made me a better human being and just in time to halt my
slide into curmudgeonism.

I bribe him shamelessly and frequently—only to assuage
my conscience I call it deal-making. Face it, negotiating is good
prep for the real world. What more basic human truth is there,
after all: if you want something, then you must give something.
Yesterday I got an almost chore-free hour in exchange for allowing Cord to watch a show. Although in truth, the terms of
this deal were a bit skewed. Once a show he likes is on, it is no

sacrifice at all for him to ignore me. The power of that media is frightening. But, you know, I watched so much damn TV growing up, thousands and thousands of hours of mostly pretty bad programming, and I don't think it fucked me up that bad. Cord doesn't watch all that much, and usually it's some PBS stuff. And I need that break; we all need a break, sometimes.

But sometimes I just need to stare out the window for a while. I've always enjoyed that. A friend once asked me what I thought about when I space out, and I said *nothing*. I forget who and where and why and how—all of it. I forget I have a brain and forget what it's for. Probably I'm subconsciously processing and updating my perceptions of space time, while the conscious part gets a powernap. Who knows, maybe I *am* suffering radiation damage from all that pre-juve TV.

During the summer, Michele's not teaching, and she spends more time looking after Cord. I drive a cab and work on the new house. When I'm home we tend the garden together, which also means we keep Cord from unplanting the starts or pulling off the leaves. He's got a sandbox and some trucks in the plot. He gets a kick out of harvesting carrots and potatoes. When we pulled them this year, it was early October and the ground surface was frozen. I broke through with the shovel.

About a quarter mile from the house where we now live are the fields that the old homesteader cleared within the birch and spruce and poplar forest. He grew hay for his horses. But nowadays the trails wind through the fields and, Michele and I go running and push Cord in a stroller. When we're done, he gets out and we play catch or fly a kite or wrestle or just lie on the ground in the sun.

Even before he could walk, pushing him around the fields, I'd hand him leaves or spruce needles or dirt or sticks. I'd say, "Cord, check this stuff out. It's called grass."

"Aksk."

"Almost, buddy. Grass."

"Ass."

"Perfect. Good job, buddy. I love you. It's called grass."

"Ass," he'd say satisfactorily, rubbing the blades between his inexperienced fingers.

I want to teach him that the power of love is greater than the love of power. Jimi Hendrix said so. I don't know if it's true, but I can hope.

I want to teach him that we are more than our collective humanity. That we are the cosmos and the black holes and whatever's on the other side.

I want to teach him to do the dishes and cook. I want to teach him how to build a house and plant a garden. I want him to know how to survive in the woods. I stay in shape 'cause I'll be sixty-two when he graduates high school, and I want us to be skiing up a glacier or playing catch or paddling down the Skoog, together. He will know that there is always an adventure to be had beyond the road system. That there is always a place to clear his head, away from the competitive clutter of struggling humanity. Yes, for the most part I like people; after all, we're in this together. But perspective is everything.

My dad didn't teach me much as far as hands-on skills go. Sometimes I get a bit of an attitude about it. Like recently Cord pulled down a shelf that the TV was on. The TV fell behind the oil heater and cracked a brass fitting that attached the fuel line. Diesel started leaking out of the supply tube inside the house, and replacing the fitting would require cutting and flaring new copper tubing, a task I was unequipped for in terms of knowledge and tools. And I realized just how many times this has happened, that I would once again need to drop everything I'd been doing and learn how to do this new thing that I may never be called upon to do again. Shouldn't some level of proficiency of this nature be a default thing that a dad gives a kid? I had friends in high school who could take a car apart and put it back together or wire a house or build a waterbed. And I got what? Pick up the phone and call somebody was the skill at 821 East Fourth Street, Eureka, Kansas.

By this time—fuel oil leaking on the floor, outside temperature rushing in—the part of my brain that prepares responses to my indignant proclamations is ready with, Yeah, but I had a dad who was always there for me, who gave me love and taught me empathy and showed me how to treat others with honesty and respect and how to live up to my responsibilities. A guy who worked hard so that his family could have a good life, 'cause, well, that's what you did.

To which the angry neurons can only reply, Yeah I know, I know, but geez, this stuff's toxic and I needed someone to hate on for a sec. So it goes. Short version, I've learned all the physical skills I have since I left home.

The first job I had involving a table saw was at the sign-making shop in Vail, Colorado. We made signs that said "Double Diamond: Experts Only" and "Cold beer and wine" and "Please do not deposit sanitary napkins in toilet." I remember this short muscled-up carpenter with a brown moustache, holding up his left hand to show the lack of middle and index fingers. He grinned wryly. "You probably won't get hurt at first 'cause you're scared of it, and that's good. You'll pay attention to it. It'll happen later when you're hungover and thinkin' 'bout the pussy you ate last night, and you're runnin' like the hundredth board of the day through that fucker. That's when it'll get you. You won't even feel it at first, it'll happen so fast. You'll just see the blood spray, but then you'll feel it all right." I maintain a healthy fear of table saws to this day, even though I have two. All these carpentry tools vibe "Respect me! Or I'll fuck you up." And I do. Still have ten fingers, two eyes, etc. (knock knock).

I started building this house ten years ago. I had just returned from a year and a half of traveling, living in Thailand most of that time. I rented a motorcycle for three bucks a day and rode it around the north of the country. Went hiking in the mountains and smoked opium and stayed with refugees who had been chased out of Burma generations ago. Ate the best food in the world for less than a dollar a meal. I lived on an island for three months and scuba dived. When I ran out of money, I taught English in Surat Thanni, a city of over a million people, and lived with a Thai woman whom I still love but will never see again.

After Thailand I ended up in Ireland with no money and no work permit. I found a job, though, remodeling a six-hundred-year-old pub in Galway for three euros an hour. I stayed in a hostel and ate PB&Js and tuna mac until I had enough money to get home.

When I got back to Alaska I was flat broke. I had left a pickup stuffed full of everything I owned parked at a friend's. So I got the truck and pitched a tent at another friend's place, Dave's, and can you guess what I did next? If you're thinking *taxi cab driver*, we have a winner. And business was rocking at the time. The Stryker Brigade was due to be stationed at Fort Wainwright, and there were massive projects going on, both there and at Eielson Air Force Base. Everybody had money. It was difficult to find a contractor willing to take on residential construction because there was so much work on base. Feeling bored behind the wheel, I could take my pick of construction jobs. It was almost enough to make a person forget that we were at war with two countries. That our soliders were coming home in caskets while perhaps hundreds of thousands of civilians, as well as those we fought, lay dead in the rubble that bombs had reduced their infrastructure to. Almost enough to ignore the growing chorus of economists warning of an imminent massive financial crisis due to shaky and fraudulent mortgages and other high-level financial high jinks.

This was when my longtime buddy Bob told me about a new subdivision, another old homestead broken up into three- to five-acre lots. Only two thousand down and two hundred a month. I picked out and purchased our lot within a week. It's the best in the area, especially since we recently bought the lot to the north, giving us nine acres with field and forest and a peaceful creek. Right now, despite the persistent snowpack—the latest in my twenty-six years here—there are sandhill cranes seeking bugs among the brown grass tips. Moose browsing the willow down by the creek. The occasional bear or wolf wandering in from the Minto Flats.

A decade has passed since I pulled the chainsaw out of the pickup and cut a driveway and house site. One month later dump trucks were bringing in gravel that Bob smoothed with a John Deere 550 bulldozer. Then he loaned me a school bus that didn't run. We towed it over and parked it next to the pad, and I moved in. By fall I'd poured the concrete posts upon which would sit the steel beams upon which would sit our home.

As winter came on, I realized that the bus wasn't going to work, that if I didn't freeze I would at least hate life much of the time. The owner of the cab company had divided his basement into five eight-by-eight rooms that he let to drivers for two hundred and fifty bucks a month. He'd fire you for sport, but beneath all that ruthlessness was a soft spot for the underdog.

The basement smelled of food on the edge and dirty laundry and Dalmatian pee and dead cigarettes. The mattress I flopped on occupied half of my room. I could hear the clicking of dog nails and the broadcasts of football games through the floor, my ceiling. But I think I needed to retreat there at the time. I was still experiencing a bit of culture shock after the year and half of traveling and that miserable room was like a deprivation tank where I could shut down and process things.

The second year I owned the land, I arranged to have power brought to a pole near the end of my driveway. I was excited to have a light to read by in the bus and to have an electric heater. I dug a trench by hand, 2 feet deep and 160 feet long back to the house site. My friend Jacob called, and when he heard what I was doing, showed up with a cold case of PBR, which has always tasted so good on a hot day. We discovered if we placed the beer in the trench, the near-frozen ground would keep it icy cold indefinitely, like a root cellar. We were so happy about this that we dug till after the midnight sun had gone down. We took a break to BBQ some moose ribs and zucchini from the garden.

I buried the cables and backfilled the trench and nailed my power box to a birch tree near the bow of the bus. That winter I lived in the bus. I slept in my winter bag with two and sometimes three electric heaters blazing away next to me. It was so cold that my hands would quickly turn numb when I tried to read by my new electric light. One day in March, Bob and Mike and I headed out from the bus on skis, bound for a week in the Minto Flats. I quickly realized that there was little difference between my life in town and winter camping. The joke wasn't lost on Bob and Mike either.

It was around this time that Julia and Ruby entered my life.

The prospect of a home was energizing. I carried a pad of graph paper with me in the cab and sketched designs and gave

people rides and smoked lots of grass. By springtime I had settled on the current design: two stories with a shed roof. The high
wall is sixteen feet tall; the lower, eight feet. The south-facing
windows offer passive solar radiance. We might put in a loft,
eventually, an office or spare bedroom looking through the boreal canopy to Ester Dome.

By the next winter I had a floor but was living with Julia
and Ruby in their house on a piece of property that adjoined
a piece her parents owned, and we made reasonable payments
to them on a kind of rent-to-own basis. Julia wanted me to
sell my property, but I had chemically bonded with the place.
I'd never owned land before and I felt an obligation, after the
years of restlessness and wandering, to develop it according to
my principles. That is to say, I wanted to leave as many trees
standing as possible and to leave the field untouched for the
migratory birds, not shit a bunch of shack-dominium rental
cabins all over it.

Out the south windows, there's a lovely, young weeping birch
trailing languid boughs with thick clusters of leaves. Dave saw
me checking it out once and said, "I just had a vision of you and
that tree growing old together and it made me smile." There's
another younger birch on the north side; in summer, leafed out,
inclined toward the house, you can touch it from the bathroom
window. I transplanted a lot of trees rather than cut them down,
moved quite a few out of what is now the garden and replanted
them in rows to allow some privacy from the neighbors to the
south. The hope being that when Michele and I are AARP eli-
gible we'll be able to garden naked without getting arrested.

To Julia the property was a symbol of my intransigence and
the limits of her persuasive power. She'd had enough of Alaska.
Selling the land would have provided a short-term windfall, a
way of getting out. The house I was building, though, had my

sweat and blood all over it. I took my relationship to it seriously. I'm kind of a softy this way, I guess. Try as I might, I cannot read *The Giving Tree* to Cord without crying. I recognize the emotion, of course. It's my dad's sentimentality, what made *him* cry after sad episodes of *Little House on the Prairie* or *The Waltons*.

Julia could never really accept cab driving as a realistic means of income, either. Yet we fought about money endlessly.

"I think I'll drive cab Tuesday, Thursday, and Saturday this week."

"So when were you planning on spending time with me and Ruby? Or is that just not a priority with you?"

"Well there's Monday, Wednesday, Friday, and Sunday. But I was hoping to get some work done on the house. We can talk about it you know. That's why I threw it out there."

"Well, I'm working Monday and Wednesday but whatever. If you'd rather go smoke a bunch of pot and drive the drunks around than hang out with us, I guess. But we need to spend time with you, too. I mean, do you even like us that much, or just enough to have sex with me sometimes? And when were you planning on tightening the bolts under this house."

"I don't know, stop fucking yelling at me. You work during the day on those days. We can hang out at night."

Her jaw would lock in a jut; her brow would transform into a granite wall. Her eyes would become daggers thrown precisely to sever my will. "Don't fucking tell me what to do. I wanna know when you plan on spending time with me and Ruby and doing stuff around our home. I'm not just gonna sit around this fuckin' house all the time, either. If I'm gonna do that, I wanna go back to school. Get my degree. Or get the hell out of this frozen wasteland. It's not all about Robby all the time. Fuck that."

At this point we'd notice Ruby had gotten up and was observing us with wide eyes and slack cheeks, so we'd bury our resentment and tell her we were just having a conversation and that everything is okay and *Are you hungry, do you want some juice?*

To be fair, I was a pretty rough piece of work when Julia and I got together. I had spent most of my life doing pretty much what I wanted to do, and she shaped me into a person capable of understanding some of the give and take necessary to sustain a relationship. She preferred a jackhammer approach over sandpaper or a chisel. The end result being that construction moved slowly while we were together. A floor one year, walls the next, then another floor. I spent three years living with this low-grade panic, struggling to protect my increasingly vested investment from the elements.

I spent hundreds of dollars on blue plastic tarps and duct tape—Alaska siding. I had dozens of containers for catching rainwater in the year between laying plywood on the roof and roof metal on the plywood. What with the dread surrounding the pace of construction and the stress from fighting with Julia, I'm pretty sure I shortened my lifespan. But I learned a lot. I learned to breathe and to accept the struggle and to remain calm and keep moving forward as best I could.

We had good times too, floated some rivers, raised Ruby, laughed a lot. Interesting, that fine line between laughter and anger. I miss not seeing Ruby grow up. She and Julia live in Seattle now. We talk on the phone sometimes.

When I say I've built this house, I mean I've built this house with help from friends. A *lot* of help. Labor-trading is an indispensable aspect of out-of-pocket construction. I've worked on dozens of friends' projects and dozens of people have lent a hand on this one.

I learned most of the carpentry I know from John. John's from North Carolina. He played linebacker in high school. His light blue eyes are direct, engaged, smoldering, framed by an unruly, yellow-going-white mane and beard. He's a veteran and pissed off about all the war we've been waging. Enough beers and he might invite a pro-war nonveteran to step outside and finish the conversation. He sings along with the bluegrass music we listen to on the job. If we bring it in on budget he'll kick me a bonus. He taught high school history before he came north.

"I liked North Carolina just fine, but I could no longer continue to live in a place that had reelected Jesse Helms six fucking times. Hey, could ya cut me one at eighty and three sixteenths."

"Sure. What, you didn't like Jesse? What are you a ho-mo-sek-shul? A Mozambiquan?"

He grins, says, "Bread and circus."

"Huh?"

"Something Lenin used to complain about. Though I think some ancient Greek fucker said it first. How the people will follow any idiot who promises them 'bread and circus.' Where I come from it's more like if you give the people a beer to drink and a nigger to hate, then they'll send you back to D.C. for decades."

John's about five foot ten, thickly muscled. I have no trouble seeing him as a warring dwarf in some Tolkienesque fantasy, swinging a battle axe through the forces of evil with a wry grin. And then, blood-spattered and drinking PBR, he'll be sitting on the tailgate of an old Ford, and we'll be laughing at the stories of our lives.

Bob might be there too. He's more toward the elfin end of the Tolkien spectrum, long and lean and subtle, more into the bow and arrow than the battle axe. We met twenty-some years ago when we were both students at the University of Alaska Fairbanks. He was studying art, and I was studying not flunking out. One summer day we put in on the Clearwater River near Delta Junction and floated the Tanana back to Fairbanks. We were gone for a week. We caught burbot from the river eddies and fried them in carbon-caked cast iron over driftwood fires. We've been friends ever since.

About that time Bob's grandfather loaned him some money, and Bob used it to buy a forty-acre homestead from an old sourdough in the valley. He subdivided and built rental cabins on the land. He sold enough of it to pay back the loan and finance another project. In this fashion he has gradually reached the point of building nice homes on lots in town in the summer. In the winter he travels. But not like a rich man. He's more likely to ride a bike across the Lower 48 and camp in farm fields or go trekking in Colombia or the Himalayas.

Bob was born and raised in Fairbanks. He remembers when the streets were dirt and the city sprayed used motor oil on them to keep the dust down in the summer. He remembers Goldstream Valley before the original settlers sold out or passed on to that great homestead in the sky. See, after the valley was stripped and dredged by F. E. Gold, it was given to a bunch of white guys, go figure, huh.

Since then a slow process of dissemination has been underway with land being deeded over to a motley succession of settlers: hippies, heavy-equipment operators, environmentalists, survivalists, slumlords, artists, college students, dog mushers, grifters, miners, wildlife biologists, and trappers. There are still a few homesteads left in the valley, but most of them are composed of swampy bottomland that is difficult to develop, which is good 'cause the critters like this part of the valley. And it's nice to live someplace where there are still critters.

It's like in *The Giving Tree* when the tree gives everything to the boy/man. I'm always hoping that the guy will realize what he's got before he cuts the tree down. That the tree is a living thing that loves him and has value beyond the worth of its severed branches. But the guy always cuts down the tree. That's what makes me cry when I read it, I think. That the tree gives everything, and the man is still alone and tired in the end. And the tree is just a stump. Maybe this house I'm building is like that stump. I hope not, though. I hope that the greatest good I can offer in exchange for what I've taken, for what others have taken from this valley before me, is this bit of acreage and some kind of giving back that Michele and Cord and I represent. Like maybe not taking everything is the best we can hope for.

Bob's an artist as well as an eco-developer. He designed the geometric tile patterns for our main floor and bathroom. He etched a sun in the landing at the top of the stairs. Sometimes in December it's helpful to have a sun or two around to remember that this darkness is temporary. That we will rise from it together.

Bob blows glass vases that make me think of the way water flows around rocks or the way wind blows around trees. He's given us a few of those that are unsaleable due to a chip here or a discoloration there. My favorite has a swirling blue color that suggests the sky in a time-lapse photograph. Michele has filled it with dried wildflowers, keeping it grounded in the cycle of life and death.

Bob sells pieces at some of the local galleries. But after renting the studio time, it's difficult for him to charge enough to make any money. What he creates is mostly for his artistic satisfaction, which works well for the piece itself but doesn't do much for the long-term viability of art in a world where beauty is subject to commercial profit. Then again it's always been this way for art and artists.

He's installing the boiler in the new house. But he's flown to Lake Clark, on the Alaska Peninsula, with his girlfriend for a week of hiking. She's a biologist who works in Denali radio collaring Dall sheep and wolves and locating them from helicopters. Last fall I showed Bob one of my favorite places, a lake on the Skoog. He and his girlfriend floated the river together and got a moose on the lake. Then they hung it and smoked it for a few days. I like to think of them sitting on that lake together, unconcerned with the pace they must sustain in town in order to meet their own standards.

When Bob returns he'll finish hooking up the half-inch tubing I ran around the floor and buried within an inch and a half of concrete slab. In winter the boiler will circulate hot water through the tubing in the concrete floors, warming them. Radiators beneath our feet, thermostatically controlled. We'll have a woodstove too. I've never been comfortable without one. I mean, what happens when the power goes out? Answer: We throw another log on the fire.

Besides, I want to go woodcutting with Cord. We'll drive out some shitty old road, slow, on a cool sunny autumn day. We'll bring a bucket for picking berries and a .22 in case we see any grouse or ptarmigan we might have for dinner. I'll show him how to notch the tree and fell it so it doesn't crush the truck (hopefully). We'll limb it and buck it into stove lengths and load it into the truck. And hopefully he'll see that there are worse ways to spend a day in this world. And hopefully when I'm an old man he'll drive the truck and run the saw and throw the rounds out near the woodshed, a rite of passage for us both.

We'll have to get a good stove, though. Things have changed in the last twenty-five years or so. The wintertime air was always bad due to inversions, a layer of warmer air above the cold air that seals and traps all the pollution in the low-lying areas, or most of Fairbanks. But as our town has grown and the price of heating oil has risen, the pollution from burning wood has gotten worse. On bad days, Fairbanks rivals Beijing in the suspended particulates count. It has become an issue of passionate testimony at the borough assembly and city council meetings. A classic confrontation of the right of an individual to heat his house any way he can versus the right of an individual to breathe air that is less carcinogenic than the cigarettes I swear to kiss good-bye every hour of my life. So we'll get an EPA-approved stove and run it wide open more often instead of smoldering. And we'll hope the poison fog of town stays to the south of the ridge north of Farmers Loop Road. And then I'll become a famous author or something so that I no longer have to go drive cab in that toxic soup that makes my throat hurt and my eyes water—symptoms I didn't experience twenty years ago.

Of course, building a house is in itself an exercise in toxicity. Insulation, sheet rock dust, concrete sealer, ABS cement, paint, stain, solder. I could still put up houses for a living, but I'm trying to preserve my health for the things I want to do, not burn it up on the stuff I have to do.

Bob once renovated a house he owns on College Road to get it ready to sell. It still had the original cedar siding on it. When he bought it, he hired me to grind away the decades of peeling paint. I wore a respirator because the dust was a poisonous death cloud. Bob took his turns with the grinder as well. Today, we laugh about wanting to save the old place in as close to original condition as we could when in reality it would have been cheaper and more pleasant to replace the siding. Come wintertime he'll head for Asia or Cuba or New Zealand and camp and ride his bike. He's paid his winter-in-Fairbanks dues. We've probably spent close to a year together on backcountry trips. These relationships, these memories, have become our lives. Often I'm struck dumb by the ease of time.

Michele's ex-husband, Bill, wired the place for us. We all went to UAF together twenty-some years ago. Bill got a math degree. He does differential equations in his head to figure out the load capacities of different circuits or the span capabilities of posts and beams. He has a daughter named Molly who's a year and a half younger than Cord. There was a picture of her in the paper last weekend at the Relay for Life, an event that raises money for cancer research. Bill has participated every year since his own father passed away from the disease. Those are his legs in the photo beside his chubby, dancing, ringlet-haired baby girl.

He's had a rough road at times, battling bipolar disorder with various medications that always work for a while, until they don't. His second marriage is ending. He seems to be winning his battle with alcoholism, but the damages are evident: a fractured hip from an accident that claimed the life of a childhood friend (the friend was driving) and a criminal DUI record. Sometimes when he's particularly manic, when the symptoms are bordering on psychotic, he says it's easier to drown the episode in alcohol. Sometimes that's the best and only option. I wonder what percentage of all the addictions in the world are rooted in similar causes. But Bill remains an inspiration to me, showing up when he says he will and fighting to stay on the sunny side of the street. And maybe his love for his daughter will be enough to muffle the sirens calling him toward madness and self-destruction.

A dozen people were on hand to lift the big second-story wall, while a dozen more barbecued brats and chickens that Julia and I had raised in a small coop we built behind her house. Wes, a retired carpenter from Wisconsin, stood below, eyeballing the angle of the wall to tell us when to nail the bracing in place because the only level had somehow gone missing at the wrong time. I can still see him down there, a can of Milwaukee's Best in his gnarled hand, swaying slightly from the buzz, squinting. And somehow he called it almost exactly plumb with just a degree or two clearance for the next wall to be raised beside it, so the big wall could be sucked back plumb and nailed off to the curtain walls.

Wes lived across the street until he moved to an island off the coast of Florida. One day he came over as I was preparing to lift the power pole and drop it into the five-foot hole I'd dug in the permafrost, pouring boiling water into it so I could posthole down another few inches. A friend had told me that the best way to do it was to pull it up with a truck while two people stood on either side of it guiding it with ropes. Wes was skeptical of the arrangement yet warily volunteered to be one of the rope guys. I took off but instead of dropping into the hole, the pole got stuck and swung viciously around and smacked Wes in the ribs, knocking him down. Panicked, I ran to help him up. Somehow he was okay, bruised but okay. It could have gone another terrible way, and that fact has since infused every decision I make and sometimes keeps me awake at night. (I can't help but wonder how many close calls our hard-working billionaires have faced, risking death and maiming, struggling to build their homes, feed their kids, lobby against health care for the poor, etc.)

When I can't sleep, it's because I'm worried that maybe there's a hole in the tubing in the concrete that's supposed to heat our house or that maybe one of the plumbing fittings will fail and start spraying pressurized water behind the sheet rock or that I drove a screw through one of the matrices of wires that will power the place or that I should have used pressure-treated wood to attach to the top of the steel beams that the floor joists are nailed into.

That's the little picture; the big picture is that our house, our way of life, has become a living memory of the web of relationships that have, and will, sustain us over the years. There's Kurt, the organic farmer neighbor who remembers Harvey Milk from the Castro District, scaling an extension ladder to nail off the trusses despite the hernia that caused him to grimace with each swing of the hammer.

And Mike, who I skied with over the Wrangell Mountains only to find that the river we planned to ski back to the road had broken, forcing us to walk and pull our sleds over rock and crossing the river twenty-eight times in the final twenty miles. Mike and I put the second floor down in the rain the day before I left to go moose hunting one fall. Another time I ran into him at the bar/liquor store as I was getting some beer to drink while I built interior walls. He was like, what the fuck, and came with me, and we got shitfaced and drank beer and built walls till four in the morning, the temps drifting down into the twenties. I helped him build the deck and railing on his house. Pretty sure we got drunk that day as well. I like to think of it as multitasking.

Mike's a biologist. And a traveler. He and Bob met in Argentina. Two guys from Fairbanks somehow choosing the same guest house half a world away. I met Mike through Bob. The three of us have skied hundreds of miles through the Alaska backcountry. After he got his master's he started a construction company and now he builds houses for a living. He writes songs, plays guitar, and sings in a band these days. We don't see as much of each other, but that connection will last as long as we do, I think.

I remember Will sleeping on the floor of the school bus as I stepped over him to make coffee and oatmeal before we went out to make the final adjustments to the forms that the concrete truck would pour into and what would become the posts the house sits upon. The posts that connect the house to the gravel pad that floats upon the sea of permafrost that is the floor of Goldstream Valley.

We borrowed the money to complete construction. This is all new to me. I've never had access to that kind of money. I thought that finish carpentry, interior doors, kitchen cabinets, and plumbing were things I did to other people's houses. Yesterday I went to Greer Tank and Welding and purchased a three-hundred-gallon fuel tank with a five-foot stand and a thousand-gallon water tank—$2,500. I realized it would take three trips to get it to the property. Or, the sales lady said, we could have everything delivered for fifty bucks—and suddenly there they were. Before the loan I'd have been thinking, *I wish I had another fifty bucks.*

But the loan comes with its own weight. I was largely debt-free before it, and I slept better. Suddenly, over the course of a few years, we are buried: student loans, the lot to the north. And there are three of us these days. When I look down my arm I see a watch and a wedding ring. And when the phone rings I almost always answer. And I can't help but wonder if this is what it means to grow up, at the tender age of forty-seven. And I decide no, that's not it. What this is is the price of not having to grow up before forty-seven.

I can't think about the miles of cab I'll need to drive in order to help pay for it all as a chore or a thing I must do to keep us out of the poor house. Inevitably that will be tempting on those days I don't pay my expenses till after midnight. But what else it is is my life and how I interact with the world. A gift I give to my son.

A thing Michele and I do together that becomes part of who we are. It's up to me how I feel about it.

Like the sacrifices my parents made for me weren't sacrifices, they were their lives. They were their definitions of righteousness. And once they thought through the choices to the truth of the matter, they weren't even choices anymore.

I think about this picture I have of my dad on a beach in France in the fifties. He was a good-looking young man laying next to this stunning oiled-up bikini babe. He didn't appear to be thinking about family values. He doesn't seem like the same guy who grounded me for sneaking drinks from their liquor cabinet thirty years ago. Now he's suffering from dementia. Sometimes he feels like his life has passed him by. Something like what I picture the old man in *The Giving Tree* thinking about on the stump in the end.

And I think about how I'm tempted to yell at the boy. Don't be a dumbass. Just stay with the tree and play in its branches and eat apples in the sun forever. But that's just not who we are, who my parents were. The sacrifices they made for me were choices. And that's what I need to tell Cord about one day.

I've been a bit of a disappointment to my parents. I never graduated from college. I don't have any money to support them like they supported me. I smoke weed and drive a taxi cab. But they came to peace with these things long ago. When they visited Alaska for the first time I took them to the Copper River and chartered a boat and pulled three huge sockeyes from the gray turbulence with a dipnet. Back in Fairbanks we had people over and barbecued the fish beneath the great wall of our new house in the midnight sun. On the way to the airport the Alaska Range broke free of the clouds and we took a detour up an old mining road to the top of Ester Dome and watched Denali rise across two hundred miles of swamp and forest. And they saw that I was all right. That I was a part of something. And they were relieved. Like my failure to find a place in this world would have been on them. And that the place I did find belonged to them as well.

And two years ago, when they met Cord for the first time they saw themselves in the way I loved my son, in the choices I was making for our family. Finally they could be proud of me, even though I wasn't a successful businessman or world-renowned journalist.

And I guess the universe is expanding, accelerating. So that in a few billion years the night sky will be black because all the stars and planets will be so far away from each other that their light will be swallowed by the darkness long before anyone can see it. And all will be cold and static and dead. So I say, let's live hot now. Let's make enough love and passion that we'll still feel it when our molecules are scattered across millions of miles of emptiness.

Funk, 2009

THERE IS STATIC. "CHRIST, you guys are walkin' all over each other. Let's try one at a time." Another burst. I hear that crease in the airwaves before it happens and key up, get through. "Go get your personal, Sherrie, at the Marlin," Smurf says. I say check.

A squawk from the radio. "I just stepped on somebody, and I liked it. Who's red City?" More static. "All right, drivers, I'm outta here in about five minutes, and I really don't care anymore. I'm on the phone." A long rumble of static like pealing thunder.

The night DJ at the public radio station is playing some old reggae, talking about a soul fire "and we ain't got no water." I turn it up, sing along, slap my hands on the steering wheel.

The Marlin is an aging plywood bar, survivor of two fires and too many owners to remember. I descend the steps into a mist of body odor, patchouli oil, dankness, and tobacco and marijuana smoke pulsing in strobe and shadows. I'm hit in the chest by a thumping bass from a white guy with a mohawk puttin' out some old Parliament, "Up for the Down Stroke." I look through the whirling dreadlocks and rolling shoulders of the dancers, see Sherrie at the bar, thirty feet away. She's a strong woman, maybe 180 pounds. Her brown hair reminds me of shredded Brillo pads, tamed by blue barrettes. She sees me and downs the last of a pint of Guinness, hugs the couple she's been talking with, heads my way.

I take a deep breath and return to the car. Sherrie gets there three minutes later.

"Hey, dude, what up?"

"Not much, girlfriend, how you doin'?"

"Oh, I'm too fuckin' busy. But I get bored when I'm not too busy. Except when I'm drunk, which I am now, so I'm good."

"Drunk or busy, huh? I see similar patterns in my life sometimes."

"Ya see, it's a fucking epidemic. We gotta tell somebody."

"All right, where should we start?"

"Well, the girls from the burlesque show are meeting at this cabin off Farmers Loop to drink and try on costumes and act sexy so we probably ought to start there."

"Okay, let's do it."

"But I wanna stop at the store first. I need ice cream and Pringles and cigars."

"By all means, then."

"Exactly."

As we drive out Farmers Loop, she talks about burlesque and how annoying it is when people confuse it with exotic dancing. "I mean I was a dancer at Reflections. But I actually danced for those motherfuckers. I didn't just shove my pussy in their face. You know, I provided some class entertainment."

"Yeah. Who wants a pussy shoved in their face at a titty bar anyway?"

"Yeah. But burlesque, you know, that's singing, comedy, melodrama, and shit. A hundred years ago, when this town was a shitty little mining camp in the middle of nowhere, burlesque was the only show in town. Sure it was sexy, but it had to be other stuff, too. It had to be theater."

"The whole package."

"Yeah."

We turn off the unlit blacktop down a gravel path, pass a lit-up new vinyl home, then turn left into a driveway that leads to a log cabin settling unevenly into the permafrost. Sherrie gives me twelve bucks for the ten-dollar meter, kisses me on the cheek, and disappears.

I call in and a new voice answers. A woman's voice: Ruby. She puts me five U. I go west and charge Peger Road, call for my option. She tells me to pick up Thrifty Liquor for Steve.

The parking lot is a scene. People are scrambling to restock before the midnight closing. Brake lights and blinkers flash in the mist, headlights, neon, and people. I lock the doors.

Deaf Betty appears by my window. Smiling and shoving an air penis in and out of her mouth, she uses her tongue to push out her cheek with each in-thrust. She laughs and points at me and then at her. I shake my head, wave.

A guy approaches. I crack the window. He asks for a dollar. I say no and he calls me a racist. I roll into a parking spot. There's a short, skinny guy struggling under the weight of an eighteen-pack of Natural Ice. I pop the locks and he gets in, and I lock back up, put the car in reverse.

"Hey, how you doin', how you been?" the guy says.

I get wary. Someone who needs something will often slip into the guise of an old friend. It makes the target want to help. I look over and I do know him. It's the same Steve I've been hauling since he assembled and maintained the radio equipment for the Alaska Fire Service when I was driving Checker Cabs. Haven't seen him in years. We exchange greetings, and he tells me to take him to Viking Apartments. He pops the top on a blueberry club cocktail without asking, hoping I won't notice or care. He's in luck.

He tells me how he's living with this woman whose husband is in prison for molesting their teenage daughter. "This went on for five years before the kid figured out that she could stop it by reporting it. I think she knew she could the whole time, but she just didn't want to lose her father. Now they both take it out on me. I'm moving outta there as soon as it warms up enough to start working on my place again."

"What're you doin' to your place?"

"See, two summers ago I was still working and there was this car that was involved in a fatal hit-and-run accident that ended up parked on my property. And it sat there for forty-two hours without my knowing about it 'cause I was partyin', you know. So when the cops found it, they arrested me for tampering with evidence. And I lost my job. About two weeks after that, my cabin burned down. Both my cats got killed. All my computer equipment was destroyed.

"Last thing I got's the land. The only good thing that came out of that pipeline for me."

"And you're gonna rebuild?"

"Yeah. Going to try and find an old school bus or something and park it up there this summer. At least try and get a twelve-by-sixteen footer up before next winter."

But he doesn't look good. His arms look like spider's legs and he's emaciated, drunk. His spinal column is collapsing and crushing the nerves. He can no longer feel his fingertips or lift his arms over his head. I wish him luck as he gives me $5 for a $5.30 meter. He uses both arms to carry his beer.

The first time I came to Fairbanks I hitchhiked. I was twenty-one, had a mountain of shit and a puppy. I got a ride from a hippie hunting guide who told me that in the winters he went to an island in the Caribbean, Antigua, which is known as a good place to have a sailboat repaired. He'd find a job as crew on a boat, sail the world, and get paid to do it. Sounded good.

The next guy who picked me up was driving a seventies Ford Pinto with no windows and no muffler. He was wearing an old leather aviator's cap and goggles with bugs splatted on them and on his face. He was smiling insanely and drinking coffee from a huge plastic to-go mug.

"I just bought this car for fifty bucks!" he said as we bolted away.

He drove fast. "I'm gonna enter it in the demolition derby this weekend." He had to yell; the sound of the engine and sixty-mile-an-hour wind were deafening.

He cranked the wheel hard to the right and the car plunged into the trees. He revved down a narrow dirt four-wheeler trail. Trees raced past a foot off either door. No seatbelts. I was terrified, sure I was about to die. The guy shot back out of the woods and onto the highway a few minutes later. A few miles down the road, smiling malevolently, he plunged back into the woods. I began to develop a theory about how the open space of this country, or the freedom that the space enabled, allowed people to evolve into shapes that might serve no useful purpose but that might be essential to something as yet unknown to us.

For a while I was a commercial fisherman. I started that career in 1988. A year later the *Exxon Valdez* rammed Bligh Reef. So I redeployed and worked on the cleanup. Exxon flew a couple hundred of us in huge helicopters to a remote finger of stone jutting into the Gulf of Alaska. We scrubbed crude from rocks. We shoveled rocks and sand into bags that we piled on a cargo net. Another helicopter came, scooped up the net, and emptied it into a barge anchored a quarter mile offshore. There were hundreds of lumps of dead seabirds and a smattering of dead otters strewn upon the beach. These were disposed of separately and never seen again.

A film crew from *USA TODAY* was on hand and documented the whole show (except for the dead critters), allowing the world to see what a fine job Exxon was doing cleaning up its mess. But after the third day, we were all fired when we got off the copter back in Homer. This despite the fact Exxon had promised us the jobs through the summer. Many of us had quit steady work for the higher paying clean-up jobs.

The beach we'd been cleaning was still buried in oil. I mean, there were trees a hundred yards from shore coated with it. The wind had picked it off the waves and splattered everything in its path. There were tide pools of oil several feet deep. And the fumes were strong enough to make people sick.

After this I got hired to wear a bright orange hazmat suit and patrol the Homer Spit for tarballs. I found three. But I looked good for the tourists. I quit after two days.

I ended up at the sea otter recovery center in Kachemak Bay and got educated on the environmental movement. I decided in the fall of 1989 I'd go to the University of Alaska in Fairbanks and try to help save the planet. It felt good to have a cause. Believing in something tempered my hedonism, my reckless motion through space and time. I could feel myself actually starting to become someone.

But first I went fishing. A commercial fisherman–environmentalist was antithetical, I knew this. But that didn't seem to stop anyone. This is one of the last industries that works directly with the natural world, and it draws people who crave contact with it. The continued viability of the industry depends on an understanding of the ocean, the fish, the weather; it depends on organizations like Exxon not dumping millions of gallons of oil into the water. People who fished weren't environmentally aware because it was hip, but because they had a relationship with the environment. Because they had invested in that relationship and depended on it to provide food and shelter for their families.

I was drawn to this simple ethos, an appreciation of the earth as that thing that sustains us. As that thing we will turn into space dust without. When we put our hands directly on it, into it, to grow crops or to fill our nets, we can understand this.

I didn't know work like fishing existed in the world. The first time I went out was on a twenty-four-hour halibut opener—a date picked at random, months in advance, when it would be legal to longline for halibut for one day. Our crew was actually up four hours before it opened and kept working for six hours after it closed, a thirty-four-hour shift. After we slept for three or four hours, we woke up and started dressing fish again.

I'd gotten the job by beating the docks and talking to the skippers of the fishing boats. Because I was green, I was only given a half share, or 5 percent, of the value of the fish we caught. The food, fuel, bait, and ice came off the top.

As soon as I was hired I began baiting hooks affixed to lengths of line (if you call it *rope* you'll be labeled a farmer, a serious slight in the fishing world) with chunks of squid, octopus, and salted herring. The line with the hooks is called *gear,* and a functional length of gear is known as a *skate.* Baiting comprises the majority of a longliner's day. When you're not baiting gear, you're maintaining it, splicing cuts, untangling snarls, removing rotten bait, replacing hooks. I've spent hundreds of hours on boats getting tossed by waves, struggling for balance, and staring into miles of line.

The most dangerous part of the job is setting the gear. First, a guy tosses a floating flagpole tied into a couple bag buoys over the side of the boat. These are tied to a length of buoy line 50 percent or so longer than the depth of the fishing grounds. A giant anchor is tied to the bottom of the buoy line, which is then affixed to a dead shot, or hookless length of line, leading around the side of the boat to the baited hooks, which are lined up in a chute at the stern. When the anchor goes over, it pulls the hooks down with it. The boat is running full throttle against the current. A guy shoves a fresh skate of gear into the chute with a push broom as soon as the last one has uncoiled into the depths. Another guy furiously ties baited skates into the train of gear going over the stern; the hooks ding against the aluminum as they go. See, you don't want to get too close. If you get hooked, the plunging gear will yank you over the rail and down with it.

Sometimes the gear floated on top of the water for a few seconds before it sank. Glaucous-winged gulls, kittiwakes, and fulmars would follow us around and try to eat the bait off the hooks before it went under. Once in the Bering Sea an albatross got taken down. When we pulled the gear, it was still there. The baited hook it was trying to pick was embedded deep in its gullet. We spread his wings and the span was a foot wider than any of us were tall. The skipper came out of the wheelhouse waving his arms and shouting at us to get that thing off his boat. He was short and muscular and hadn't shaved in a week, and his face was stained with the coffee and cigarettes he consumed religiously while staring at the screens of the sounders, radars, GPS. He was infantry in Vietnam. When his third tour ended, he bought a guitar and played folk music at festivals across the Lower 48. He became a fisherman 'cause it was the only job he could find that made his adrenaline flow the way it had in war. And he was superstitious about that albatross, so we threw it over the side and kept pulling gear.

I never did any hunting or fishing growing up. Then suddenly there I was on the deck of a seventy-five-foot boat, knee-deep in dying fish as big as I was, their gills spread wide as they asphyxiated on the cool air. They sloshed to and fro as the boat was tossed by the swell. Blood spatter on my face, in my hair, viscera lost beneath hydraulic cables. Most of it had a purpose: To provide food for people, to provide income for myself. But much of it, the by-catch, served no purpose whatsoever and this incidental death bothered me.

I thought about the breaking waves the albatross had skimmed, the fish he'd pulled from the ocean, the other albatross who learned to fish by watching her, the birds' pure pursuit of life a stark contrast to the slaughter at my feet.

So we threw the albatross into the foaming chop. I knew that the ocean would re-absorb it, that it would be taken up into new life. But it still felt wrong. Somewhere on some forsaken rock sticking out of this remote sea, a tiny albatross was waiting for the dead bird to return with a feast of puked-up fish. And whether the universe cared about the fate of this family or not, I did. And I've had to make my peace with that.

We fished way out along the Aleutians, halfway to Siberia, where steep conical volcanoes rise from the slate blue water and currents from Hawaii and Antarctica surge between them, getting pinched into tight rollers as they rise from the depths of the Pacific to the Bering Sea.

The islands are mostly andesitic stratovolcanoes formed by the subduction of the Pacific tectonic plate beneath the North American Plate. Many are highly active with trails of smoke, steam, and ash drifting from their summits. This is the northern boundary of the Ring of Fire, more than a hundred islands spread across twelve hundred miles of North Pacific. On a few of the islands, foxes or cattle had been left behind, vestiges of abandoned dreams of fur farming or ranching. But the vast majority of these islands are home only to the seabirds and thick-stemmed brush that grows close to the ground so as not to be torn away by the constant scouring of the wind.

Other boats fished out there as well, but we were all swallowed by the immensity of it and rarely showed up on one another's radar. It wouldn't have surprised me if a fire-breathing sea monster had writhed up from the depths to swallow us, or if we'd sailed off the edge of the world, where the oceans spilled off the map into space.

Sometimes killer whale families ate the black cod off the hooks we'd spent hours and hours baiting, and all we could do was watch as they devoured our profit margin and frolicked and dove thirty feet away. Once a big male breached next to the boat and the wind blew the spindrift in our faces. I believed he was saying thanks for the fish. Then he was gone. Sixty miles from shore and the chopped swell of stone blue water was all we could see.

At the end of such a day I would be torn between gratitude for the total awesomeness of what I'd witnessed and disgust over the sour feeling of working for free. We'd have to spend the next day or two moving to a new location, far enough away that the whales couldn't lock onto our hydraulics. And we wouldn't be making any money while we were doing that, either.

I remember standing outside with Will at the back door of the Salty Dog, first bar you come to off the Homer docks, twenty-some years ago. We were smoking a bowl with a guy from Louisiana who told everybody his name was Hound Dog. He had "fuck you" tattooed across his knuckles and "coon ass motherfucker" running up one arm. He'd been fishing in the Bering Sea and was telling us what they'd done when the whales took their fish. "I got cap'n's 30.06 out his cabin and shot the mo-tha fucka, he was just right next to da boat like dey do. I emptied the whole mag in 'em. Steal my motherfuckin' fish motha fucka!

Then another one came ova and started nudging dat first one, and I shot dat bitch, too. Fuck doze fuckin' tieves."

No one said anything for a minute. Then Will said, "Well, fuck it then, why don't you go shoot some people or something? I mean you murdered thinking, feeling beings. For what?"

"To save our fuckin' fish, man. I din't do all dat fuckin' work for nuttin'."

"Oh, so you're a fuckin' hero, huh. Big hero shootin' fish in a fuckin' barrel, is that it?"

And there they were, standing a foot apart, unblinking, fists clenched.

"I don't have to listen to dis shit," Hound Dog mumbled as he turned away. "Fuckin' greenies don't not even know."

"Fuckin' murderer," Will replied.

I've always loved this about Will. His inability to shut up. His disregard for his physical well-being when something needs to be said. Like the time he and I were on our way back to Alaska after we'd spent several months being homeless in D.C., protesting the first Gulf War. We were at Sea-Tac, traveling across the tarmac aboard a shuttle crowded with people in suits and trench coats smelling like cologne and sipping Starbucks lattes. I noticed Will had that telling stony expression on his face. Then he asked, loudly, "Do you people know that your tax dollars are paying for torture and murder in Central America? I mean is any of this"—he gestured at the shuttle's cozy interior—"okay while that's happening?"

Silence.

"I know it, but what can I do about it?" a man asked.

"I don't know. I'm asking you. It seems like we should be doing something, though. Doesn't all of this feel wrong to you?"

Silence.

I'm not as brave or selfless as Will—but then again, even he appreciates that a disagreement on a boat in the middle of the ocean isn't advisable. I mean he and I worked with some tough characters. A former heavyweight wrestling champ from the state of Washington. He was six four, 260, and always heavily armed. We worked together on a boat named after a region of Norway. He was a dangerous human being. He defied the skipper's no-gun-no-booze rules on the boat, had a 9 mil in a shoulder holster, a .32 in his Xtratuf. He'd bring two hundred airplane shot bottles of Canadian whiskey on a two-week trip, sneak them all day long. We were too scared of him to tell the skipper, whose back we were busy smoking marijuana behind. One time he grabbed another deckhand by the ears and started shaking him back and forth, slammed his head into the wooden ladder that led from the fo'c'sle to the deck. It was obvious to everyone how easily this guy could have killed Paul. Will was reaching for a cast iron pan to swing when the wrestler let go. Paul fell to the floor like a wet towel. The guy looked scared of himself for a while after that. Like he was aware he was only partially in control of the enormous destructive power he wielded. In port he'd go to the bar with his guns and four very sharp knives strapped onto different parts of his anatomy. He would consume large quantities of cocaine and whiskey. Nobody ever messed with him. You could just tell. He was a hell of a deckhand, though, and the skipper knew it.

His best buddy on the boat was a guy named Chris, who'd dropped out of his final year in med school to become a commercial fisherman. The two of them were drinking at the Porpoise Room in Homer one day. Chris was on the pay phone trying to score more coke and couldn't resist urinating in the potted plant sitting there. He got caught and thrown out. So the two of them decided to rent a limo, buy more coke and booze, and go to a whorehouse in Anchorage, 240 miles away. (Anchorage had dozens of such places just a few years ago. Pipeline residue. They're almost all gone now.) They were missing for two days, and we had to delay our departure waiting for them.

When it's your wheel watch on a fishing boat and everyone else is asleep and you step out of the wheelhouse to take a leak, you stare into that cold water, thousands of feet deep and more expansive than all the continents put together and know that if you fall in the boat will continue on autopilot, and the last thing you'll see before the waves take you down will be the running lights of the boat leaving you behind, hours before anyone knows you're gone.

Out on the deck I'd grip a steel cable so tightly that it still has the imprint of my hand on it. And, yes, it was completely fucking exhilarating to be there, with death as easy as letting go, or losing your grip.

Eventually I had to quit fishing. I had carpal tunnel syndrome so bad I couldn't make a fist. I could no longer straighten my spine. And I still had plans for this body, rivers to float, mountains to explore. I'd stopped going to college because I still didn't know what I wanted to do with my life. I was lonely. I was drinking too much, writing about things I'd written about before but no closer to knowing what I wanted to say. I decided that my peripatetic and largely improvisational life was serving a perspective that was already gone—which is another way of saying, I was finally growing up.

I drove a cab five days a week for a year. I saved a big stack of cash that I hid in an abandoned freezer behind the cabin I was renting. A month after 9/11, I left for Southeast Asia. I had no return ticket. But a year and a half later I came back to Fairbanks. I bought the land, had a kid, got married.

I haven't had time to worry about perspectives for a while. I'll be a different person when I go to bed tonight than I am at this moment. Maybe someday I'll read this and know that it's utter bullshit. But for now I know that the truth moves around a bit depending on where you're observing it from. And if you spend your whole life trying to pin it down—or running away from it—you'll wake one day and find it's gotten away from you. And you'll be looking for tracks, hunting ghosts.

Ruby's telling a driver to pick up at the Boatel. She's been dispatching since the seventies and her voice commands your respect, whether you like it or not. "Who was next, please?"

It takes me a couple of tries to get through but when I do she tells me I have another personal call, a P.C., at 99 Bentley Drive. I catch my breath, say, "Check and good morning."

"Good morning, 29. Can I help the next car, please?"

Two minutes to get to Bentley Drive. I knock on the door. She answers wearing the same dress as the last time with a huge army green coat over it so when it's zipped up all I can see are her bare legs extending down and slightly apart. Elliot is bundled beside her. She smiles, and I see that she has covered a bruise high on her left cheek with some powder. "Call a cab?"

"Yeah, we're ready. Can you help me carry this?" She hands me a small duffel. Her eyes are a little glazed from alcohol, and she's looking at me with her head hanging, slightly cowed.

"You're not taking her nowhere man. Put the bag down. Get the fuck outta here."

The guy steps into the entryway with his little eyes on me. He's big and angry, shirtless and shoeless. "I mean it, man. Move on. This ain't your business."

"She called a cab. It's up to her to tell me she doesn't want it," I say over my shoulder. "You coming?" I say to her. She pushes Elliot out the door and swings it closed behind her, starts running for the cab.

The door opens before it latches and the guy is after her. I hear the door slam. He makes it about halfway to the car by the time we're in. He stops and yells, "Motherfucker!" Bare feet on negative-forty-five-degree concrete will do that. "Fuck! Fuckin' cunt, get back here." The guy gimps back to the house.

He pulls on the door but it doesn't open.

"What're you waiting for? Get out of here," the woman shouts.

She's sitting in the front seat. Her legs parted slightly. Beneath the green coat she could be naked. "He's locked out. His feet'll freeze."

"He's an asshole, man. He hit me. See that, he fuckin' hit me!"

"Okay, but I'm not down with . . . with being responsible for him losing his feet or . . . or worse."

The guy comes to the cab. "God dammit man let me in! I can't feel my fucking feet! Please. Let me in."

"Do you have a key?" I ask her.

"Yeah, but I'm not giving him my extra key. It's my fuckin' house."

"Bullshit, I pay, too. C'mon, Des. I said I'm sorry."

"Give him the keys or I'm gonna let him in," I say.

She pulls the key with a flourish from one of the coat pockets, dangles it in front of the window. "You mean this? Would you like to borrow this, Willard? How're your feet doin', you little bitch ass piece of shit."

"They hurt, Desi. Please."

"Why don't you bend over and I'll shove it up your ass?"

"All right I'm letting him in." I move my hand to the power lock switch.

"I'll give it to him. Fine." She flicks the key out the narrow window crack and it lands in shallow snow at the edge of the driveway. Willard goes down on his hands and knees and paws at the area. Comes up with it. Lurches back to the house. "Satisfied? Can we go now?"

I wait till he gets the door open. Put the car in reverse. "Go where?"

"Gloria Street, so I can drop him off at my mom's, and then to Arctic Bar."

"Okay."

We get halfway there, and she says, "I should've told you before, but I don't have any money."

"Great."

"Listen, I'm really sorry, but we had to get outta there and I didn't know what else to do."

"No, that's all right. But I'm not taking you to the bar."

"I can't stay at my mom's. She says I can't if I been drinkin'. She'll take Elliot, though, she say."

"What's she gonna do, though? She gonna make you stand outside? Freeze to death?"

"Maybe you got some place we could go, huh? Maybe we go have a little fun and then you can take me to Arctic." She puts her hand on my right thigh. When I look at her I can see down the coat to her breasts tapering to aureoles. I can feel the heat rising up from between her legs and I'm getting hard and forgetting to think. Feeling the attraction pulling at my viscera, riding that wave of sensation. Inhaling the sweet noxious love chemicals.

I look in the rearview mirror and watch Elliot staring out the window, writing his name in the frost his breath leaves on the glass. I hear myself saying, "I can't."

"What, you have a girlfriend, huh?" She removes her hand.

"Yeah. We have a kid." I feel myself rising to the surface.

"Oh. Well, good for you. A boy or girl?"

"A boy. This is your mom's house here, huh."

"Yeah. So you can't take me to the bar, huh?"

"No. Sorry."

"It's all right." I carry the duffel to the front door and wait until they go inside. Driving away I say, "Fuuuck."

Street signs covered in hoar frost materialize from the fog. I say the names in my head as I pass them. *Blanche, Bonnie, and Brigit Streets. Rosella, Katherine, Mary Leigh.* Cab legend has it they're named after prostitutes who worked the area when the roads were just trails: The trail to Bonnie's, the trail to Katherine's . . . The industry was shut down in the fifties, when the army threatened to ban its personnel from the city limits unless the town did something about its gambling and prostitution.

The main district was downtown, near where the bingo halls and the post office stand today. By most accounts the women who worked there were treated decently by the rest of the community. Their business was largely considered a necessary thing in an outcast mining town, something that would exist whether it was legal or not. The girls registered with the city, paid an assortment of fees and fines, and received regular blood tests.

Cab 9 is telling the dispatcher that his fare went into the Safeway on Airport a half hour ago and he doesn't think she's coming back. Thinks he got ripped off. Wants Ruby to give him a position in the West. "United 9, I'm holding calls in that zone if you're ready to move on."

"Yeah, I guess I'm ready to move on."

"Okay, get the Lonely Lady for Cinnamon."

"United 9 check."

It takes about three minutes to get through. Ruby puts me seven north. I think how impossible it would be to call for help when the radio's snarled up like this. Like it is every Friday and Saturday night. When there are too many buttons on the board for a dispatcher to keep track of. When a driver might have a little money.

Be careful, I tell myself. Remain calm and be careful.

It seems like a card game, sometimes. There are cards that say go and take so-and-so to bingo or to the airport or the bar or wherever. Collect this much money—or don't. There are cards where your car breaks down or your fare gets swiped by another company. Cards where you'll get laid or at least high. Cards where you assist people with wheelchairs and groceries and bikes. There are death cards, too.

I remember two, the last one early in the morning. I'd been one of seven drivers on the road but I'd gone home. The call came about an hour after that. The driver was found stabbed to death a few hours later. He was a great guy, the kind of guy who'd help somebody when they were down. His name was Mike.

The night spins. A short, muscular, drunk GI wearing a Texas Longhorns sweatshirt is angry about being deprived of the adrenaline rush of kicking down doors in Baghdad. Tells me to fuck off when I ask him to put his seatbelt on for the gate guards. Tells me they don't even have seat belts in the Strykers, the armored assault vehicles from which the brigade takes its name.

There are phone lines ringing on top of each other in the background. I can feel the frustration of the drivers waiting to clear.

A woman goes to the Stop 'n' Go and back for chips, candy, and sodas and talks about her kids developing personalities without pausing for breath. Inside I'm screaming, "What makes you think I care!? Please, please, please stop!"

A ninety-seven-year old Inupiaq whaler goes to the emergency room.

"United 26 go," Ruby is saying.

"Ee-gul twenny sik, I led West at Aw Jay."

"You're red West at R.J.'s . . . step inside and see the bartender, she's got one for you."

"Ee-gul twenny sik che."

Phil is from Laos. Cab is his second language.

I get sent to the Birch Park low-income housing. A young, light-skinned black man wearing Dub, South Pole, and Triple F.A.T. Goose comes to the car after a few minutes. He gets in the back passenger side and pulls his hood down to reveal thin dreds. He says, "Hold up," into his iPhone and looks at me. "Uh, yeah, can you take me to Sheridan Apartments?"

"Sure can, man." And we're off. The kid goes back to his phone, maybe twenty-three years old. He's got a fine-boned face, a sweet smile. Smells like good weed. "Yo niggah what?—Oh hell no.—What he want.—What you mean five-oh?—Oh.—Hard or soft?—Not right now, I don't. Maybe in a hour or two.—Peace." He puts the phone down. "What up, man?"

"Drivin' around in circles, ya' know. How you doin'?"

"'Bout the same. You wanna smoke a blunt?"

"More than I want my next breath."

"Yeah, huh?" Laughing.

It's strong skunky bud, and by the time I drop him off, I've forgotten most of the tension that's accumulated over the evening. He pops the money off a fat roll of faced bills grouped by denomination. A working roll.

The night DJ is finishing up, reading the temperatures from around the state. "It's fifty-seven below in Fort Yukon, forty-eight below in Tanana, fifty-two below in Arctic Village, fifty-one below in Fairbanks. Tomorrow look for temperatures of forty-five to fifty below during the day, goin' as low as fifty-five below tomorrow night, people." He lets his smoked, gravelly voice extend the syllables into long seconds. "So stay home and stay warm, and if you do have to go anywhere better plug that car in now. All right, Fairbanks, it's been a peach. Gonna turn you over to the capable hands of Bob Parloche for jazz through the night. Good night." The airwaves cut to the middle of some old Coltrane. I feel the car slide around the ice like an extension of my central nervous system. Call red South. Get sent to Reflections.

I almost hit a King Cab in the parking lot fog. I note he has a fare. Wonder if it's my trip. Almost say screw it and call it a dud rather than get back out in the cold. But I go in.

I force my way through a bunch of GIs waiting to pay the cover in the entryway and get buzzed through. I'm hit by loud electronic music. Dominique is standing by the door and towering above three nervous-looking white guys. Dom is an African American man maybe six foot six and three hundred pounds. He points to the three guys as soon as he sees me. "These are for you," he says.

I'm distracted by two dancers wearing G-strings and playing pool with a couple construction workers past Dom's shoulder. When the girls pass each other they kiss. Their nipples brush together.

"Hey, I said these motha fuckas, man, you don't get the girls. They still gotta work." He's grinning at me out of the corner of his mouth.

"Oh, yeah, right."

"Now you guys got to get the hell outta here. And don't bring this bitch back."

The two younger guys are helping the oldest to his feet, to the door. As they go through, he turns to Dom. "Yo my niggah, be cool brother."

Dom lowers his eyes and shakes his head. I can see the slightest trace of a smile there when the steel door slams.

Outside the two younger guys are trying to fold the third guy into the cab. "Goddamn you crazy fuck, you tryin' to get killed?"

"I think he's tryin' to get all of us killed," the other guy says.

"Oh, whatever. You guys are a bunch of nervous Nellies. I just got outta jail. That's how they talk to each other in there. So I talked to 'em like that, too. 'Yo my niggah, yo!' you know."

An African American man has just left the bar. He stands between the front door and the cab composing a text message. He looks up when he hears the N word. His eyes linger on the drunk man who is oblivious to his presence.

"Listen, man, you're not in jail anymore." I say. "So if you really want to go around shoutin' that word, then go for it. But if you want a ride, let's go. Shut the door. We're busy."

"Whatever. All right." He looks up briefly and sees the man standing by the door looking at him. "Yo my niggah! Deuces!" he calls, gets in the back, shuts the door.

The man continues to stare at him as I back the car up and roll away. Watching until he's obscured by fog.

"Comet Club, my man," the drunk guy says.

"Fuck, Larry, let's just go home. I'm going home, anyway. Gonna get killed hangin' out with your ass," the second oldest guy says.

"Oh, shit. You're kiddin' me man. I just got out of jail! We gotta celebrate! Don't be scared. They think it's funny when I talk to 'em like that."

"What'd you do?" I had to ask.

"My fourth DUI," he laughs. "And then this punk cop, couldn't've been more than twenty, not old enough to shave, he tries to get tough with me when he's puttin' the cuffs on. And I turned around and clocked him. Man, he went down. Shit. Next thing I know I'm on the ground with a shotgun in my ear." He laughs.

He appears to be in his mid- to late sixties. How's he made it this far? "All right man, Comet Club," I say.

"You pussies really goin' home?"

"Yeah, tired but alive."

"I think I'll quit while I'm ahead too."

"All right, cabbie, here's five bucks, get these two home and it's all yours."

"Uh, it's six bucks now. Probably be around eight by the time I get 'em home."

"You bitches broke? Shit, all right, here's two more." He hands me the crumpled up bills. The other two get out a couple minutes away.

I call my number. Ruby puts me two City, and I roll over to Kodiak Jack's to see if I can flag anyone. L.M. is at the entrance to the parking lot in United Cab 1. I pull up next to him. He wears a NASCAR cap over short, sandy hair and wire-rimmed glasses with fat lenses. His eyes are like blue half dollars behind them. A friend once told me there's nothing wrong with his eyes, that he wears the glasses to better see the facial cues that give away the true motivations of others.

"What's up?" he asks when I pull up.

"Not too much, booked about $200, you?"

"About that. Did you hear her give Denali Way to Cab 50?"

"I think so, yeah."

"Yeah, well, I watched him drive by with a carload of people at the same time he checks the trip."

"No. shit, huh. What'd you do?"

"I went and picked up the trip. And I took him to channel two. Told him he wants to fuck with me, I'll go to the bank, take out my expenses, spend the rest of the night taking every fucking trip of his I can get."

"Way to go."

"Fuck him." There's a Ford pickup that wants to get around us. It's jacked to the sky and set down on mud tires that would fit a loader. The horn honks.

"What the fuck? Like this guy can't get around." L.M. opens his window and waves. The truck takes its time even though it has a couple feet on either side. It stops when it clears cab one, and two young guys with military haircuts stare back at us through the Confederate flag sticker that covers the rear window.

"Look at these two, still pissed at Lincoln." He pulls a two-million candlepower spotlight from between his front seats and blazes it into the big Ford. The two occupants duck. He pulls out a blued steel Beretta nine millimeter and racks one into the chamber, taps it on the roof of the cab. "You got somethin' to say, motherfuckers?"

The truck spins its tires and slides sideways out of the parking lot, spraying us with gravel.

"Jesus Christ, man," I say.

He's laughing. "What I thought," he says.

Ruby sends him to bingo. L.M. says, "Later," spins a 180, and is gone.

She tells me to pick up Bobby's.

It's still busy, people standing around the bar. A trio of keyboards, drums, and a bass plays softly to my right, lulling the din of conversation. Lights half dimmed. I smell the good Greek food and start to salivate. My stomach clenches. I feel light-headed, shake it off. Shout, "Taxi-cab!"

I take a couple in their forties to a house on the north side. The guy and I talk football for a minute, and then he and the woman murmur back and forth. I smell his expensive leather coat. Her sweet perfume.

Class distinctions get blurred here. The nearest Nordstrom may be 360 miles away, but this town has its share of little black dresses and strap sandals. They're probably behind the Carhartts and Xtratufs in the closet, but they're there, like rare birds, flitting from a private party in the hills to Lavelle's Bistro to a condo in the west end. Then put away until the next trip to Seattle.

This is pretty much a blue collar town, but it's a small tank and we all swim in it together. That is to say nobody comes here to be a member of the Fairbanks elite. The wealthiest guy in any room may be wearing the filthiest clothes.

When my mom visited, we went to a nice restaurant, and she noticed how some of the people wore sport coats or ruffled dresses, while others sported torn work clothes and baseball caps. And the two groups were often seated at the same table.

It reminded her a little of Eureka, Kansas, where farmers, bankers, ranchers, judges, and roughnecks could often be found in the same room having a drink together. My mom was an English teacher before she married dad. She used to diagram sentences she'd overhear on the back of the paper placemats. She'd make us do it too. Like a game, having dinner and diagramming some sentences.

-:::-

I get sent to Shenanigans. When I get there I have no memory of checking the trip or driving to it. I'm just there and aware that someone inside needs a ride. The entrance is an unlit door in the backside of Reflections. I go in.

The room is the size of a tractor-trailer van extending away from the door into a murky area at the far wall. The half closest to the door is split by a scratched plastic bar. Behind the bar a heavy woman wears a black leather vest over freckled skin that has not seen the sun in many moons. The woman's biceps would look good on a college linebacker. She keeps a sawed-off 12-gauge loaded with six rounds of double-aught beneath the cash register. Enough firepower to wipe out the entire bar if she has to.

"Hey Lola, you call a cab?" I say.

"Hey, fuckstick, your cab's here. Drink up and go home," she yells toward the back. The tattoo on her right arm draws me in, a blue-lashed eye inside a star staring from the left socket of a cracked and fading blue skull. When Lola lifts something with that arm, it looks like the eye is leaping from the socket.

"Now, barmaid, is that any way to talk to the man that's been fillin' up your tip jar all night?" It's a big voice.

"Yeah, thanks for all that. Looks like mom'll be able to have that operation after all. And if you ever call me barmaid again, I'll cut your nuts off and throw 'em in the deep fryer." She pops a kernel of popcorn into her mouth.

"In England they call them barmaids, not bartenders. If you called one a bartender it'd be an insult."

"Yeah, and if we were in England, I'd be callin' you a wanker instead of a fuckstick, but we ain't in England, mate. And you two told me to call a cab, and now he's here, and it's time for you to go," she replies. "Guy spends a week on an oil rig in the North Sea and thinks he gets to change the American language," she says to me as she grinds a pint glass down on the sink brush and winks.

"All right, all right, we're moving. Thanks."

Before I see the people behind the voice, I walk back to the cab. I don't see it so much as remember where it is. The temp is slowly falling, nudging fifty below. I let myself be carried away by a jazz musician dead more than thirty years. I jump when the door pops open.

"Hey, chief, how ya' doin'?" the big man inquires.

I look over my right shoulder and see a pair of Carhartt-covered arms pushing and folding a thin resistant woman into the backseat. Her head smacks against the top of the doorjamb. "Ouch, motherfucker, shit. I said I don't wanna go yet." She falls into the cab and swings futilely at the arms while she talks.

"Oh c'mon, babe. Rog is at the Club A.K. Rog and Reno. They're waitin' for us there."

"Fuck Rog and Reno. I ain't seen you in over a week and you're goin' right back up north and all you wanna do is go get drunk with Rog and Reno. What, you wanna go home and fuck Rog. Is that it? You go queer on me over there?"

"Ahhh, fer fuck's sake, Glenda."

"Hey guys, I don't care what you end up doing, but you gotta shut the door. I can't keep the cab warm. So get in, and I'll take you somewhere. Or get out. But we're busy. I'm cold. Let's do something."

"You hear that, honey? The man's busy, so let's just go have a couple at the AK, then we'll go home."

"A couple, huh. Like you ever had a couple in your whole life." She rolls on her back and kicks at the man with both legs. Connects with his stomach.

"Ooooomph!" he says, doubles over. "Fuck! Fuckin' bitch!"

"Ahhh shit. Listen, just get out, okay. Just get out and shut the door please."

"It ain't cold, motherfucker. Fuck you. I don't even wanna be in your pussy cab, anyway. Never asked for it in the first place. She scoots herself out the door to the big guy leaning back against an idling El Camino. "C'mon, big man, take my ass home and fuck me before I explode, you hear?"

"Christ, Glenda. Can't a man have a drink with a buddy without it bein' such a big deal?"

He grabs each of her arms in his long fingers and lifts her off the ground, tosses her. She lands in a snowbank in front of the car. He slides into the backseat. "Fuck! All right, driver. Fuck her. I'm goin' to the Club AK."

"Uh, listen, maybe this isn't gonna work. Why don't you just call another cab?"

"Fuck that shit, man. That bitch, my wife, is psycho. You're a cabbie. I need a ride. Look here's twenty bucks. Keep it and take me to Club Alaska, please."

I take the money. When I look the woman is no longer in the snowbank, just the imprint of where she landed. "All right." I put the car in reverse and look at the left rearview mirror as my foot leaves the brake for the gas. "Fuck!" I gasp and slam my foot back down on the brake.

"What? What now?" the guy says.

"Your wife. She put her head under the tire."

"Who gives a shit. Fuck that bitch. Run 'er over."

"Oh, okay. Great idea. Why don't you go get her."

"I ain't gettin' her. Here, here's another twenty, run 'er over."

"Christ." I don't take the twenty and get out of the car.

"Uh, ma'am, listen, it doesn't have to be like this. Why don't you get back in and I'll take you home."

"Go ahead and run me over. I'd rather be dead than married to that asshole." She coughs on the exhaust cocoon wrapping around her.

"God dammit." I grab her by the shoulder and elbow and pull. She rolls and kicks and hits my shin, almost takes out the knee. "Fuck." I kick back reflexively, not sure where, and start pulling again, protectively.

The giant's hands wrap around my biceps. I'm off the ground and tossed like a bag of laundry over a Celica. I hit a Dodge Ram and slide to the ground. When I try to breathe, I can't. *I don't believe this*, I think. I try again and get a little air. Try again and get a bit more and wonder if I can get it back before I pass out. I sit there for what seems like several minutes before I'm breathing normally.

I'm aware of being very cold and slowly get to my feet. My hands are numb and of no help. When I'm up I shove them into my pockets and look to the cab. The man and woman are leaning against the Celica in a passionate lip-lock.

I shake my head to clear it.

"I love you, Poochie koo," the giant is saying.

"Oh, my big, strong brute. You saved me from that bad man, didn't you?"

"I did, and I'll do it again. I love you, Pooch. Let's go home."

The woman makes a sound like a sexually aroused lioness. "Oh big man, you gonna fuck my brains out?"

"I'm gonna fuck you like you ain't never been fucked before."

I slide around the front of the Celica in a crouch. I creep past the space between the Celica and the cab and around the front of the cab to the front passenger door. I open it and jump in and hit the power locks, slide back into my seat, and let the heat hit me. I put the cab in reverse.

I call in. Tell the dispatcher I got a no-go, and I'm red South. "You're two South," she says.

I head north on Cushman. When I cross Airport Way, I'll be in the city, and she's holding calls in the city. Timmy, Cab 99, from Thailand crosses before me and gets sent to Kodiak Jack's, leaving me one South. As I'm approaching Airport with the mike in my hand, Ruby tells me to pick up at the Goldrush Saloon for Michael.

I pass Kodiak's. Flashing police lights in the parking lot throb red, blue, and yellow in the fog. The top-lights on the taxis outside the door look like illuminated dorsal fins.

It takes five minutes to get to the Goldrush. The parking lot's overflowing with Navigators, Expeditions, Yukons, and Escalades. The plywood bar is thumping like a subwoofer to a rap artist I don't know.

There's a scrum by the door. A dozen African American men grab and punch into the center as it moves to and fro. A woman in a lime dress slit to the hip and hangin' low between her breasts swings a purse with vicious accuracy into the fray. A woman in a satiny red number screams for it to stop. People stand around watching and laughing.

Two men approach the cab from different sides of the fracas. "This cab for Leon?" "This cab for Michael?" they say at once.

"It's for Michael, actually."

"All right, I'm ready to get the hell out this motha fucka. These niggahs here just plain stupid. Hey B, where you goin'? You can jump in this one you want."

"Uh, I'm just going over here to Twenty-Seventh Avenue."

"Shit yeah, we can drop you off on the way."

"Where we goin'?" I inquire.

"My brother here goin' to Twenty-Seventh, and then you can take me over by Aurora."

"So, Leon, right? You callin' it a night?"

"Yeah. I like to beat the rush at closing time. How 'bout you?"

"Naw, I ain't done yet. I just gotta decide. I got three bitches I could go visit. I'm thinkin' I'll go with that Becky tonight."

The other guy laughs. "Gonna get that Becky, huh."

"You seen that too, huh. That's some funny shit, yo. Where you from, Leon?"

"I'm from Tampa, but I've been workin' construction up here a few years now."

"No shit, huh? I just did four years in the Florida pen. I know all them gold-toothed niggahs down there."

"This your place, man?" I say to Leon.

"Yeah, this is it. Thanks." He hands Michael some money for his fare.

I say thanks as he shuts the door.

"Where on Aurora?" I ask.

"Offa Dogwood, man. How 'bout you? You must get them Beckys all the time, huh?"

"I don't know man. What's a Becky?"

"Oh, it's this new video on the Internet. You know how black women they don't like to suck dick, right?"

"I never knew that."

"Yeah, most of 'em don't even do it. But you find one that do? She gonna get down on the motherfucker. But, anyway, in this video it be talkin' about gettin' a white girl, a Becky, when you wanna get your dick sucked. It show the back uh this white girl's head goin' up and down. Fuckin' hilarious. So, shit, you probably get yourself plenty uh Becky just drivin' around pickin' bitches up, huh."

"It's happened, you know, not so much anymore."

"Oh yeah. You in love, huh? I can tell."

"Well, yeah, I love her. But there's more to it. We have a kid. She's a good woman, and we're, like, in this together, now. I don't wanna fuck that up."

"No, I feel you man. That's good that you see it that way. I respect that. I'd like that myself, someday. But for now I just got out four years in the pen, man. I got some catchin' up to do."

"Hell yeah you do. This where you're goin' here?"

"Yeah, this it. Here, B, keep the change, yo."

"Thanks, man. Enjoy that Becky."

"You know I do."

Ruby puts me six North so I go City. "Ten oh four on six," she says.

I say, "Check."

I park in front of the small house, old Fairbanks. Sixty-year-old cedar siding, wood-paned windows revealing a tidy living room, an arctic entryway, a Metalbestos stovepipe smoking lazily. Subtle contortions in the roofline reveal the enduring surrender to the permafrost. A vinyl home across the street. I honk the horn. A young guy steps in front of the window and waves. I wait. The guy comes out with his girlfriend. He opens the back door for her, sits in front with me.

He's got short black hair, in his early thirties. The set of his features says "sardonic appraisal." The girl has short blonde hair. She's perky and cute. "Hi," she says cheerily.

"Hey, how you guys?"

"Yeah, we're good. We've been drinking. Is that okay?" The guy says.

"Yeah, that's allowed. I'll be keepin' my eye on you, though."

"Ya hear that, honey. Keep your shit together."

"Okay, I'll try not to kick any ass, but you know how I get."

"She's an ass-kicker," the guy says to me confidingly. "But I think you're safe."

"I feel better. Where you guys goin'?"

"South Noble."

"All right."

"What you reading," the guy says, pointing to a book sticking out of my backpack.

"It's a mystery about this African American private eye in LA. in the fifties and sixties. This one's during the Watts riots."

"The Watts riots, huh?"

"Yeah."

"My dad was a cop in this state for twenty years. But before that he was in the National Guard in California. He was one of the guys that got sent into Watts to quell the riots."

"Wow, that must've been something."

"Yeah, he used to talk about it. Like they were all gung-ho to go in there and kick ass. But when he got there, it was like 'Wow, these people are really poor. I see why they're pissed.'"

"That must've been tricky."

"Yeah, I mean, he was pretty sure they wanted to kill him too."

"And that's how you ended up in Fairbanks, huh?"

"Pretty much."

There's a pause, and I say, "How 'bout you, you reading anything?"

"I'm reading a book called *Player Piano*."

"By Kurt Vonnegut."

"You've read it?"

"Yeah, that's the one where machines do the work, right?"

"Yeah. The people don't have anything to do. But they live a long time."

"And there's suicide clinics?"

"Yeah, you get a free meal with your suicide."

"Yeah, I read it. That was a good one. This you guys on the left here?"

"I think that's our house in that fog," the woman says. "And you have been such a good cab driver that . . . do you like blueberries?"

"Yes."

"Well we're going to give you our last mini blueberry pie. He makes them. They're delicious. The blueberries are from Ester Dome."

"Wow, thank you very much. It looks awesome." They pay me and they're gone.

Ruby sends me to the Midnight Mine for Tommy Lee, a regular.

The Mine is half packed with young Fairbanksans. There are no GIs here. After the Strykers came home from their first deployment, there were so many fights between locals and soldiers that the bar banned the military from the premises. A waterfall fountain near the front door adds refreshing humidity to the dry winter air.

I find Tommy in a bowed head conversation with a drunk woman. He looks like Mark Spitz, somewhere between the age of forty and sixty. A black leather trench coat, slurring words, smoking. The woman slides off her stool, and Tommy helps her with her coat. They lean against each other as they stumble to the cab.

Tommy holds the woman's door for her. The woman's a little older than he, I guess. I take them to 1300 on Nine, a duplex. They're kissing when we get there. He hands me a ten and says keep it.

I get sent to the Big I. The Pogues are playing on the outdoor speakers, "If I Should Fall from Grace with God."

I go inside and shout cab for Rikki, but my voice doesn't carry far through the music and people. I ask the bartender if she knows who called. She says no, but she asks the other bartender who talks to the bar back who points to some women sitting at a tall round table between the bar and the backroom.

I ask them if they called, and they say yes and look surprised that I'm here, and I smile and head back to the car before the song has ended.

They're in their early thirties. The thin one with brown hair is helping her friend, who wears a heavy wool trench coat, across the ice. She appears unsteady. They get into the backseat.

"Good morning. How we doin'?" I say.

"Christ, it is morning isn't it?" the brown-haired woman says.

"For a little while, now."

"Well, I'm just awesome, how 'bout you?"

"I'm not quite awesome, but I'm not too bad."

"Well, I guess that'll have to do."

"Where you need to go?"

"I need to take my friend home to Hamilton Acres, and then I'm going to State Street." The woman in wool is snuggled into her friend and wiggles her fingers at me and tries to smile, but it looks more like a grimace.

On Minnie Street the conscious woman says, "Yeah I was the DD tonight for some friends from work, but I got tired of cartin' their drunk asses around. Told 'em to call a cab 'cause I need a drink. And my friend here, well her husband's an asshole, and a co-worker. And so somehow it falls to me to get her home, but whatever. It was time to go, anyway."

"Where do you work?"

"DOT. I'm a heavy equipment operator."

"You like that?"

"Yeah, I do. I love it, operating the machines I mean. The bureaucracy can be kind of a mess. Sometimes I have to resist the temptation to accidentally dump twenty yards of gravel on the supervisor. You know."

The other woman pushes herself away from her friend. She says something I can't hear. The friend says, "Uh, I'm sorry, could you pull over or something. I think my friend's about to puke."

I wrench the wheel to the right, slide to a stop on the side of the road, turn on the dome light. The woman has her hand over her mouth. She's pale and retching, flailing for the door handle. I roll and reach back and find it, pop the door open. She throws herself at the opening. She makes barfing sounds, her body tensing, flowing, relaxing. Her friend leans over and pulls fallen locks of blonde back from the stream. I gag on the smell of hydrochloric acid, fruity sugary shit, and alcohol.

"Aaahh honey, you gotta quit doin' this. She strokes her friend's hair as she holds it. "That's right. Get it out. I'm sorry about this, driver. Thanks for being patient."

"Hey, no problem. I'm just happy there's none in the car." I turn the meter to time.

"You know, no offense, you seem nice enough, but I'm young, got some money, a good job. I like men. I'm not gay, I mean. But fuck if I can understand marryin' some man just cause you're supposed to be with somebody, you know. I'm fine with dying alone as long as I made the most of what I had. You know what I mean?"

"Yeah."

"He's still at the bar with that other girl right now. Shouldn't this be his fuckin' job?" The woman finishes and pushes herself back into the car. Her friend pulls on her shoulders until she's leaning against her. She shuts the door. There are two more stops on the way to the sick woman's house, the last is nothing but dry heaves.

"Hey, thanks again," the woman with brown hair says in front of her house. She pays me twenty bucks and tells me to keep it.

I say thanks, tell her to take care. She gets out. She's gone.

Rows of houses stream past in the fog. They're thirty feet apart, connected to thousands of miles of other rows. All of us struggling our whole lives to understand what the hell all this is. I'm wondering, Does anyone get to get it in the end?

A female driver tells Ruby that the people she was sent to pick up on Eighteenth didn't need a ride. "They just wanted to bum a cigarette," she says.

"Oh for goodness' sakes. We'll remember that when they call back. You're back two South. I had another one dud out in front of you. Who was next?"

She sends me to the Golden Nugget Hotel. A guy gets in. He pulls down his hood, and I see he's about fifty. I say hi, and there's no reply. The guy is smiling gently. Making the motion of writing on his hand. Making the motion of speaking but shaking his head no, pointing to his ears.

I hand him a business card and pen and he writes 1215 Bunnell then hands the card back. He holds a plastic bag filled with Styrofoam containers that smell like fried chicken, french fries, soup.

I almost write, "You can pay me in chicken," but he pays in cash and shakes my hand and gives me a wai, like they do in much of Asia, bowing slightly with the palms pressed together, as if praying.

Ruby tells a driver to bring her a liter of coke, some beef jerky, and a pack of cigarettes before she dies or refuses to pick up the phone again.

She tells me to pick up Duke at the Elks, and I say check. I park in the handicapped spot in front of the glass doors. The bartender buzzes me in, and I walk to the bar and shout taxi cab to the dozen patrons. A shorter guy in a leather jacket with salt-and-pepper hair and an oversized mustache raises a finger as he wipes beer foam from his upper lip. "Right here, buddy," he says.

"Be right outside." I say.

"You know where Roland Road is?" he says in the cab.

"Yessir."

"Excellent, take me there."

"You got it." He lives in the hills above the university, a nice cab fare. "So how was your night?"

"Oh, it was all right. Just had a little hold 'em tournament at the bar."

"You do okay?"

"I made the final table. But those cocksuckers gave me the beatdown after that. Oh well, try again next week. I was gonna drive home but it'd be just like those cocksuckers to pull me over and fuck me in the ass, you know what I mean."

"Yeah, they really screw you to the wall and leave you there, anymore."

"No shit, fuckin' cocksuckers, so I called you."

I decide to count; between his fellow Elks, the cops, his wife's lawyer, environmentalists, and the Dallas Cowboys he uses the word *cocksucker* thirteen times in the fourteen minutes it takes to get him home. He tips me $1.30 and I thank him.

Ruby sends me to the Oasis. It's an old Dairy Queen filled with neon, pool tables, and cigarette smoke.

I go through the double glass doors and shout, "TAXI!!!" A bunch of drunk dudes in snow machine jackets look at me like I'm a lunatic. Like they might have to kick my ass to protect the innocent. Flushed girls in tight jeans and leather jackets look at me like I'm covered in feces. Everyone looks away at the same instant. Nobody seems to need a cab. I leave.

Back in the taxi I call in the dud. Ruby sends me to the Boatel. I put the car in gear and have that out-of-body feeling again. Me, the people, the destinations, and the stories—we're a part of something else, bigger, uncaring. Like we're blood, and a complex organism is pumping us through its veins and capillaries.

Killers, 2012

I met Neal on a boulder that had come to rest at the base of a cliff beside the Copper River, where it enters a canyon. It's over a quarter mile across and a hundred feet deep; the surface is rent by whirlpools and upwellings. I've seen uprooted trees sucked beneath its gray chop and ejected six feet into the air, a stone's heave down the river. The torrent drains the expansive ice sheets of the Wrangell Mountains, bores through them southbound, plunging to the Gulf of Alaska.

Neal saw me below from the trail that clings to the canyon's crumbling walls. Saw me struggling to hold my dip net at the end of a ten-foot pole in the current of a back eddy that flowed upriver with more force than most rivers flow down. The fiberglass pole bent around a rock brace sticking a foot above the water. Every ten or fifteen minutes I'd pull the net to shore with the silver flash of a sockeye salmon slashing within. When the fishing is slow, it's easy to convince yourself that this is a ludicrous pursuit, that no fish could live in this turbidity. But that would be a mistake, for they're here, every summer, reliving the odyssey of survival pioneered by their ancestors, outcast trout, fifty thousand years ago.

Neal worked his way down the steep rocks with his net. He called down, "Hey, how you doing?"

I was impressed by his youth. He looked as if he hadn't yet graduated high school. His build rangy, about 180 pounds stretched taut on a six-foot-five-inch frame. "Howdy," I responded, certain I had seen him somewhere before.

"Looks like you're doing pretty good."

"Yeah, this is a pretty good spot, long as there's not an earthquake."

He gazed back up the rockslide, poised upon itself and waiting for a shift. Then he gazed upriver to the blinding glare of the ice- and snow-cloaked Wrangells. "Yeah, well, if it was easy, everybody'd do it, right?"

"Yeah," I agreed with a smile.

"Hey, would you mind if I wait here and fish this spot when you're done?"

"Not at all. I mean you can fish here now. There's enough room."

So he came down to the water and pushed his net into the flow, and we shouted above the river's roar. He told me he'd dropped out of high school in Vermont a couple years ago, loaded all his possessions into a worn Toyota pickup, and headed west and eventually north. "I always heard Alaska had the best hunting and the kindest weed, so I thought I better check it out for myself."

"And what have you found?"

"Pretty accurate, so far."

He told me he drove a taxi in Fairbanks, and I remembered where I'd seen him. He had painted a Crown Vic camo and turned it into an unaffiliated cab, taking trips on his cell phone and flagging off the airport and the bars. He told me he was a hunting guide and was working on getting his outfitter's license, which would enable him to open his own guiding business.

We kept in touch after that day, chatting in cabs when business was slow. He eventually got his outfitter's license, bought some land, and built a small lodge, client cabins, and a sauna on the banks of the Itkillik River. He bought a Super Cub. And he became a successful businessman and eventually quit driving cabs—though he was in the habit of pantomiming someone injecting narcotics whenever he talked about it.

"I miss the hustle. Miss that seamy underbelly, that raw capitalism. But these guys, the clients, they have real money. And I want that money. I mean it's nothing to them to drop twenty-five, thirty grand for a chance to kill something. And they tip too." Neal is an intuitive capitalist, could sell water to fish.

A few years after Neal got his outfitter's license, he called me and explained that Henrich, his friend and ace guide, wasn't going to be able to make it for the upcoming season. He and his wife were going to have a baby, and Henrich was going to stay in Norway. Another of his guides was starting a construction company in Fairbanks and wouldn't be able to make it either. He asked if I would be interested in guiding during the fall season.

Michele and I talked about it. She thought it might be a good opportunity for me to make some money while at the same time providing a fix for my wilderness deprivation. During my bachelorhood, I was in the habit of spending two or three months a year in the Alaska backcountry. It was what I did: drive cab and go on trips. But after the birth of my son, I was relegated to a couple weeks of moose hunting and a road trip to the Copper River each year. I love my family, but I missed being in the country. I was okay with this arrangement, knowing it wasn't permanent but that it was necessary. But Michele could sense my bottled longing. She told me that I should do it.

I've always been a little disdainful of the guided trophy-hunting gig. I'm a meat hunter. I don't really give a shit how big an animal's horns are. I hunt to fill my freezer with organic meat and to hang out in the woods. Sure, there's a thrill in the hunt, the kill. But it's kind of a heavy thrill. One that I don't want too much of. A thrill with some sacred responsibility, some ritual of gratitude. But it's also a lot of fucking work. And it's the gradual immersion into the backcountry and the care of the meat that constitute the vast majority of a trip.

This was the crux of the decision: do I give up two weeks on the Skoog with Jacob to shepherd multimillionaires around the Brooks Range. Michele and I were barely keeping up with the bills, and the pay would be a decent raise from cab wages, and I'd probably have the chance to get back to Fairbanks a couple times between trips during the two-month commitment. And because the clients rarely took more than the cape and antlers, I would still get the meat. And the Brooks Range is awesome.

Cord, Michele, and I drove up a month before the first sheep hunt. We parked on the side of the road and climbed a mountain and camped in a dry gravel slough strewn with driftwood. The next day we drove into Neal's camp. His cabin, which doubled as the lodge, was a shed-roofed three-sided log structure with a loft—a prime example of Interior Alaska architecture. There were four smaller structures of the same style around a gravel loop, the occasional skinny tree stump poking through the rocks. There was his red-and-black Super Cub, an orange Kubota tractor, a suburban, and an array of Toyota pickups in varying stages of repair. The drone of a generator seeped into the silence of the stunted boreal forest that ran several hundred yards to the base of a mountain and then continued halfway up before yielding to brush-filled gullies, tan scree slopes, and dark rock outcrops. Neal's porch is a good place to set up a scope and glass the mountain to find sheep, bears, wolves, caribou.

Neal had invited us up because he wanted to discuss the details and responsibilities of the job I would be performing for him. "You do realize that you're jumping right to the front lines of the guiding profession here, don't you? I don't say that like I expect your gratitude or anything. I mean you're doing me a favor basically. But most guides have undergone years of being packers. For free usually. So it's a pretty good opportunity for you, if you like it, for something you could do for years to come." He was splayed on a leather couch beside the wood ladder stairs that led to the loft. He wore slip-on sandals, old blue jeans, and a sweatshirt that read "The Boatel: A sleazy waterfront bar."

Bonnie was frying black bear steaks in a large cast iron skillet. She had frizzy orange-blonde hair and was skinny, young, and barefoot. She wore old jeans rolled up to her knees, a gray half shirt that looked like it had been cut to length with a broken bottle.

Cord was probing the thawing carcass of a medium-sized cinnamon black bear laid atop a blue tarp spread in the center of the plywood floor. He was in awe.

"Yeah, I realize that. I'm psyched to check it out. Psyched to get out there." I glanced out the window. "But it couldn't be any other way, you know. I can't afford to do anything for free, anymore. This is America, man. The money's gotta keep comin' or shit starts falling off."

"No, I know that. You're doing me a favor too. I'm just saying that I like you, Rob. I like Michele."

"I like you too Neal," Michele said over her large black coffee cup.

"And Cord is so goddamned cute I just wanna pick him up and hug him, like, every time I see him."

Cord looked up. "Bear?" he said, pointing to the carcass.

"That's right, buddy. Your dad and I are going to take the skin off that bear today. You wanna help?"

Cord squealed. "I help, Nee-oh." He pumped his little fists and resumed his examination of the bear.

"Oh, Jesus. He said my name. You're so damn cute. I want a kid. What do you say, honey, do you wanna have one?"

Bonnie guardedly looked over her shoulder. Raised her eyebrows as if to say, *motherfucker I might love you, don't be fucking with me, but maybe, someday.* "But what would Kay say?" she said.

"Who?" Neal smiled slyly. "You know I love you, baby, my dirty south-side skank." He slid off the couch to hug her from the rear in a fluid motion.

"Well, when you say it like that—" She allowed herself his tenderness.

"No, I really like you guys," Neal continued. When I told Bonnie you were coming, she took out some stew meat, and I said 'No, I actually like these people, let's eat that back strap.' And I can tell already that you're going to be good at this. I mean more than half the battle is just managing the clients. And that's where the taxi cab experience comes in. These hunts are a lot like a cab trip, they just last longer. You're not gonna have any problem. Just remember, be their buddy. Listen to their stories about their kids, or the whores they had the other night, or the elephant they killed in Africa. Whatever. But always keep that invisible barrier between you." He passed his hand down over his face in a motion like a slow karate chop. "I mean, you're their guide. You're in charge. You have to always maintain this professional distance. Always remember that we're on the same team. I mean if the trip's not going well, they'll try and turn you against me. Get something out of you that they can use against me. Don't give them that."

"I was wondering about that. Like what happens if we're just not seeing any animals. I mean I'm sure we've both been on trips where you just don't get anything."

"That's where those trophy fees come in. Most of these guys have tags for more than one kind of animal. And you can apply the more expensive permits to any of the less expensive ones. I mean if you can't find a sheep, shoot a bear or a wolf or a caribou. It takes the pressure off. And then if you do get that moose, then they have to pay extra, a trophy fee, for that other animal. There must be dead animals, Rob.

"But, God, don't take any sub-legal ones. We'll look at some different sets of sheep horns later, but if there's any question in your mind, don't shoot it. I would much prefer that you come back empty-handed than come back with a sub-legal animal. Then we have to go to the troopers. There are fines and black marks on my record. So don't do that."

"Okay."

"You'll do fine. Just remember," he passed his hand down over his face, "the invisible shield."

After lunch Michele took Cord for a nap, Bonnie did the dishes, and Neal and I went to work on the black bear. He showed me how to cut around the eyes without cutting off the lids, how to go under the ears, through the nose, behind the lips, and around the toes and claws. Tedious work.

A few weeks earlier, he'd left camp bound for Fairbanks, for Walmart and Sam's Club, in order to fill the Suburban with dehydrated, canned, and otherwise preserved foods for the upcoming season. He saw the bears on a bluff. "I knew they were a little small, but I wanted one of those capes. Those are the first cinnamon ones I ever saw. I mean I'd seen these two before, but they were either out of range or I was busy or something. One would've been fine, but if there's two—" A shit-eatin' grin was smeared across his face. He spread his arms, palms up, in the universal gesture for 'Hey, who am I to go against Providence?'

"Then me and the kids drug them down the slope and threw them in the 'burban." (*Kids* is how he referred to two twenty-year-old guys he'd recruited from a guiding school in Wyoming. They were to serve as meat packers for the upcoming season and had been up there for several weeks already, digging wells, clearing land, cutting trail. Their pay was their airfare, shack and board, and the experience of the trips they would go on.)

Bonnie cut in, "So there I was, kind of psyched for a couple days to myself. Maybe I'll go for a hike, write some letters, do some reading. When I see Neal coming back down the driveway. I'm like uh-oh. And sure enough they pull right up and jump right out and bring these two bears in and lay them on the floor. Neal's all like 'Hey honey, you're so hot. Would you pretty please, with cream and sugar, cape and butcher these bears while I'm gone.' And then they leave again."

"She did it though, had it done and in the freezer before we got back," Neal said with a touch of pride, even awe, in his tone. "But I had her leave the head and claws on this one so you could get a little practice."

"I stayed up all night," Bonnie said. "Had it done before the sun came up the next day. I still had time to go berry-picking before they got back."

"How's the berry picking this year?"

She moved to a chest freezer in the arctic entry. Pulled out a gallon Ziploc stuffed with frozen berries. "You know, since I've never really done this kind of stuff, I'm not sure what constitutes good, but we've got five bags this size put away already."

"Wow, that's awesome. All blueberries?"

"One of 'ems cranberries." She was smiling, happy with herself, youthfully radiant.

"How'd you end up with this guy? In this place?"

"Well, you know, he broke up with me two days ago. So other than the part about us still sleeping together and carrying on exactly as we were before, I'm not really 'with him' anymore." She paused to sip coffee from a giant mug that covered her face when upturned. With a sheepish, conflicted expression, Neal stared hard down into his coffee until it went away.

"But after I got my degree in sustainable agriculture, I was looking for an organic farm to do an internship with and I found this place outside of Fairbanks. When that ended, I hung around for the winter. I put up flyers advertising for housecleaning and cleaned houses for a while. And then I met Neal at The Marlin."

"She took me home, bro. It was awesome."

"The next day he's like asking me to go back to his camp with him. And that sounded way better than cleaning houses. I mean I didn't really stay in Alaska so that I could clean houses in Fairbanks. This is my great Alaskan adventure."

"I hope it turns out well."

"It already has."

Michele, Cord, and I left the next day, and two days later Michele and Cord got on a plane to Montana to visit grandparents, great-grandparents, aunts, uncles, and cousins. I drove to the Copper River and caught forty salmon, which I filleted, vacuum sealed, and froze. I began insulating and putting a vapor barrier on the new house. Michele and Cord returned two days before I left for the season. That good-bye was hard.

It rained most of the way up to Neal's. The gravel road becoming a muddy goat track that wound over the hills and through the endless forest into the heart of wild country. The leaves began to go gold the farther north I went, and the deciduous trees were eventually absorbed by the spruce.

I arrived at Neal's in the dark. He was waiting for me by the airstrip that ran alongside the access road to his property. Standing under an airplane wing to avoid the rain, he was tense. "I've already got two clients and guides out. I don't really like that I'd never met either of those two guides before a couple days ago. But I don't see what choice I had. They flew out this morning. Your guy is here. His name's Don. He seems like a real nice guy. And I got you a packer, his name's Val. But here's the thing with Val: he's a registered guide in Wyoming and Montana. He's guided trips in Africa. Part of what he's doing up here is working on a certification in Alaska. So you guys will kind of be co-guides on this trip. Don doesn't know this, and he doesn't need to know this. It should all be seen as going through you. Val knows this."

His eyes were bugged wide and focused intently on me, like he could forcefully imprint his words upon my subconscious. "Okay," I said. "How you doing?"

"Oh, I'm freakin' out, bro. I mean I'm always a little nervous at the start of the season, but this year, with all the new guides, it's worse. How 'bout you? You ready?"

"Fuck yeah. What's the schedule? Pack up and get out of here tomorrow?"

"Yeah, tomorrow afternoon'll be fine. I'm gonna have you guys hike in from the road. You'll have to go at least five miles to get out of the pipeline corridor. But there's a long mountain back there, just out of the corridor. We've been seeing sheep on it all summer. Thing is, there's really weird winds all around that mountain, and there's no airstrip, so you gotta hike in."

"Okay."

"You wanna go look at some maps, have a beer? Your client went to bed already."

"Sounds good."

"Don't worry, your guy seems real easygoing. It'll be fine."

"This is why you're waiting for me in the rain half a mile from your place." I smile as we coast to a stop at his cabin.

"Yeah." He grins sheepishly. We chuckle a moment.

"So you got any food in here?"

"Yeah there's moose chili on the woodstove. Bonnie made it today. C'mon."

The next morning Don was on his second cup of coffee at the table downstairs. He stood up grinning broadly as I entered. Six foot five, 200 pounds, white hair and mustache, wire-rimmed glasses that magnified his blue eyes. He pumped my hand. His was large and meaty, the grip firm but not crushing. I could feel his excitement in the motion of the shake. Bonnie was making pancakes and frying sausage. Val was also at the table with coffee. He was six feet tall, 190 pounds, and thirty years old. He was lean and broadly muscled with a stubbly beard and 'stache. His brown eyes danced with his wry grin, confident and intelligent. His nose had been broken, flattened at some point, probably during his high school wrestling career in Colorado. We made eye contact through our invisible shields as we shook.

Don and Eric were talking about one of the heads on Neal's wall, a big ten-point buck. The interior walls were cluttered with trophies, draped with the pelts of dozens of wolves, wolverines, bears, martens, lynx, and foxes that he'd trapped or shot.

"We used to have one just like that back East," Don said, pointing to the buck. "You'd never see him close or out in the middle of a field, though. He was always back in the brush a little. Yeah, that's a nice deer." Neal looked sheepish.

After we ate, Val and I went to the food shed and packed two weeks of food for three people into our packs along with tents and stoves and pans in with the bullets and knives and radios. "I'm gonna have a hell of a time fitting an animal in here," I mused.

"We'll have to get out there and start eating some of this shit." Val smiled.

"I guess we're going back next trip, so we could always make a cache."

"There ya' go."

Val told me about his Denali ascent while we sorted. We loaded the heavy packs—and Don's much lighter pack—in the Suburban. The difference in weight was an aspect of the job, hired mule. Bonnie served caribou burgers for lunch, and afterward we got in the assault vehicle and drove twenty miles to an old mining road that deteriorated into a trail a couple hundred yards in, where it crossed a creek. Neal came with us for the first part of the hike and carried Don's pack. The creek was high from several days' rain, we crossed it nine times on the way up. The lower crossings required the removal of shoes, socks, pants. The upper ones could be skipped across on rocks or downed trees.

The trail faded and branched into game trails before disappearing entirely. Neal peeled away and returned to the Suburban. Don, Val, and I were at the bottom of a V-shaped drainage, climbing along the walls to avoid the more thickly brushed floor. The hike took time, but it would be light past midnight. We broke free of the trees at ten; the sun was already banished from the floor of the fissure. Polychromatic tundra clung in thick layers to what would otherwise have been a landscape of shattered schist and limestone falling in geo-time from the broken spines of upthrust bedrock.

We decided to head for an outcrop near the top of the ridge above us that was still smoldering in the sun. The tundra on the steep walls made for difficult walking, not unlike postholing in deep snow. Val and I got up before Don, and I doubled back to carry Don's pack while Val set up tents and a stove and retrieved water from a small hole in the tundra. We ate rehydrated food from foil pouches.

The GPS informed us that we were only four miles from the road. It was illegal to hunt within five miles of the road; the no-hunting boundary cut through the westernmost slice of the mountain rising to the east. "How you doing, Don?" I asked.

"Oh, I'm about done the fuck in. I don't see how you guys do it. I mean I've been walking with a pack every day, all summer, getting ready for this." He paused to pop four ibuprofen. "I'll be fine, though. Just need a good night's rest."

"So no blisters or sprains or anything?"

"Not that I know of. No, I'll be fine. Fuck, it sure is beautiful here, though. This is great, guys. What I wanna know is what's the matter with that Super Cub back at camp. I mean I've had a pilot's license for thirty years, and you could put a cub down on one of those ridges up there."

"He told me the winds can be kinda tricky back here for landing. But they've been seeing animals when they scout it."

"Hey guys, I got some sheep," Val said.

"Where?" I asked.

Without taking the binos off his face, Val said, "Up on that face. About a third of the way up. You see where it starts to turn into a waterfall?"

"By where those snow patches are?"

"Yeah. You see that one snow patch to the left that kind of looks like . . . like an upside-down wizard's hat or something."

"Yeah."

"Go down from that and like kind of going into that gully . . ."

"Yeah, oh yeah. There's a few of 'em there."

"No bone, though."

"Lambs and ewes?"

"Lambs and ewes. You see 'em, Don?"

"Yeah, I think so. Boy they sure blend in with that snow, don't they?"

"Yeah. This is good. There'll be rams around here."

To be legal, a ram must have horns that make a complete 360-degree curl, so that the tips of the horns reach back around to the bases. Or if one or both of the horns has been broken off, or broomed—what older sheep sometimes do when their horns start to interfere with their ability to eat—then that sheep is legal. And finally, if a sheep is at least eight years of age, it is legal, but this is nearly impossible to verify until after the animal is dead and the annual growth rings on the horns can be counted.

Don told us that his daughter was a graduate student in natural resource management at the University of Alaska Fairbanks. "We were up visiting her when I met Charley. He's the other guide I've gone with in Alaska. I was supposed to go on this hunt with him, but he's gettin' kinda old and doesn't really like to climb mountains and fly airplanes anymore. Not that the plane part's any different with Neal, I guess." We laughed. "And I know what he's talking about when it comes to getting old, too. Right at this moment, I'm right fucking with him on that." He laughed again.

I liked him. He laughed often and spoke in a rural New England drawl. Too loud, though, I'd have to caution him on several occasions. People from the East Coast speak loudly.

He told us he was a retired electrician, a thirty-eight-year member of the IBEW. He and his wife, who was a retired teacher, had started buying up vacant properties in their hometown thirty some years ago. They remodeled them, brought the wiring up to code, and turned them into rentals. "I don't even know how many of 'em there are right now. But the town's going to hell these days. We'd like to sell 'em all and just go live in our Florida house, but nobody wants to buy right now 'cause of the financial crisis."

"Is that why the town's in decline, 'cause of the recession?"

"No, or I'm sure that's sped things up, but we've lost our manufacturing. There used to be a big refrigerator factory there and a big glass manufacturer. Well, they're still there, but they're a lot smaller. A lot of people have packed their bags. About the only people left are the niggers, 'cause they were all on welfare anyway, so they don't really need the jobs."

Val and I were silent. Then I heard myself saying, "You know, I had an uncle who was a black man. He was a really good person. And I gotta say I find it a little bit offensive when I hear that word." The uncle part was a complete lie, made up on the spot, as if my invisible shield was giving me super bullshit powers. Val was looking at me, suppressing a wry grin.

Don was looking at the ground. He looked at me all sheepish and said, "Geez, I'm sorry. I shouldn't have said that. I didn't mean anything by it. I have lots of friends who are black."

"Hey, no big deal. Don't worry about it." A lot of white people throw the word out there. And if you call them on it, they usually claim they didn't mean anything by it. But they say it with such relish. I suspect that when they find a sympathetic soul they throw racial epithets, the way monkeys hurl feces, against the wall for hours. I see the whole N-word-baiting thing as a kind of radar for bigots.

"I'm gonna hit it," Val announced.

Don claimed the small two-person tent, Val headed for his bivy, and I decided to sleep outside between two crags in the rock outcrop. It was a cold night, and I regretted not having a warmer bag. But there had been no room for it.

One thing about sleeping outside: I wake up early. I packed my stuff, made instant coffee, and wrote. I shook Val and shook Don's tent and made instant oatmeal. "There's a bunch of sheep over there now," I said. We raised binos and counted twenty-seven sheep by the waterfall, where we'd seen four the night before. It was a large nursery, all lambs and ewes. They were just within the five-mile corridor. Sunrise tinted everything rouge. Small cumuli spun lazily around the black mountain.

We headed east, away from the corridor. We climbed over a rib reaching from the tundra toward the summit of the mountain. We saw two rams as soon as we entered the hunting area. They were five hundred yards up the mountain from us and were luxuriating on green, gold, and red orbs of lichen. We dropped to our stomachs and put glass on them. I busted out a sixty-power spotting scope that Neal had loaned me. He'd gotten it from a former client as a tip. Thing retails for $3,000.

The sheep, wary but not yet alarmed, were looking at us. We looked at them for a long time and decided that the bigger of the two was a seven-eighths curl. The other three-quarters. We spent a little more time to see if the bigger one's horns might grow another couple inches, but it wasn't happening and we pressed on. The season didn't open until the following day, anyway. We had left early to get past the five-mile corridor by opening day.

There was a lake at the top of the drainage we were trudging up. Neal had had success hiking up from that lake in the past, but he had been flown in. The lake was another four miles, and we were hoping to concentrate our efforts a little closer to the road. The tundra was deep, and beneath it lay loose rocks making the walking difficult. We set up camp on a stone pedestal at the bottom of a steep valley that swept down from the summit ridge like slashed flesh. We decided that in the morning we would leave most of our food and gear at this spot and run up to the ridge and see what we could see and be prepared to bivy.

We were relaxing, glassing after dinner. "Holy shit, guys, I see something. Something big. Holy shit, is that a big grizzly?!" Don said.

"Where're you looking?" I asked, taking down my binos to see where his were pointing.

"On the other side of the valley, up the creek. Do you see that big pile of rocks, at the bottom of that steep gully? And then there's those gold leaves. Just this side of those. He just went behind something, he's like, a thousand yards."

Val picked him up before Don had finished speaking. He was like the Doc Holliday of binoculars. "There he is. He came back up again over by those spruce."

"Yeah. He's really blond, huh? Pretty good sized, too."

"Wow," Don said. "That's the second grizzly I've ever seen. This is great, guys. I'm gonna try and get some pictures." We watched him until after midnight.

The next morning I found the bear browsing the berries down in the brush of the valley floor. He was moving back up the drainage, toward the lake. It would be legal to shoot him in fourteen hours. We decided to stay high on the mountain slope and follow the bear. If we could hang with him until midnight, there would still be enough light to take a shot. We stopped occasionally to eat energy bars, pilot crackers, and smoked oysters. We drank water scooped from rivulets in the tundra; we glassed. There were quite a few sheep scattered about the peaks on the far side of the valley, but we saw no full curls.

The lake sat in a cirque surrounded by steep scree slopes that stretched to high ridges shoved against the cold blue sky. The bear cut around the far side of the lake and slipped into willow and moraine. We looked for two hours without seeing him. Then Val found a bear on the far side of the lake, ambling back our way. It was a different bear, darker, bigger. It moved slower, more deliberately, vibing, "This is all mine, and if you're here, then you're mine too."

We watched him for an hour until he slid into some dwarf birch between us and the lake. We looked for another hour until suddenly the first bear, the blond one, burst from the brush in a hurry, loping several hundred yards back down the valley and looking over its shoulder from time to time. It slowed to a walk directly below us, 250 yards away. It was 6:00 p.m.

The wind drifting down the valley had been perfect for following the bear up the valley, but now it would be trickier. We would have to stay ahead of or even with the bear. So back down the valley we roamed. By ten o'clock we were getting excited. Perhaps we would get to take a shot.

I was conflicted. I enjoy watching wild animals. Killing them is . . . exciting. But it's also sad, for me anyway. I had only done it for meat up to this point. I liked that bear. We'd spent the day together, and I felt as if I knew him a little. My first thoughts upon seeing him were not, "Let's kill it."

But it was my job. And it would take the pressure off the rest of the hunt and make the client happy. Val could pack the hide back to the road and be back with us in a day or two. We weren't going to eat it. We didn't need it. But I'd taken the job and I was ready to perform it, like the song my carpenter buddy John likes to sing when the conversation comes around to it, "Water boy, water boy, bring that bucket round. If you don't like the job, put the water bucket down."

The bear dropped behind a swale in the floor of the valley, and we lost sight of him. We glassed intently. I saw a flash of blond down by the creek. It was the bear, running at full throttle away from us, across the creek. The sun-reddened mist of his splashing hung in the air. We watched him until dark, for more than two hours, and he never even slowed down, ran up a fucking mountain, throwing gravel in his wake. Impressive.

"Oh well, that was exciting, anyway. And cool as fuck, too," Don said back in camp over his bag of food.

"I can't believe he just ran over that mountain. What a fucking badass," Val added.

"Yeah, I wonder what tipped him off," I said.

I slept out again. Saw Polaris for the first time in three months and a green blur of aurora smudged the northern horizon.

Next morning we climbed the rib that camp was on to the long, curving summit ridge of the mountain. We walked west, climbing outcrops to scope down into the high basins opening below us. We came to one where the headwaters of a northbound creek began their journey. There was a group of twenty sheep six hundred yards beneath us, where the initial headwall of the valley leveled into a meadow. Nine of them appeared to be rams, and three of them were around the full curl of the law.

We crept down a lichen-heaped slope until we were above them. We could not get any closer without taking a wide detour down a steep slope of loose big rocks. We lay on our stomachs and peered over the edge of a sheer drop. They were head butting and using each other's horns to scratch themselves and rubbing against and leaning on one another. Val ranged them at four hundred yards. "But that's really only two hundred yards, 'cause you're shooting straight down," he said.

"Oh yeah, I've heard that before," Don replied.

"Yeah, it's true," I said. "When you're shooting horizontally, like at the range, the path of the bullet is perpendicular to the pull of gravity. It drops quicker; there's more force working against it than if you shoot down. 'Cause then the path of the bullet is closer to the direction of gravity. So the path of the bullet isn't altered as much."

"Yeah, whatever, you guys just want me to take this shot so we can go home, I know." He was grinning ruefully, as though this were a minor betrayal he'd been expecting.

"You know, Don, we might not be able to get any closer to them than this. See how they've situated themselves out in the middle of that meadow. They're like five, six hundred yards away from anything that we could hide behind. See how every one of them is looking in a slightly different direction. I mean their eyes are right up there with the eagles, Don, and all they do, all day, is look around for things that might try and eat them."

"Yeah, dude, I mean . . . this ain't the east coast," Val added.

"What's that supposed to mean."

"It means take the shot man, we might not get another chance. Don't think about it like a four-hundred-yard shot. It's a two-hundred-yard shot."

"It's true. I've done hunts where you don't see any full curls. This is a good opportunity," I said.

"Oh, you guys are gonna make me do this, aren't you?" He reluctantly got himself ready to shoot, Val built him a gun rest out of rocks, and I watched the sheep through the scope.

They were bunched tightly together, shifting their positions around. It was difficult to find the full curls through the scope, and then more difficult to keep track of them. And he couldn't shoot into the group because a miss could hit one of the other sheep, so I strained to follow the full curls and waited for one of them to separate himself, waited close to three hours before a big one ambled away to exploit some virgin willow. "Okay, there he is. Shoot him," I said.

Boom! The bullet shattered a rock a couple of feet past the ram into shrapnel. The sheep jumped as one and bolted forty yards away and mixed themselves all up again. Don had compensated for the drop of the bullet as if it were a four-hundred-yard shot. We sorted through the new arrangement, located the full curls, and waited until another one separated. They butted heads and scratched each other in the sun. We only had to wait an hour.

But Don missed the second shot. The sheep ran to the far side of the valley and out of range. Sunset colors began to stain the mountain orange. We returned to the summit ridge and set up a bivouac camp in the rocks. There was no water nearby. It was below us, below the cliffs and rock slides, down in that meadow where the sheep happily munched their browse. We boiled much of what we had left for dinner. I called Neal on the sat phone, checked in, and brushed my teeth.

I didn't sleep much. I had left my camping pad at base camp in an effort to go light, so I slept on my pack wedged between some rocks. Sunset blurred the sky red. The temperature dipped into the teens with a breeze. We were surrounded by long-ridged peaks wrapping around each other like squirming otters in a crimson sea. We waited for the sun to reemerge a few degrees east of where it had slipped behind the northern horizon.

We had oatmeal and drank the rest of our water. We crept along the back side of the summit ridge until we came to the top of a long low hump that reached from the ridge down to the meadow where the sheep were just becoming visible. Four of them relaxed atop a rock pinnacle at the edge of the meadow. The rest were spread below. We crawled and slithered down the headwall of the valley, keeping the long low hump between us and the sheep. It took four hours of silent stalking to get within a hundred yards of them and another hour to get Don into a good shooting posture, to pick out the legal ram on the rock, to make sure we were looking at the same ram.

"Shoot him," I said.

Boom! The sheep stumbled forward, slid headfirst off the pinnacle into the rock slide it rose above. The rest of the sheep were in a panic looking in all directions for the source of this deadly intrusion. Don stood up and yelled, "I told you I'd get you, you fucking dickhead!" shaking his fist at the sheep, smiling. The rest of the sheep saw us and started running off down the valley.

"Hey, Don, calm down, buddy," Val said. "We're probably gonna hunt here next time too. Probably gonna hunt these same sheep."

"Oh, yeah, sorry," Don said. The hit sheep was attempting to stand up.

"Shoot him again," I said.

"No, don't shoot him again," Val said. "It'll fuck up the cape."

"But he's not dead yet."

"He will be. He hit him good."

We made our way over to him. It took us about twenty minutes, and the sheep was dead when we got there. We spent over an hour posing and taking pictures with the kill. I was going crazy inside. I like to start the butchering right away, get the meat cooling as quickly as possible. But that was not our priority. Val told a story about a deer hunt he'd guided in Wyoming. How he'd caped the deer on a mountainside and then kicked the carcass off a cliff. "Cape and kick," he said grinning. He talked about submerging the meat in the creek to cool it.

"We can't do that. It'll ruin the meat. It'll leach the blood out, make it more prone to spoiling," I said.

We hauled the sheep down to the meadow and laid out our bags. I fried sheep in sheep fat on a camp stove in some aluminum foil recovered from the bottom of Val's pack. I could only cook a few pieces at a time, so we cooked and ate for two hours, drinking lots of water from pockets in the tundra. We decided to walk down the valley and then climb over a ridge to the south and contour around the slope of the mountain back to the valley we'd hiked up from the road.

Val and I climbed the mountain early the next morning to retrieve our base camp from the other side. We rested there long enough to consume a few thousand calories and then climbed back over the mountain. Carrying his gear and a sheep shoulder, Don headed down the valley to a small lake. Val and I stopped at the camp in the meadow on our way back and loaded the rest of the meat onto our already heavy packs and staggered down to the lake where thin wisps of smoke rose from Don's fire. The tundra was deep and spongy and wet, and it was eleven by the time we made it there. Don had water boiling for us, and we poured it into the bags of freeze-dried ingredients to make our dinner. Don set up the tents while Val and I ate. We were too tired to offer much in the way of conversation.

The following day we hiked out. Our packs were heavy, and the ground was soft and tussocky and the tussocks fell over when we stepped on them wrong. We went down a tributary of the creek we had hiked up and that was a mistake. The brush was thicker and the slope steeper. With our heavy packs getting snagged and rifles getting pulled off shoulders we slithered through the morass of fallen trees, interwoven willow, and attack alder. It took us four hours to go a mile and a half.

I have a vague memory of Neal picking us up in the Suburban. We returned to the lodge and ate and got drunk and slept for two days.

-:⁘:-

Neal was freaking out. Two of his new guides were waiting for a plane at an airstrip to the north. But the wind was wrong, and several pilots who had tried to get to them decided they could land, but as far as taking off with a load, they weren't interested. Neal pleaded, cajoled, and yelled at the guides via sat phone. He urged them to hike ten miles down the river to a lake where a floatplane could extract them in two or three trips. But the guides, along with the young unpaid packers, were resistant to the point of hostility. The clients were furious and were threatening to sue and say bad things about Neal at the big hunting conventions over the winter. Their families were calling Neal. Calling other pilots and outfitters. One of the guides called the troopers who in turn called Neal. A prayer vigil website was spawned. Neal, the nerve center of this concern, was constantly on the phone or deep in brooding thought. The fact that the clients had each gotten a sheep was often lost in the confusion.

I went home for a couple days and ate and slept and played with Cord. I was impressed by the workload of guiding, the kind that broke a human down quickly, especially one my age. The physical toll was similar to commercial fishing, which I had stopped doing a decade previously 'cause I wanted my body to last a while.

I was impressed by the pressure I had felt when selecting a sheep and getting Don a shot at it. It was not easy to tell the difference between a full curl and a fifteen-sixteenths curl from four hundred yards away and it was solely up to me to choose a legal animal. The focus of the client and Val and Neal and the Alaska Department of Fish and Game like a lens magnifying the energy of the sun till it burned.

The day after I returned, Neal drove me and Val to a nearby airstrip. "This next guy is a very accomplished hunter," Neal was saying. "I booked this hunt at the big hunting convention a couple years ago, and I haven't seen him since, so I'm not sure what to expect. But this is what I know: He's some kind of oil and gas tycoon from Texas. He has his own jet that he was going to fly up here, which I'm a little in awe of, actually. But it ended up having some mechanical issues, so it's being worked on and he flew commercial. But this guy already has one grand slam and he's working on his second."

A "grand slam" is awarded to those who kill the four main types of sheep found in North America: Dall, desert, stone, and bighorn. It is a fantastically expensive accomplishment.

"He's hunted all over Africa, Canada, the Lower 48. And he's pretty high up in the hunting community, and I really want him to say nice things about us when he gets back. He could send us a lot of business. So, you know, treat him good."

Within thirty minutes a small jet from Fairbanks touched down, disgorging a handful of tourists onto the gently heaving asphalt. Phillip was easy to pick out. He was six foot four with short brown hair and a great Roman nose, and he carried a polished stainless steel gun case. He had intense dark eyes and a posture that was erect and solid, like you could take a straight edge and place it on his back and it would touch his waist, shoulders, neck, and the back of his head. His expression was somewhere between a superior sneer and a warm smile. It felt like it could go either way with equal ease.

We drove back to the lodge, and Val and I packed for the trip while Neal and Phillip sorted through the paperwork. We ate salmon tacos and planned to head back up the mountain by six. Phillip's friend Gary had come for a hunt also. Because the first two guides were still stranded at the airstrip, Neal had flown in a new guide. His name was Sean, but he liked to be called Shawnee. He was quiet and Christian, had a large family waiting for him in rural Northern California.

I could tell Shawnee liked us despite our heathen ways. He was a certified hit man of a guide and had been selected three times to guide the Governor's Cup hunt, an auction held annually for a tag to hunt sheep in the Chugach Mountains, north of Anchorage, where they grow big but where the hunting pressure is strong and thus access restricted.

Phillip and Gary had been out drinking late in Fairbanks and had closed the Midnight Mine the night before. Gary elected to spend a night in camp recovering, but Phillip was ready to go. Phillip was ready to kill, kill, kill.

Neal drove us back to the drop-off point, and we headed up to sheep country. We found a full curl ram two miles off the road. "Now tell me, Rob, is that a shooter? Is that the kind of animal you'd tell me to shoot?" Phillip asked.

I was staring furiously through the spotting scope trying to form my opinion. "Uh—"

"Does he look like a nice one?"

"Yeah, he's a nice one."

"How many inches do you think he is?"

"I'll guess thirty-eight, thirty-nine."

"Do you get forty inchers up here?"

"Yeah, we do. But we're north of the Arctic Circle so it's not as common as in the Chugach. But we definitely do. And I tend to estimate conservatively."

"Can I shoot him?" he asked, excited, his eyes glassing over, staring at the sheep. I could feel his primal longing, the death gene strong in this one.

"No, he's within the five-mile corridor."

"Those tips go a ways past the full curl. I bet he's over forty," Val said.

"They flare out a ways too," I said.

He was on a two-hundred-foot dirt cliff that had been cut by the creek that ran along its base.

"That's a nice ram," Val was saying reluctantly. We continued up, checking back on him from time to time, hoping he would head up the well-worn trail to sheep country. He eventually disappeared into some brush at the top of the bluff. He had water and willow close by. He reemerged, charging down the cliff, down the creek, out of sight. We found a moose cow and calf drinking from the pool nearest the edge of the bluff.

Val found a couple griz down on the flats while I heated water for dinner. A lone bull moose, eight hundred yards away, pushed his head below the black surface of a pond and held it there long enough that the ripples calmed, the energy absorbed by the water.

I thought about the obsession with death. Couldn't feel it. I was here on a job and numb to the vagaries of passage from this world. When I kill something, I feel sad and heavy, albeit exhilarated and relieved. I thank the animal and apologize and promise to honor him, to sing songs about him, as the last oxygen leaks from his blown apart lungs.

Phillip said, "I wanna snipe that motherfucker from five hundred yards out." He told a story about a stone sheep hunt he'd done in BC. The guide had caped the sheep atop this stone pinnacle where Phillip had shot him. Then he'd kicked the carcass down a seven-hundred-foot cliff. "The meat was completely fuckin' shredded, I mean there was hardly anything left of him," he laughed.

I thought about the blond griz amid the crimson and gold tundra, watching him with Don all night, waiting for midnight to kill him. Remembered the bear sprinting two thousand feet up a mountain until he faded into the bino background near the top. He'd been romping, digging up squirrel holes and roots, swiping berries, just rambling around eating, sensing, being the world.

It rained all night, and we awoke within a cloud that had swallowed the ridge. When the mist cleared, we saw the big ram on the bluff below us, but he was scrambling down the bluff to the creek.

A wolf howled in the distance. It was answered by another, closer, just beyond the bluff. A gray, cream, and tan motion moved through the trees up top. A large black wolf stepped out of the spruce to the edge. It dislodged some rocks which rolled down the bluff and landed behind the sheep. The sheep bolted toward us at a dead run. The black wolf faded back into the spruce. Another howl rose from the shadows, close.

"Holy shit," I said, moved down to the tundra to see if I could catch sight of him.

Then he burst into view twenty yards below me. He was massive. We locked eyes and froze for a second. He lowered his head and charged. I dove out of the way. He missed me by a couple feet, continued up the mountain. We lost sight of him as the trail wove around the rock outcrops that studded the ridge. We followed him up, pausing to shove camp into our packs. The ridge dropped down to a cradled belt of tundra wrapped round the lower flanks of the mountain. The waterfall where we'd seen the large nursery of sheep with Don was directly in front of us. We sat among the rocks and glassed the mountain for a couple hours without seeing the big ram.

Phillip and I headed down to collect some water. I found the ram a couple hundred feet below the summit. We walked toward him, he was more than a mile away. He stood up and shuffled around. What eyes! We retreated and took the water back to camp.

After dinner Val spotted a griz a mile across the tussocks, and we set out after him. We crept around boulders up a ridge behind him. He sprinted out of a depression below us, and we ducked. Phillip was on one knee, sighting in the bear who was looking at us over his left shoulder. The bear started running again. "That's a small one, isn't it?" Phillip said.

"I doubt he'd go five feet squared," I replied. The bear came to a stop again, two hundred yards away, broadside.

"Nope, I ain't shooting anything that small," Phillip said. The bear bolted and was gone. We walked an hour and a half back to camp. Sunset lit curtains of virga orange, purple, and black above the white limestone peak's cruel curves.

The next day we saw that the big ram was still at the top of the mountain. We loaded two days' worth of food, cookware, and sleeping bags and circled behind the peak, hoping to come down on him from the ridge he sat below. We climbed as clouds came down and settled upon us, and then we crept along the ridge in silence and fog all day, never sensing our elusive prey.

At the end of the day we came to the top of a high basin. There was a pass at its apex that led to the backside of the mountain and to a hidden crevice of the sprawling massif. This cut flowed down into the creek where Don had gotten his sheep. We'd looked up into it on our hike out and remarked on its beauty. There was an arête across the crevice from the pass that separated the two forks of the valley. The big ram was on top of that arête, looking at us. The steep boulder slide slopes that formed the crevice swept down to fields of tundra and moraine and a small lake. There were nineteen sheep milling around down there. We lay on our bellies in a strong wind and watched them until dark.

The big ram wasn't on the arête in the morning. We found him among the lambs, ewes, and young rams on the crevice floor, twelve hundred vertical feet down. We devised a stalk, picking out rocks in the slide we could hide behind. We would have to crawl and slither down the steep, loose slope. Two stretches of a hundred yards would be mostly in the open. I was beginning to think we should wait and watch a while.

But Phillip was pumped. He had that killing gleam in his eyes. We descended, and the sheep spread out. Some seeped into the big-bouldered moraine above the meadow. From above they were slow, white specks milling among the charcoal, green, and blue landscape. We'd been hoping to use those big boulders to stalk the ram, who was in the meadow. The wind shifted and began to lazily waft down. I realized this wasn't looking good, that we should retreat and wait for a better opportunity, but Phillip was in charge mode, and it was all I could do to keep up.

Nine hundred yards away a young ram on the far side of the meadow stood up and looked at us. The rest of the group immediately stiffened, stopped eating, started looking around, and responded to the stimulus like a flock of birds into a fluid turn. The big ram began ambling toward the arête from his bed near the meadow's far edge. We were pinned in an open area above a large pyramidal boulder. "Let's get down there while he's walking away and not paying attention," Phillip said.

From behind the rock, we watched as the big ram walked slowly and easily up the cliff. A ewe, two lambs, and a young ram walked up the valley and stared at us. "That's the alpha ewe," Phillip said. "We oughta just kill her now. That's what we do deer hunting. We pull up to the field and the first doe that sticks her head up we fuckin' blast her and we're done with it. She's the oldest and the smartest. Look at that, fuckin' cunt, starin' right at us." She was pissed, stomping rocks loose, glaring.

We sat and waited until the ram lay down in the saddle atop the arête between the two forks of the creek. Four younger rams moseyed up and sat in the cliffs below him. The rest of the sheep made their way to the lower reaches of the cliff, ready to make their escape. There was a hierarchy. The ewe stared and stomped and stewed. We retreated up the steep slate and rotten schist. The rocks crumbled under our feet and sometimes we slid down farther than we'd stepped up. The force of the wind increased as we approached the pass and poured through it like a cold river flowing down on top of us.

We had only brought two days' worth of food, and we liked our camp high on the ridge that winds the length of the mountain. I headed back to our cache camp of the previous day to grab more supplies. As I walked down the basin opposite the pass from the one the sheep were in, side-hilling and skipping from one boulder to the next, the flanks of the mountains splayed out beneath me. The colors of the tundra ran together like spilled paint and plunged into vertical gorges lit gold by the afternoon sun. I walked through a group of forty lambs and ewes in the spongy tundra below base camp and got within forty yards of a dozen of them while making no attempt to conceal myself. They scurried to the cliffs of the west face of the mountain where a spring gushed out of the rocks.

I got back to the saddle about six hours after I'd left. Phillip and Val had moved jagged rocks around to form a wide, flat area beneath an overhang. As I approached, Phillip was tearing up moss with a rock knife and tossing it to Val who laid it across the rocks to create a soft sleeping platform. Phillip worked with aggressive zeal, turning over huge rocks and throwing moss like he was getting paid by the piece. The man never carried more than his bedroll, gun, spare clothes, and a cool rock he wanted his geologists to analyze, but he worked tirelessly to contribute, desperate to be part of the group. When he saw me coming, he ran fifty yards down and grabbed my pack.

Over rehydrated food he was saying, "You know, I've had twenty-some airplanes over the last thirty years. Right now I've just got the jet and a Cub. I was gonna fly the Jet up here, but it was having some issues with the navigational system so I had to leave it in Seattle to get fixed. I think I'll go get it after this and go visit my son, he's on a wrestling scholarship in Minnesota. Then maybe I'll fly it up to BC, do a stone sheep hunt. Or maybe I'll just go to Vegas and relax for a few days. See a girl I know there." A shit-eatin' grin slid over his features.

"Anyway, I think I'm gonna have to get a second Cub. See the one I got's on floats, and I have to change over to wheels or skis every year. It's such a pain in the ass."

"Yeah, that sucks," I said. Val and I exchanged a glance from the corners of our eyes, grinned subtly.

Red-stained cumulus were tossed above us and above them high cirrus blurred over a deepening azure sky. When I woke to piss there were whorls of emerald and bone northern lights. I lay in my bag and watched them and smelled the fungal earth until I fell back to sleep.

The next day we were socked in. In the dense mist we walked a ridge to the other fork of the creek, where Don had shot his sheep. The wind built and blew from the east at forty to sixty miles an hour. It rained and snowed.

The fog began to lift and we wedged ourselves into cracks in the ridge to glass out of the wind. Our light raingear had reached its saturation point. When we continued and came around a corner, a huge wolverine shot out from a hole in the ridge and saw us. Just twenty feet away he stopped and faced us, sniffed, then he shot down the slope into a chaos of broken boulders. Phillip had his rifle up and roaming the rocks should it show its shaded hide again. "Was that a wolverine? Can I shoot it? I've never seen one before."

"No, season doesn't open for another week." Phillip lowered his gun slowly. We all stared down the mountain toward the only wolverine any of us had ever seen.

We found sheep down in the basin where we'd found Don's ram. But the visibility was too poor to see if one of them was the big guy.

We set up a two-person tent in the sharp rocks. The wind howled and flattened the tent, so we built a rock wall around it to lessen the impact. Filthy and soaked, we got in and laughed a little about whatever series of life decisions had led us to this point.

I hiked down to find water. The rain and snow, hitting like paintballs, dissipated as I descended and was a steady drizzle by the time I reached collectible agua forty-five minutes later. Then I headed back up, into the paintballs.

Val slept in a shallow cave that night and came to the tent early. He was cold and wet and muddy. It was sleeting and foggy. We had coffee and oatmeal and devised many plans. Val decided to head down to get some dry clothes from our cache camp. He needed to dry out and warm up. Phillip and I waited for a few hours to see if the weather might break so we could glass the area we'd worked so hard to occupy but had yet to see. When it became obvious that it wasn't going to clear, we shoved our wet shit into our packs and headed down. We would meet Val at the confluence of the two forks of the creek.

The descent was treacherous at first. All the rocks were covered with wet snow and ice. But soon we were below the storm, and the slope began to level out, and it was a pleasant walk down the valley. We glassed many sheep clinging to its walls, though none were full curl rams.

Over a fire of fat dead willows, Val told us how he'd gone camping with his fiancée before he'd come up for the season. "We were lookin' down into this valley in the morning, having coffee, and I'm like, 'Oh, what's that? I think I see sumthin'.' So I get my spotting scope set up and get it focused on the other side of the valley. I had hung up a sheet there with 'Will you marry me?' written on it in big letters before we left. So I got the scope set up on that and I say, 'Yeah, I got sumthin', look at this.' And she did." He paused, grinned smugly.

"So, what'd she say?" I asked.

"She said yeah."

"Hey. Congratulations," Phillip said.

"You romantic bastard," I grinned.

He smiled smugly and told us they were going to live in a suburb north of Dallas over the winter after he finished his Alaska hunts, guided horseback deer and elk hunts in Montana, and went elk hunting with a buddy in Colorado.

Turned out that Phillip lives a day's drive from the town Val will be living in.

"You'll have to visit," Phillip said. "We'll go deer hunting."

That will give Val a chance to admire Phillip's gymnasium-sized trophy room for himself. It contains a small mountain and a log cabin. The mountain displays full body mounts of sheep, goats, and bears scaling its heights. These keep company with more than two hundred other trophies. Phillip told us about building the log cabin with his own hands, explaining with zeal and in great detail how he'd cut the logs, leaving the bark on for a more rustic look. At one party he'd hosted there were more than seventy guests in the trophy room, drinking tequila from the bar. He also has a skiing room and a hunting room where he outfits his trips, though these rooms are smaller and lack bars and mountains.

The next day, after a good, dry night's sleep, we sat in the rain all day glassing up the same basin we'd been looking down two days before, through windows in the fog and drifting clouds.

Phillip was getting frustrated. I told him about Val's plan to go start a fire and dry out again. "Somebody should go and look up that other valley," he said testily.

I agreed and hiked back to the creek we'd come down the day before and crawled the last few hundred yards to some gray boulders sitting in the green swale of the swerving down valley. I counted nineteen sheep, eleven in a meadow just above me, eight more in the cliffs, no full curls. Pockets of snow were plastered onto the ledges and rough spots of the mountain, smoothing the terrain into soaring relief. They had a fire going when I got back. We dried out again.

The next morning we woke to snow. Big flakes mixed with freezing rain. The snowline was down to a couple hundred feet above camp. Phillip and I made coffee and oatmeal in the tent. We talked about kids. He and his wife have raised three boys. "You just teach them right from wrong, Rob, that's all you can do. I knew my boys were gonna smoke dope, drink. I just tell 'em be smart about it. Don't be stupid and be doin' it in a car or some huge party that's probably gonna get busted.

"Fuckin' weather just ain't gonna give us a break, is it?" he said.

"It's looking pretty ugly up there. Makes the sheep harder to see too," I said. "Now there's millions of white dots up there."

"Yeah, no shit. Damn."

One side effect of bad weather and being bivouacked in tight quarters for hours was the stories. Phillip had dropped out of college and started a rock band with some friends. They drove around the country in a van. "We hardly ever knew where the next tank of gas was coming from. We had an agent, and he'd book us in bars, and we'd pick up our own gigs in between. My dad said I was fucking nuts to do it, but I'm glad I did. I felt really free during that time.

"When the band broke up, I went to work for my dad in the oil and gas business. I stayed with him long enough to learn how things worked, then I started my own business. I've got over a thousand wells now. Back when I started with my old man, back in the eighties, he told me, 'Son, I don't know what you're gonna do when the time comes, but I would learn how to do something different. The oil's almost gone, and they're not makin' any more of it.' But here I am. And with all the advances in technology, we're lookin' at hundreds of years of reserves."

"Is it mostly the fracking that's driving it?" I asked.

"It's all because of the fracking."

"What about those people that can like, light their tap water on fire and stuff?"

"I'm sure some of it's true. But, ya know, people want their power. Without it there'd be a big population crash. At this point I think they're a little less willing to deal with that."

"Yeah, I guess so."

I opened the tent to view the snow-flecked cloud interior but instead found that shotgun patterns of sunshine were burning through the vapor, touching the ground around us. Phillip's resigned demeanor was replaced by the killer's gleam I'd come to know.

We hiked down to some bluffs ascending a high ridge above the creek and started climbing. Phillip saw some rams go over the ridge and we followed them. We found two full curl rams below the spine of the ridge on the large black rocks falling, in geo time, to the sea. Neither was the big one we'd been following. We never saw him again.

We crawled behind a boulder two hundred yards away, and I built Phillip a rock pile to steady his gun. He lay on his stomach and sighted in the bigger of the two sheep, gut shot it. Val, watching through the binos, told him where it hit, and Phillip put one through the ram's heart. We ran over to him, bloodied and still on the black rocks.

Then Val saw a griz coming up the basin and turning into the valley to the west of us. Phillip was excited and wanted that bear too. He re-sighted the rifle using a rock a couple hundred yards across the slope with Val calling out: "High," "Low," "Left," and "Right." We jogged over to the point on the ridge where Val had last seen it and looked down a steep drainage to a skinny willow-lined creek slicing through humps of olive- and auburn-colored tundra. After a half hour Phillip and Val began trudging back to begin photographing and butchering the sheep. I found the griz in the brush at the bottom of an arroyo on the far side of the creek. She was digging roots and Arctic tundra squirrels and de-vouring berries. She was very blonde and carefree, lazily piling on the calories before the dark season came down. I watched her for a couple minutes, wanting very much for her to survive this encounter but knowing she probably wouldn't. She had a blonde dreadlock in the middle of her back that flopped around as she ambled—a young, happy, hippie bear. I felt like a real asshole as I chased Phillip and Val down and got their attention with a twenty-yard *ppssssst*. The gleam came back into Phillips's eyes, and we jogged back to the ridge.

We ranged her at three hundred yards and descended a rocky rib until we were within two hundred. She was licking a paw in the midst of a crimson blueberry patch. She resumed her course down the drainage. Beyond her the land cascaded down to open valley, fuzzy mist drifting above the gnarled vegetation, doz-ens of square miles flowing to thousands more. The immensity of this fundamental truth like an arrow through us all. *Boom!* Phillip hit the bear in the ass with the first shot. She spun a three sixty and bit at the point where the bullet had entered, like she was gonna fuck that bullet up. She kept going down the valley. I leveled my rifle on a mound of rocks and waited for her to stop. Phillip missed a couple times and then hit her in the chest. I saw blood blow out onto the tundra. She kept going. She leapt across the creek, into the brush, out of the brush. *Boom!* Phillip hit her again and she rolled slowly back into the creek, onto her belly and facing downstream, to the water, trickling now, to the sea. I found myself wondering if this water would make it to the Pacific this year or find itself frozen in some massive eddy on the lower Yukon. Wondering how finely diluted the bear's blood could be before it became something else.

We went to her and performed another exhaustive photo shoot ritual. Then Phillip and Val headed back to the sheep, while I stayed behind to skin the bear. I was two thousand feet below the notch on the ridge that we had cut through to get to this side of the mountain. The land angled sharply up, clad in alder and dwarf birch in the V-cut of the drainage, then naked gray boulders piled to the edge of the ridge that pressed into the liquid blue of the sky. Sunset lavenders and orange had begun to form in the north, where the distant bank of the Koyukuk River pushed against the scarped limestone. I worked as fast as I could, ended up cutting the tip off one of my fingers. In my haste I left a bit more meat and fat on the cape than I should have, left the skull and paws attached. The trophy was incredibly heavy as I began the long climb up the mountain in the gathering darkness. I descended the steep lichen-covered slope in the dark, occasionally slipping, falling, grabbing at alders, exhausted. I could see the campfire in the distance. I crossed the creek, my senses on alert for any noises that might be stalking me.

I came into camp and laid down and unclipped the pack, leaving it where it fell. I cooked the sheep ribs Johnny James style. Phillip was giddy, like a kid, at the primal camaraderie. He and Val pulled the griz from my pack and arranged it with the sheep so they were beside each other, in the glow of the flames. "This is what it's all about. This is the best," he said. And the ribs were succulent.

Phillip talked about hunting baboons with AK-47s from helicopters in Africa. On one of their family trips there, he'd woken his son up one morning: "He was, I think, fourteen at the time, and he looked at me all sleepy and said, 'Honestly, dad, isn't fourteen animals enough?' And what could I say but, 'Yeah, son, I guess it is.' And I let him go back to sleep. I got a really nice buffalo that day, though."

The night sky was an explosion of stars tinted by pale aurora to the north. The temperature dipped into the teens and covered the tundra in frost. We slept in. In the morning, Val and I went to work on the trophies. I removed twenty pounds of meat, fat, and gristle I'd been in too much of a hurry to get to yesterday. There was no need for me to pack those pounds back to the road. In fact, with the added weight of our camp, I would be carrying more weight to the road than I'd carried over the mountain the night before. And we still had to stop and collect our cache camp on the way out.

Phillip cooked sheep tenderloins in bear grease while we worked. He told us about his friend Jay who lived in Nevada. "Maybe you've heard of him. He won the Remington Award a few years ago."

"What's that?"

He looked at me incredulously. "It's only the most prestigious award in hunting."

"What, like whoever kills the most shit in a year?"

"It's more of a lifetime achievement award. It has more to do with how many different species you've taken. And Jay pioneered a bunch of new hunts, like in Senegal and the Ivory Coast, for species no one'd even heard of at the time. We met each other in Tanzania. We've both spent a lot of time in hunting lodges in the upper Midwest, and there was a game of euchre going on at this hunting lodge we were at. Well, euchre is a Midwest hunting lodge kind of game, and he and I partnered up and kicked ass on everyone else in the place. We've been friends ever since.

"He used to own a big chain of banks, had branches in all fifty states. He sold out in '07."

"Just before the crash. Did he see that coming?" I asked.

"He doesn't talk to me about stuff like that, but I wouldn't doubt it. He's a pretty shrewd operator. He's got a four-hundred-thousand-acre ranch in Nevada. He's got like ten Suburbans there for his guests to use. We load 'em up with beer and food and drive around and shoot deer and coyotes out the windows. We have contests to see who can shoot the most. I usually win. I jump over those other motherfuckers and shoot 'em out their side. I don't give a fuck," he laughed.

"One time we took one of the Suburbans and stuffed the fucker full of five-gallon gas cans. Then a dozen of us opened up on it from about five hundred yards until ka-fuckin'-boom! That was so fucking funny."

I tried to laugh along with him, but I was preoccupied with the math: if a Suburban could hold fifty 5-gallon gas cans for a total of 250 gallons then that would cost $1,000 and power my Toyota for eight months. I managed a few chuckles. There was my tip to consider.

We headed for the road in the late morning. We climbed over a steep rib plunging off the summit ridge. The sun was hot, and we shed layers rapidly. But the other side of the rib was still swathed in fog and six inches of snow on the jumbled rocks. We added the layers back on as we slipped and slid along.

On the one hand, I very much wanted to hate Phillip. He killed for no reason. He flew his jet from a week at his condo in Vail to the big hunting convention in Reno to his girlfriend's home in Dallas. He called African Americans niggers, people of Middle Eastern descent were Osamas, Hispanic people were spics.

But I couldn't quite manage hate. Neither Val nor I ever responded to his race baiting, and he phased this out of our interactions. He very much loved his kids, and I couldn't help but feel that one who is capable of love is not completely irredeemable. He wanted to be friends with us, with people. He was basically a nice guy outside of his reprehensible attributes, so I couldn't hate him. Which is good 'cause hate is poison. Cancer.

But I did see in him something I came to see in all the clients I'd meet, though never as strong as in Phillip. I call it the killing gene. Some fundamental genetic necessity fascinated by death, by killing. This trait has been enshrined during our shared evolution from swamp jizz to sentient space explorers. The hunters and warriors occupying positions of prominence, getting the hottest girls. These people are extremely competitive and smart, and they want to bury you in the game of capitalism. Part of the reason they're so into hunting is because it's no longer legal to deal with you, a human from another tribe, in this way.

Bonnie met us by the creek where Neal had left us ten days before. We threw our gear and meat into the back and within minutes were hurtling down the packed gravel road at sixty. It was always a rush to hit the road after days of hiking without a trail, the miles suddenly whizzing by with carefree ease.

Bonnie told us that Neal had booked Phillip on a flight out that night. She also told us that some guy had shot up a Batman movie near Denver, that a bunch of people had been killed or injured.

Phillip said, "Oh, no. You know what that means, don't ya? Pretty soon they'll be trying to push new gun control laws down our throats, take away our guns. The NRA's gonna be mass mailing everybody, fund-raising." Nobody responded.

According to Bonnie, she and Neal had broken up, so she was going to Hawaii to harvest a plant that had hallucinogenic properties. Since the drug form of the plant was so new, the production of it was unregulated. "Neal's ex is coming up to cook, so good luck with that. I don't think the woman can fry an egg, but whatever." A tear slipped out of the corner of her right eye, and she wiped it away before it broke across her cheek.

She told us that the group of sheep hunters were still stuck. That they still refused to hike down to the lake. That Neal had been air-dropping them food. That the clients had been calling the troopers. That the clients' families in the Lower 48 had been organizing Internet prayer gatherings. That Neal had nicknamed them the Donner Party.

"Well, fuck, that sucks," Phillip said. "I was hoping we could all get drunk together tonight. But I guess if my jet's ready, then I could be wheels up and outta Seattle by tomorrow."

"Neal's got beer and whiskey at camp. We could down a few before you go," I offered.

"Yeah, I guess that'll have to do. Well, shit, it's been good hunting with you guys. We did good, huh?"

"Yeah, yeah, we did good," I said, entirely unsure what that meant.

Shortly after his plane popped into the blue horizon, I entered the sauna back at the lodge. It was two hundred degrees in there, and I let the bad chemicals go and rinsed with cold water from a nearby spring. Bonnie served sheep backstrap, sautéed onions and carrots from the garden she'd started, and homemade mac and cheese. Afterward I went to one of the guest shacks and slept for fourteen hours.

I spent the next day sipping whiskey and fleshing out Phillips's bear. Val shared the whiskey with me and worked on the sheep hide. It was slow, painstaking work, the meat drying millimeters thin against the hide. The hide is delicate, and you don't want to be putting holes in some guy's $20,000 trophy, but you can't leave any flesh on there or the fur will slip and leave a bald spot. Bonnie showed me how she cut the thin flesh layers into grids of tiny squares, which she then scraped from the skin; she showed me how to tie the paw bones and sever the last knuckle from the claw. How to cut the pads on three sides to leave them hinged on to the hide. "I guess most taxidermists don't even use the real pads anymore. They use, like, synthetic rubber and shit."

"Yeah, those guys have displays at the conventions. It's pretty fuckin' crazy. They have eyes, teeth, fur, claws. They could probably make a bear if they wanted to," Neal said. He was pacing, looming, pacing. Nervous energy pulsing in waves.

I used an old wine bottle Neal had found on a mountain twenty years ago to turn the ears and the nose. I split the lips. I poured forty pounds of salt onto the skin and spread it so the surface was covered evenly. Two days after Phil left, I was finished.

Meanwhile, the lodge was frenetic. The Donner party had decided to walk to the lake and get rescued rather than eat themselves. Neal was uncertain about what to expect. "They've turned against me, Rob. It happens. You keep doing this long enough you'll get these kind of clients who will try to turn you against me. Derrick I'm not so sure about. He seems to be playing some kind of middle way game, which I can totally understand. They've been out there for close to a month now."

"That's a long time to wear the invisible shield," I said.

Neal smiled. "Yeah, I like you, Rob. I like having a cabbie up here with me. So I think I'm gonna keep Derrick. But Gary and the two packers, fuck them. They're fired as soon as they hit the ground. I've got cash to pay them off. Gary's got a truck here, but I'm thinking I'll give the packers a ride south a ways and kick 'em out. Say good fuckin' luck. I'd fuckin' fire Derrick, too, if I could find another guide in like two days. Which I can't. I've been trying, believe me. I've got a guy to do Gary's next hunt, but I can't find anyone else right now. So Derrick can keep his fuckin' job. For now."

I nodded at the stainless semiauto he was wearing in a holster on his belt. "Expecting trouble?"

I'm not sure what to expect. The clients fuckin' hate me, but I think they'll be so happy to be back, they'll forget all about that in a couple minutes. Gary and the packers . . . I guess I'm not expecting any trouble but . . . my spidey sense is tingling a little, I guess."

Neal and Bonnie walked out of earshot and had conversations that escalated to arguments then collapsed in tears. I had two days until my next client got there. I drove home. I gave Bonnie a ride. She told me Neal bought her plane ticket and gave her a thousand bucks. "Just so he wouldn't feel so guilty about dumping me, but who cares, I haven't been able to work the whole time I've been up there. Been working for Neal, really."

"Hell, yeah, girlfriend, I'd say he got off cheap with you." She punched me in the arm, sniffled, wiped another lone tear from her puffy red eyes. She told me about her older brother back in Baltimore who has twice been pronounced clinically dead of a heroin overdose. She'd never known her dad, and her mom had checked out emotionally. "Personally, I think she's waiting for him to go ahead and get it over with before she can move on. I just couldn't stay there and watch it anymore."

The reentry to home life was a blur, and soon I was driving back up. I had a twenty-five-year-old guy named Shim with me. Neal had hired him as a packer. He'd been packing luggage in Denali all summer. He was from Arizona.

When we got to camp, there was a Maule parked in the driveway next to Neal's Super Cub. Lance, the new pilot, was sitting at the folding table poring over aviation maps. His T-shirt had a picture of Bubbles, the character from Trailer Park Boys, on it. Underneath the picture was written "HOPE," in the style of Barack Obama's '08 campaign. Chantalle, his girlfriend, was on the couch, her legs curled under her, studying for her nurse's exam on a laptop. Lance was short and stout with a moustache that descended to his jaw. He was African American–Canadian. Chantalle was Alaska Native. She was thin and willowy with long black hair that fell below her shoulder blades. She wore hot-librarian glasses and looked at me over the tops of them when we were introduced. Her smile was pleasant but reserved. They lived in Dillingham, a village on Alaska's southwest coast. Lance flew commercial service there, and in his spare time used the Maule for outfitter hunts.

Val and Shawnee, the Christian guide, sipped coffee at the table with Lance. Looking sheepish and clutching his tea, Derrick sat on the couch between Chantalle and Neal, who was talking on the phone. Neal's ex, Kay, was dumping stewed tomatoes into a pot of burned caribou burger. She served it with cool, pasty noodles, called it spaghetti.

Neal called her "the hot mess." Told everyone that was her nickname. She looked at him like she could kill him. Or fuck him. Or both. "Don't call me that," she said temptingly.

"The hot mess," he repeated slowly.

They'd been together for years but broke up in the spring. Bonnie had come along in the interim, but Neal and Kay kept a thing going in Fairbanks. She worked for the state. She had an office. She and Bonnie had known about each other. The summer had been an anguished, unspoken competition. I thought about him calling Bonnie "a zombie prostitute from the south side" one morning when she lay sprawled in her cutoffs and T-shirt across the leather couch.

Time to take a break. I went to the shed and packed my next trip. If the weather cooperated, I would fly out in the morning and set up camp, inflate the raft, get ready to float a river. My client was scheduled to arrive in the afternoon. He wanted sheep and moose. Neal decided Shim would go with me as a packer.

In the morning Lance dropped Shim and me off on a strip of gravel bar 150 yards long. The big Maule touched down, and Lance winced at the sound of a rock smacking into the aluminum belly of his plane. He swerved around a drift-scoured tree half buried in sand and brought the plane to a stop twenty feet from the water. We tossed gear from Lance to Shim to me. Lance left quickly, the empty plane leaping off the beach within a few seconds.

Shim had played college baseball in California and converted to Christianity. He didn't drink or do any drugs, except hot chocolate, he confessed, grinning. His long sandy hair was cinched into a ponytail poking out the back of his baseball cap. His boyish face was offset by a scar running from his right eye orbital, along his jaw, to the point of his chin.

He set up the tents. I inflated the raft and assembled the rowing frame and oars. We built a big fire and hauled great armloads of river wood.

We glassed the arid country: mesas, buttes, and arroyos. Found a few lambs and ewes a couple miles up the opposite side of the river. Grotesque limestone escarpments eroded into melting faces and a lopsided buttress. I noted how autumn was well advanced here, the riverbanks rippling gold and orange, while in Fairbanks it was still a few splotches of yellow in a field of green.

We heard the hint of Lance's motor at the periphery of consciousness, droning into a roar as the powerful plane dropped back onto the bar. A tire touched the surface of the river, setting off rooster tails of arcing water spray. The plane lifted, then settled on the beach in a burst of loess.

Nick hopped out. Lance introduced us. "This is fuckin' awesome, man. I'm pumped. This is great."

I felt a bit assaulted by his enthusiasm. Like I might need to work a little of that off. But I liked that he was awed by the country, by the flight. That he could be moved by beauty. This was his first time to Alaska. He was forty, from the upper Midwest. He was twenty-five pounds overweight, but he looked like he could get around all right. He had olive skin and floppy black hair and a fleshy nose and brown eyes. He and his younger brother and some partners owned an engineering business in their hometown. "At first it was just me and Biff. We tried to make it work for the first few years, working like over a hundred hours a week. But we just couldn't keep up. I guess it wasn't working anyway. I got divorced. I got cancer. Anymore we never put in over eighty."

His brother had gone with Val and Shawnee back to the mountain Phillip and Don had hunted. They were hoping to run into the big guy Val, Phillip, and I had lost track of. Nick's dad, who owns a dairy farm and still gets up at three thirty every morning to milk the cows even though he's seventy, had gone with Derrick to look for a moose. Nick and his brother had bought this hunt for their dad as a birthday present, his dad having always dreamed of big moose.

In the morning, we pushed the fourteen-foot raft into the swift current. "You guys put some glass on these mountains," I said. "It's gonna be hard for me to look too thoroughly and steer this boat." The big empty country was laced with sheep trails. After lunch we climbed a mountain to see what we could see. I pushed the pace hoping to bring Nick's sheep fever down just a bit. Patience is key. It's actually a standard guide tactic: if in an area with limited game, hike the crap out of your client, and at the end of the trip he'll be so happy just to get away from you that he won't mind going home empty- handed. Nick was pretty out of shape. He fell far behind us and doubled over, hands on knees, gasping for air. Shim and I went ahead, climbing outcrops and pinnacles, putting glass on every surface of the multi-crenellated country. We saw nothing. Nick caught his breath, kept coming, caught his breath, kept coming. He was embarrassed, but he was having a ball.

Back in the boat we floated down, surrendered to the flow of something grander than ourselves. It began to rain heavily, and we pulled over since clouds had obscured sheep country. We set up camp on a muddy gravel bar, ate our nutrition-in-a-bag flavor-of-the-day.

A buddy of mine, Bob, and I were packing for a trip once and joked about taking all the stores out of their packaging and dumping them into a big tote and writing "FOOD" on the side of it. Just dip your cup in there and have some. Maybe add some boiling water, maybe not.

The country smelled of decomposing willow, wet lichen, damp fur. By morning the rain had stopped but the clouds remained. Wolves were howling from the red and orange vegetation that clung to the banks of the river as it wound away from us. I pictured them prowling through the branches for eggs; ears, nose, eyes a part of this place as surely as the brush through which they came, their ethos like the conscience of the harsh country.

It was the opening day of moose season. Nick wanted to focus on sheep. There was a creek we'd make it to that evening where Neal had found sheep before. It's difficult to access, unless you have a boat. Nick and Shim had hot chocolate, and I had coffee. Over our instant oatmeal Nick talked about how many hours of his life he's spent at a computer screen submitting bids, designing structural supports, acquiring permits. "I can't even tell you guys how good this feels. Like I'm getting a fresh start or something."

We floated most of the day, stopping to climb hills and glass the mountains. We stopped at some lakes too, and I scraped the brush with a moose scapula hoping a bull might come out to challenge me. The sandbars were transected with the tracks of caribou, moose, griz, wolf. An animal came out to drink, here. Another preying at night there. Hunting is a game of probability and chance: float past enough beaches and the odds are that one of them will have an animal on it. Improve your odds by being on that river in the early morning or late evening when the critters are the most active, by calling to them, by obtaining a wider vantage.

I wondered what the odds would be were we to stay in one place and watch one spot for ten days versus floating down a river for ten days, constantly reevaluating our tactics based upon new data, fresh stimuli. We floated on, waiting for that union of preparation and opportunity, otherwise known as luck.

It becomes a workout to stay present, to fend off the impulses to go inward, to let focus dissolve in the river, to relish some sweet memory or suffer a cruel recrimination. Or both at the same time. It is life, after all.

We began to see lambs and ewes up high. Found two half-curl rams, the first rams of the journey, in the early evening.

We made it to the confluence with the creek Neal had recommended as pale gold and crimson began oozing over the azure horizons. I conferred with him on the sat phone. He told me Nick's brother, Biff, had got a nice ram with Val and Shawnee, and that if we had a chance we should hike up the right fork of the creek and follow it to the head of the valley and take down the camp that the "Donner" party had left behind.

"I don't know if we'll have time for that," I said.

Shim spotted three young griz, all about the same size, coming over the mountain across the river from camp, a mile and a half away. One was dark, one dark and blond, one blond. I speculated that they were siblings, juveniles. Eventually they would go their own ways, but for now they wrestled and dug for roots together, separating and regrouping when one found something interesting.

As dusk came down and the bears faded from our scopes, we sat around a fire and listened to the lap of the river, the cascade of the creek. Nick told us about hunting mountain lions with dogs in Montana: the dogs tree the lion, a bit later the gasping human gets there and shoots the lion out of the tree. Shim and Nick discussed hunting coues deer and mulies in Arizona. Shim, speaking with the determined enthusiasm of youth, said he wanted to kill every kind of deer there was. He had guided his dad to get his first deer in twenty years. On to the next topic: bow hunting. I was sick of hunting stories. I sat by the fire pretending to listen, while behind my invisible shield I detached and roamed the cosmos. Before turning in I scraped the brush with the scapula, did some grunting.

I was up at four thirty under a three-quarter moon and the far-flung spray of gaseous fireballs, a tossed array of opaque clouds. A moose had walked to within thirty feet of our camp during the night. We packed three days' worth of supplies into backpacks and headed across a flat expanse of willow pressed with moose tracks and stunted spruce. Shooting stars cut across the morning sky.

After sunrise Nick spotted a group of sheep up the valley, below timberline. I put the scope on them—rams. They were on the other side of the creek from us, a mile and a half ahead, perched halfway up the steep slope in spruce that thinned into shrubs and bushes a hundred yards above them.

I told everybody to drop their packs, get their pants off, find a walking stick. We had to cross the rain-swollen creek, and it seemed best to do it now while we were still a ways away from the sheep, in the cover of the boreal. The current was cold and fast, cloudy and green, up to my balls. My bare feet slipped on the worn-smooth rocks. I braced myself with the walking stick through the deepest current, tried to imagine the journey of these molecules, caught up in a continental cloud of vapor, blown across the North Pacific onto this far north aggregate of cast-off crust. Conveyed over five mountain ranges until, like a salmon that could no longer contain itself, it burst and poured off the mountains in creeks and rivers. Getting sucked up by plants and lapped by bears. Almost carrying us away in its rush.

Nick crossed the creek holding up his white boxers with one hand, bracing with his walking stick with the other. I could hardly stand to watch as he crossed the deepest fastest section, ready to jump in after him should the current pry him loose.

It was unbelievable to me how these guys showed up to hunt north of the Arctic Circle in September with cotton clothes, inadequate raingear, no hat or gloves. I'd have to go through their packs before we left, taking out bath towels and stacks of hardcover books, inserting stocking caps, long johns, and neck gaiters. Though wealthy and competent in many ways, they were often helpless here. I'd have thought it kind of comical were I not responsible for bringing them back to the road system in a condition similar to the one they arrived in.

We continued through the moss, lichen, spruce, and willow. Soon we were side-hilling across the mountain in a crouch, stopping to glass the sheep—horns and white coats—through the trees. Two hundred yards away we identified several full curl rams within the group. The shot would have been through trees and brush, and Nick didn't want to take it. We stayed put.

A breeze stirred from no obvious direction. I watched five sheep huddled for warmth in a depression in the slope. A three-quarter curl stood with his nose in a puff of wind. The others stood within a few seconds. They ambled slowly away from us, pausing to eat, passing over the next rib of the mountain.

I decided to wait. We ate a candy bar, went back for the gear we'd stashed a quarter mile behind. Waited some more.

"So, you had cancer, huh?" I whispered.

"Yeah, I started shitting blood a few years back."

"Like, a lot of blood?"

"Not a lot, but sometimes a lot. So I went in for one of those colonoscopies, and they found some polyps. A few months later I had intestinal cancer."

"No shit?"

"No shit. A lot of people I know were like, 'I ain't lettin' 'em shove that thing up my ass.'"

"Sounds better than colon cancer, any day. I gotta do that. I hear it's recommended around fifty."

"That's what they say."

"So'd they go in and get 'em?"

"Yeah, they got 'em all out. It hadn't spread. I was going through my divorce at the time too. It was kinda tough. But really, there hadn't been anything there for quite some time. She wasn't happy at all. She got remarried to this guy who makes tree stands for bow hunting. She's happy now. She's great with our kids, you know. It all worked out for the best.

"Then I got together with this other girl. I used to go out with her in high school. But she moved back East and hooked up with this military guy, married him, you know. But she walked out on him. He was a jerk. Got rough with her, you know. She divorced him. I love her. She's a great gal. She loves my kids."

He asked me about Michele. I told him about her first husband, his struggles with bipolar disorder. How he was wiring our house. We both chuckled. "Life's a funny thing, huh?" I said.

"I couldn't explain it if I tried."

"You wanna go and see if we can find those guys?"

"Yeah."

We tracked the group of sheep around the mountain. Their small hooves left clean prints in the metamorphic grit. The trail ran into gnarly eroded cliffs, the walls of steep gullies plunging off the mountain. We descended to the tree line, thinking about camping, not wanting to push the sheep. Shim spotted one on the next ridge. The others soon joined him. We set up the scope and watched them for two hours. There were nine sheep. Six of them were full curls. One of them was a much heavier animal than the others. His horns were broomed off, but they still reached inches past the full curl. An awesome ram.

We descended and continued around the mountain till we were in the trickle drainage below the gorge they were above. The sheep descended cautiously into the gorge and disappeared behind outcrops. We dumped our gear and crept tree to tree toward the gorge. It took thirty minutes to get inside the walls of the gully, where jagged jumbled rocks and the detritus of a thousand flash floods clogged the way. We climbed up a smooth gray boulder to a narrow ledge that looked back across the gorge to its rim. Shim gave Nick my pack frame, and Nick balanced his rifle on it, sighted in boulders.

A minute later a sheep walked out, then another and another, 350 yards out. One of them looked legal.

"There he is," Shim said when the big one stepped out.

"Shoot that sheep," I said.

"What's the range?" Nick said.

I pressed the range finder into Shim's chest, who had his ears plugged, not wanting to take my eye off the big sheep. "What's the range?"

"What," he said, unplugging his ears.

"The range."

"I got him at 322 yards."

Nick fired, gut shot the ram. He ran fifty yards and stopped broadside to us. Nick fired again.

"Six inches high," I said.

He fired again. "Six inches low," I said.

Boom! I heard the next shot hit him in the chest. Watched the fur and smoke blow from his ribs. He didn't flinch. Didn't stagger. He turned toward us. *Boom!* Nick hit him in the neck. That did it. He stumbled, rolled fifty feet down and died.

"Oh, boy! Holy shit! That was something!" Nick blurted.

"Nice shooting, bro," I said. I know, it might not seem like it. But imagine kneeling on a narrow stone ledge with the rifle propped on a backpack, sighting in a target more than three football fields away. From that distance the sheep looks only slightly larger than the point where the reticles come together in the scope. Your heartbeat, a blink, a breath—all are enough to move the crosshairs away from the kill zone. It's often not a perfect shot, but once it's begun it must be finished. And Nick did that well.

"Fuck!" he said.

We hiked up to the sheep. It was tough going, a hard forty-five minutes. We took the requisite photographs, posing the sheep on rocks. Stacking rocks to pose the sheep on. Holding up his lolling head. I felt disrespectful. We could see the lakes on the other side of the river framed within the grotesquely eroded walls of the gully. The rouged light of sunset moved in the brush we'd walked through that morning. Inside our drainage, the shadows gathered darkness the way a filter gathers dust.

"It kinda makes me just a little sad. Just think of the stories he could've told," Nick said.

"Yeah, I hear you." I said. "But he was old. It was his time."

"Yeah," Shim said. "He was griz food in a couple years, max."

"But I know what you mean. It always makes me sad to kill an animal, this beautiful creature," I said, stroking his white fur, the side of his head.

"I think there's something wrong with you if it doesn't," Shim said.

"Just think of the pussy he got," Nick said.

"The heads he bashed," I said.

We observed a period of silence.

It took ninety minutes to cape and butcher him, taking special care around the eyes and lips, the skin thin and delicate beneath steel blade. Shim carried the meat down in four game bags, two pairs tied together and draped over either end of a stick he bore upon his shoulders. I carried the hide and horns and gear.

We made it back to our stuff in forty-five minutes and set up camp in the dark. Rehydrated chili mac, horn admiration, ibuprofen, bed.

In the morning, I tagged the skull. We hiked two and a half miles to our river camp, where we ate seven sheep steaks apiece and then cooked the ribs and ate those too. It was a lovely day, no rain at all for the first day of the trip. Rainbow shreds nestled in the limestone mountains looming over the river. The second night out, the river had come up four inches. Now it was starting to drop.

Nick paced around talking on his sat phone, coordinating work orders with his manager back home. Around the fire, I coaxed more out of him. I like listening to people. I like to be reassured that we're really all just winging it. That no one secretly carries the answer to the great riddle of the universe, or the question for that matter. That maybe we're all just infinitesimal pieces of it. That our lives all tumble like rocks rolling off mountains rather than carefully plotted journeys unto death. That we're all susceptible to revelation and circumstance.

Nick had gone to school for dentistry, optometry, and biology before he took a summer job surveying for the state. After working for a private company, he earned an engineering degree. "When we first started, all the people who owned surveying companies were these old guys. Most of them were still using map and compass. And there's nothing wrong with that. I mean it works and all. But there was a lot of new stuff available. You know, computers . . . satellites. So I was like, 'Fuck it, let's use the new stuff,' and our business fucking exploded. And I almost worked myself to death. But I take vacations now. I live with my family now." Robots do the surveying, prepare 3D imagery, and run the heavy equipment; all the operator does is control the speed. Nick hires people from his hometown, people without college degrees, and trains them to do the work.

"Yeah it's kind of funny. We spread the money around pretty good. Everybody gets a nice Christmas bonus. At first people'd be showin' up for work on their new Harleys and shit. Now, I see their wives driving around in a new minivan, kids in it."

-:::-

The next day we were on the river by sunrise, the surface a metallic orange hue reflecting the clouds. We stopped frequently to look at lakes, scrape brush, climb hills, put glass on the country.

Around midday I checked in with Neal via sat phone. I told him we could use candy bars, cocoa, and some of the Crown Royal in Nick's cabin. Three hours later Lance roared out of the sky, dropped a box with candy bars and cocoa, no Crown. "Sorry," he giggled over the radio as he fumbled the box and dropped it on the far side of the river.

"No problem, man. Thanks for coming."

"Congrats on the sheep." Then he was gone.

We climbed a slope with a gorgeous view of seven lakes. There were tents on two of the lakes, probably dropped by floatplane as there were no boats in the river. Probably the dumb fucks who'd blown off a box of ammo earlier in the day. We floated on.

We found a big lake with the freshest moose sign of the trip around it, but there was a Taj Mahal of a camp there too—three wall tents, a canoe with an outboard. We floated on.

We stopped at a willow-crowded sandbar. A slough wrapped behind it. Fresh moose tracks were on the upriver end. Griz tracks the size of volleyballs on the lower end. There was a lake atop the bank through some willow and scraggly spruce. We sat in a harrowing north wind and watched the lake through the evening. I could feel Nick's resolve faltering in the blow. He and Shim went back to the boat to make some cocoa. I climbed a tree and watched until my hands and feet were numb and then went back to camp for food and cocoa. I returned to check the lake every fifteen minutes. We all came back for the last look of the day. Saw nothing. Shim was barefoot. He'd left his shoes and socks drying by a small fire.

"That's my dream, man, to hunt barefoot someday."

"I like you, Shim. You're like a hippie Christian athlete or something. And I mean that as a compliment. I'm part hippie, myself, you know."

"What, would you bowhunt?" Nick asked.

"Oh yeah, man. For sure."

"Guy's like Spicoli on Jesus." Nick laughed. Called him Sitting Bull.

In the morning I was on the lake alone before sunrise. Watched the light coming down the mountain, turning the world scarlet, orange, gold and casting black shadows beyond umber outcrops. The north wind was still relentless, mojo sapping. A cow bawled tentatively up the river. I answered. Sat in the wind. The tops of the mountains were powdered with snow.

When I returned to camp, Nick didn't seem to care about the moose wailing I'd heard on the lake. He was pulling back, preparing himself to leave without a moose. "So what's the plan, buddy? Just float on down lookin' for some better sign?"

"Well, I heard a moose this morning. There might be something around here. But if you feel like heading for the takeout, hunting the river, we can do that too." We left an hour later. By lunch he was ready to call it a trip. There was ice coating the branches hanging in the tributaries. The mud riverbanks were frozen hard. The river became rocky, shallow and swift. We ran a class II rapid in the early afternoon.

Lunch rejuvenated him, though. He started seeing fresh tracks, and we stopped at a big lake that sprawled below towering snow-plastered ridgelines. There were moose trails circumnavigating it and meandering off into the boreal. We scoped it for hours, three sets of eyes from three separate vantages with the same result: no moose. Shim found a big black bear high up the rock-pinnacled slopes of the mountain behind the lake. There were muskrats and buffleheads swimming around the shallows,

bubbling the water, keeping us company. The last glare of sunshine caught a patch of snow atop the ridge and turned it orange
while the rest of the world was cloaked in twilight and shadow.
Before sleep I scraped the willow, spruce, alder and grunted bull
challenges like a maniac.

I woke before I could see the lake. Took a thermos of coffee down to the edge and sat in the cold darkness. Shim came
down and we spoke in hushed tones. "Was that your stomach?"
I asked him.

"No."

"Do you hear that?"

"Yeah, I think so. Is that a moose?"

"Yeah. I think so."

The moose was doing a low burping echolocation. I started
calling back to him. The burps became more consistent, seemed
to be coming toward us around the lake on the upriver end after originating against the wall of the mountain beyond. I went
back to camp to let Nick know something might be talking to us.

"Let me lace up my boots. I'll be down there in two minutes,"
he said. I went back to the lake and scraped and called.

"Let's walk around this way. See if we can meet him over there
somewhere." Shim and Nick nodded, excited. At the north end
of the lake we could tell the moose was close. I scraped . . . he
scraped. Then we saw him in the brush, twenty-five yards away.

"Can I shoot him?" Nick asked.

"Wait. I haven't seen both sides of his antlers yet." To be legal
this moose needed to have an antler spread of at least fifty inches
or at least four brow tines on one side of the antlers. I was pretty
sure he was legal just by the way he came in, steadily but also
patiently, confidently. He shifted, and I saw the other side. There
were only three tines on each side but the spread was close to
sixty inches. "Put him down," I said.

"I don't have a shot right now," Nick said. I raked the bush and he moved out a little ways. "Shoot when you can," I said.

The moose burped and I burped back, scraped. I watched him lower his left antler and scrape some willow.

Boom! The moose bolted right, came out broadside left. *Boom!* . . . *Boom!* He stood steady a moment and then reared up on his haunches and went over backward. He lay there with his last breaths. The exhalations a release of pressure rather than a bold stroke.

Nick jumped on me and gave me a hug. I held him off the ground.

Shim had gotten the whole thing on video. Within a year it would be viewed online by tens of thousands of people. I wish I could take that part of it back; the voyeurism seems disrespectful. The moose's death had been a pact between the four of us, not a YouTube moment to be consumed and shit back out across the digital cosmos.

"You got one ready?" I asked Nick.

"I'm empty."

"Put one in," I said.

I went to the moose. Helpless, dying, leaving this world—for a while. "Easy, buddy," I said. "It's okay, easy, thank you. He looked at me confused and then he lay down his great head. I waited till he was still. Till there hadn't been a breath for a couple minutes. I stroked his nose and whispered an apology, a promise to sing songs about him the rest of my days. It took five hours to cape, quarter, and butcher him.

We ate and loaded up camp and pulled the raft a hundred yards upriver to the moose. We loaded that raft heavy. Meat piled above the thwarts and gunnels. We were on the river by three. I rowed for six hours, with only a brief break for food, until my wrists and elbows were jelly. The warm sun melted away, and it got windy, cold. It began to snow. We had a driftwood fire beside the river. We sang the moose's praises. "They use that thing like a hand. Like they know every point on those antlers the way we know our fingers," Nick was saying.

I wanted to share with Nick and Shim the feeling of caping a moose and a sheep for a taxidermist, as though I were an old hand at it when in fact I'd never done it before Neal had hired me. But to divulge this would mean lifting my invisible shield. It was getting stuffy behind that thing. The glass was fogging up. I wanted out. I kept my mouth shut, though, and allowed myself to be carried away by the cold wind and flecks of snow and warm smoke.

The next day we rowed a few miles down the river until it emptied into a lake that was several miles long and a mile wide and contained by high mountains. Sheer cliffs rushed up from the water for hundreds of feet. There were sheep on them. Forlorn gatherings of black spruce, tangles of alder, expanses of green, maroon, and gold-blotched tundra rose to the ridgelines. Cabins scattered around the shore. The airstrip where Lance would land when he came to get us was there too. With a north wind pushing us, I didn't want to overshoot it and then have to battle back against it.

Two guys were standing on the beach next to a fire, scoping the cliffs above the north shore. I rowed over to them. One guy was tall and olive skinned with a long beard and a menacing disposition. I could feel the potential for violence within him. He grinned at us as though he were thinking of cutting us up and using us for wolf bait. The other guy was short, clean cut, extremely nice. Like way too nice. I didn't trust him. He reminded me of Michael J. Fox's evil twin. They were hunting guides. They didn't know where the airstrip was. They couldn't answer any of our questions. They told us their boss would be down in a minute, but it was clear that they wanted us to leave. We did.

Later, over a large bottle of Crown, Neal would tell us the troopers were after their employer. "Those two guys are multiple felons. Their boss has several assault convictions of his own. He's a fraud, too. Sells people hunts and then never picks them up at the airport. He can't get any pilots to fly for him anymore. That's how I got that area where the guys got stuck waiting for the plane, when they took his license one time before."

The next guy we met motored out to us in an inflatable. He pulled us the final two hundred feet to the airstrip and then hauled our gear up to the strip in a trailer he pulled with his four-wheeler. He was from Fairbanks. We gave him a pile of meat for his trouble. We washed the raft and broke it down and hauled it up with the rest of the gear and sat and ate and waited for the aggressive rumble of Lance's Maule coming through the mountains.

"You ever hit a woman, Rob?" Neal asked.

"No. How 'bout you?"

"Yes. Since you asked."

"What happened there?"

"Which time?"

"Pick one."

"She pointed a pistol at me."

"Chambered?"

"Safety off, finger on the trigger. It was with this woman from Anchorage. She could get pretty emotional."

"Jesus, I guess."

"Ask me about the other time I hit a woman."

"What about the other time you hit a woman?"

"She pointed a pistol at me."

"Was she fucked up?"

"Just crying and stuff. Hey, can you pull over? I think I see a sheep up there."

We were driving north, looking for sheep. Neal could only hunt legally if he didn't have clients in the field, which was the case on this day but would not be so the next. This was his only day of sheep season. He had a subsistence permit that would allow him to shoot one within the five-mile pipeline corridor. "I enjoy irony, Rob," he was saying as we rode along, me driving. "Like when I'm doing those big hunting shows in the winter, selling hunts, and I'm set up in this huge room, and there's all these millionaires and billionaires walking around with their entourages of prostitutes and shit. The place just reeks of opulence. People who aren't incredibly rich don't get to come. And everybody's drinking, and there's all this money and ego, and it's all about this sheep, who at that precise moment is on some cliff in the Brooks Range getting blasted by the wind and snow. At least I think that's irony. Either way, I enjoy thinking about that when I do those shows. Keeps me from getting too disgusted. Hey, can you pull over, I see a sheep up there."

Neal went after the sheep. The day waning, I refused to join him. I'd been out of the field a day and had another client coming in the following day. I wanted to be back at camp stuffing my face and sleeping. My whole body hurt at once from the season. I'd been running up and down mountains with heavy loads for a month and a half. Neal hadn't told me we were going hunting. He'd only asked if I wanted to go for a ride.

I was eating those shitty soft granola bars, and they were making me queasy. I had no weed or cigarettes, and I was pissed sitting there on the side of the road waiting for him. I used the time to write in my journal. I wrote till I was sick of it, turned the truck on, and shone the brights across the river Neal had crossed on his way to the mountain he had to climb. I watched for wolves cruising the willow, heard four gunshots from the mountain. I wrote some more.

Neal returned to the truck at 11:15 with a big full-curl ram. I grabbed his pack as he was climbing out of the riverbed. It must have weighed 125 pounds. Neal was cold, wet, exhausted, hungry. He kept asking me to turn the car heater up till it was in the nineties in the truck. I told him I had to turn it down or it would put me to sleep. He was trembling too hard to drive, pumped, having left the camp drama behind for a while. Pumped from something real. I recognized that killer gleam in his eyes. He apologized for holding me up. All I needed to hear. We returned to camp and feasted on the heart and backstrap.

Twelve hours later Lance and I roared down from the clouds, touched a rocky bar, bounced several feet into the air, came back down, bounced a foot, came back down, did a little hop, came back to earth, and rolled to a stop. We had flown over a giant bull in the middle of a lake 1.4 miles downriver and found another legal bull in a different lake a mile upriver.

Shim and I inflated a small boat and clamped a twenty-five horse Yamaha to the transom. We hooked up a gas tank and primed the motor and fired it up. The boat and motor belonged to Lance, who used them to guide fishing trips in his spare time.

Soon Lance came back with the client, an emergency room doctor named Lewis from Northern California. He was unimpressed with Alaska, the flight through these far north mountains, the presence of a massive bull so close to camp. It was illegal to go after that one at this point because we'd all flown that day, and state law required that we wait until the day after flying to kill an animal, this a response to unethical hunting guides running animals to exhaustion then landing and shooting them. It's still okay to shoot wolves from airplanes. But that's a whole other controversy.

Lewis told us he'd been to Africa eight times. He spoke quickly, seemed a bit hyper. He told us he'd done his residency in Detroit, dealing with multiple gunshot wounds every night. Now he worked the night shift at the hospital back home. "Yeah, we deal with a lot of alcohol stuff, a lot of schizophrenia. They never have their episodes at noon. It's always at midnight."

Then came a story about an unknown powdered drug that had killed several kids in the town he lives in. Several other kids who tried it had been committed to mental institutions where they would likely spend the rest of their lives. The DEA had taken a sample of the powder for analysis but as of yet had been unable to identify it.

I found myself disturbed, unable to think of anything else but what an uncertain journey raising my son would be. How the love I felt for him was like an extension of my physical self. If that were to be severed, I wondered, would I bleed to death? I felt a loss of control and then surrender remembering what a wild thing I'd been through my teen years. Drinking to unconsciousness, doing any drug that was put in front of me. I remembered the fear on my parents' faces whenever I'd leave the house.

Lewis showed us pictures of impoverished African men he'd hired as hunting guides. They wore duct-taped flip-flops or no shoes at all. I could see their ribs through the holes in their shirts.

He seemed not to notice the country. We were in the lowlands, the river winding through mud bluffs and snarled willow. Low mountains rose a mile back from the turquoise water. I told him about the big bull we'd seen downriver.

He shrugged. "All right. Let's go put a bullet in him." He was overweight and his movements were oafish. He threw his garbage on the ground, and I picked it up.

Shim was happy. He had his Bible and toothbrush, two items he'd been missing on our previous trip. It began to rain.

By morning the rain had turned to big flakes of snow that stuck to the muddy ground. We were rowing down the river by six and reached the shore proximate to the oxbow where we'd seen the big bull before seven. The lake was surrounded by dense brush, and it was nearly impossible to move quietly through it to get to the lake. Lewis broke sticks and branches. He'd pause and let loose huge sighs, like air brakes on a tractor trailer releasing pressure. Shim and I exchanged glances, like, what are we gonna do with this guy?

I called a few times and received exactly one cautious grunt in response. I could not get the moose to say anymore. I decided not to push him, to be patient. It was early. We found a spot to watch the lake, an old bend of the river that had silted up and was cut off from the flow. We sat there in the snow until it turned to rain, and we sat some more before heading back up-river. Lewis had brought no raingear, no rubber boots. He had cotton clothes, leather gloves, a baseball cap. I called Neal on the sat phone and told him to get a package together and fly it out.

The outboard gave us trouble on the way back to camp. The plugs were fouled. I took them out and cleaned them and then pulled the starter cord a bunch of times to drain the cylinders of the oil that had leaked into them. We didn't have enough oil and the motor wouldn't start, so we beached the boat a half mile below camp and walked up, had lunch. I called camp and told them about the boat and the lack of oil. Lance would be by to help as soon as the weather cleared.

Hiking upriver on game trails, we checked some other lakes. Lewis was breathing like a freight train and breaking brush like a bulldozer. We got back to camp after dark in a cold mist. The boat had been brought to camp. There was a note on it: "Call before using."

I called. "What were you guys doing so far upriver from camp?" Neal asked.

"Looking for moose."

"What happened this morning, with the big bull?" I told him. "Okay," he said, with a note of hesitation, nervousness. "That prop's pretty fucked up too. I got a new one ordered. It's gonna get flown up from Fairbanks. We'll get it out to you as soon as we can."

The raingear had been delivered, and Lewis put on dry clothes. We had a fire. Lewis talked about putting a ninety-eight-year-old man with an aneurism on life support. "We used up all the blood in the hospital on him because the relatives wanted to keep him alive. Try doing that in England or Canada. Don't get me wrong, but it's messed up to put those kind of resources into a ninety-plus-year-old with kidney failure. But socialized medicine has its drawbacks too. Somewhere in between the two systems there's probably a reasonable compromise. But things are so screwed up in this country, I don't know if we'll ever get there."

Lewis was clearly still decompressing from his job.

"I shot a baboon one time in Cameroon," he said. "The black guys wanted me to do it. They asked me to. The first thing they do with it is throw it on the fire to singe all the hair off it. Then a guy cuts the ass off and eats it. It's pretty much all fat."

"Was it like raw or what?" Shim asked.

"Pretty much. Those guys pretty much ate that whole baboon that night. Our tracker was the one who ate the ass. He was the village witch doctor. Like, one guy below the chief."

We got into our tents, out of the rain. Lewis was up for hours listening to a book on tape, still on the night shift. It was raining when we awoke the next morning. We had instant oatmeal and headed down the river and sat on the oxbow all morning. Lewis listened to his book on tape, *The Rise and Fall of the Third Reich*. He did not once pick up his $2,000 binoculars to examine the willow and cattail lake border. He left his rifle laying on the moss in the rain. I leaned it against a spruce tree.

A cow in the grass at the far end of the lake plunged her head and neck into the still, black water and pulled up huge mouthfuls of the grass. She glanced into the trees nervously. We stayed and watched her into the afternoon and then watched the lake for an hour after she'd gone.

I decided I liked Lewis all right, though he was probably the kind of doctor people talked shit about.

"I like being an ER doctor because I don't have to deal with people. I mean I have to deal with them, but I don't develop a relationship with them, which is fine with me," he said back at camp sitting by the fire in the drizzle. He was calm and weirdly hyper at the same time. He'd probably be a good guy to have work on you were you ever to show up in the ER with a gunshot wound.

I scraped the spruce and willow around camp. Shim had said that he'd heard a bull scraping and grunting the last two nights. I found his tracks in the sand, circumnavigating our camp. He'd probably come to investigate the noises we'd made breaking the dry branches off the bottoms of the tree trunks for the fire.

We went upriver for the evening hunt. We stopped at a small lake close enough to the river that Lewis couldn't make too much noise getting to it. I told Shim where to sit by the river to glass up and down it. Told him to come get us if he saw anything. Lewis and I crawled into a thatch of cottonwood saplings at the edge of the water. I told him to turn his book down as I watched the lake. Shim ran to us out of breath. "I got a bull," he panted.

We ran back to the river. The bull was five hundred yards up-river with his ass pointed at us, his head in the brush. We were upwind of him. His ears swiveled around and pointed directly at us. He was a big sixty-plus-inch bull, his neck bigger than any of the trees along the river. He went into the brush.

I decided to go at him and see what happened. The five hundred yards that separated us was an unruly tangle of brush to beat through, a treacherous tussock field with moats of water encircling the grass clumps. It took an hour to get to where we'd seen him. The brush he'd disappeared into lay between the river and the small lake I'd seen the second bull on when we'd flown in. We crept through the brush—though, of course, Lewis could not creep quietly. He broke brush and exhaled with a sound like an air compressor releasing its load.

We sat on the shore of the small round lake a while. A nearly all-white cow stepped out of the strip of brush between the lake and the river. Lewis rested his rifle on my shooting stick, aimed at the trees behind the cow, and was ready for the big guy to step out. He never did. Eventually the cow turned back into the tangled branches and was gone. She did it so effortlessly that it seemed like a magic trick, like pulling a moose out of a forest.

The texture of the lakeshore had been created by the hoofprints of many moose. We sat in the brush and watched the portal to the fourth dimension into which the cow had vanished until dusk and then headed back to the boat. We split up by the first lake. Lewis and I went to retrieve our gear, and Shim headed to the spot where he'd seen the bull to retrieve his things. We were to meet at the boat. But Shim didn't show.

As I walked to the boat I thought I heard him shouting, a weird yelling, panicked and twisted by the upriver wind. I wondered if he'd seen a moose, but when we got to the boat he wasn't there. I heard more of the strange noises. I shouted back, but it stopped. Lewis and I figured it would be nearly impossible to get lost between the place where we'd separated and the boat. We discussed the very fresh, large griz tracks we'd been seeing along the shore, and the fact that Shim had no gun. We called to him and scoured the riverbank for over an hour. I began to fear the worst, imagined my hippie Christian athlete buddy being dragged screaming into the bushes, partially eaten alive, buried for later. I made the call to return to camp, hoping for a different scenario. I figured if he wasn't there, I'd call Neal and maybe the troopers could get a chopper in the air that night.

Lewis and I talked about whether a bear would have drug him into the tussocks or the brush. Lewis seemed bewildered that this could be happening on his vacation, as if medical emergencies weren't part of his contract here. I was going over what I might say at the memorial service as I drove the boat home in the dark, bouncing off rocks and beating up the prop.

And then we came around the last corner, and I saw a big fire at our camp. I was pissed. "What the fuck happened? How the fuck did you get turned around? We totally fucked that area up for hunting with all that yelling!" Shim took it and apologized. Then I realized that it happens, that it had happened to me. We were smack in the middle of one of the largest swaths of wilderness left in this world. You need only let your attention wander a few moments and look up . . . lost. Panic can set in quickly. And the only thing Shim could be sure of was that camp was downriver. I apologized. We made dinner.

The three of us stood around in the rain eating our food from foil pouches and discussing how moose memory works. How long one might remember our yelling. I posited that they were intelligent critters. Lewis said "Really? They seem pretty fuckin' stupid to me. Not like a whitetail." And I had to stop myself from telling him to fuck off. I didn't say anything for a while. I was becoming aware that part of me didn't want him to get a moose, didn't feel he deserved one.

Before we turned in I said to him, "Yeah, it's always a heart-breaker when one gets away. But we've seen four moose in three days. There's plenty of time left. I think we'll be all right." He stood up and walked away without saying a damn word. I wondered if he was Asperger's light. It made it easier not to loathe him.

The next day we drove the boat far up the river. We saw a mottled gray-and-white wolf with long legs trotting over the stones at the entrance to a slough on the east bank, forty feet away. I told Lewis he could shoot him. He waited until the wolf was on the bank and partially obscured by the grass and willow. He missed. The wolf ducked and then sprang into the forest. He was gone before Lewis could get a second round ready. We got out and inspected the ground for a blood trail, but there was nothing. I wanted him to get that wolf to take some of the pressure off. But I was glad he missed it too. Didn't feel we had the right to end its life so Lew could have another head for his wall. My feelings about my job were getting complicated.

We sat on the lake where we'd seen the bull the night before. We heard a cow calling. Loons and buffleheads paddled across the surface, which reflected the golden crowns of the birch, willow, and cottonwood. It began to rain. We headed back to camp. Lance and Natalie flew in with a new prop, but it was the wrong one, a twelve spline instead of an eight. They would have to get another one sent up from Fairbanks. They left tea, raingear, sardines.

We hunted the lake downriver that night. We came back up in the dark, getting repeatedly stuck in the shallow, rocky current. Shim and I kept jumping out and pulling the boat free, walking it around sleeper rocks. We were soaked and shivering by the time we got to camp.

Lewis had remained dry in the boat with his new raingear. I could not dismiss the image of him being borne in a litter across the African savanna by a bunch of "the black guys." Saw them setting him down and pointing to a lion, a giraffe, an elephant. Saw him shooting it and returning to his perch while his servants went and retrieved his trophy.

That night he talked about doing his training in Detroit. An electronics plant there had laid off twenty-two thousand people the week before he arrived. Again with the multiple gunshot wounds every night. "We'd have to cut their clothes off, and I couldn't even tell you how many crack vials spilled out of their pockets and broke on the floor. It killed my empathy. It really did. And I haven't got it back. I wonder sometimes if I'll ever get it back, and then I realize that I just don't care that much. And that maybe that's the most fucked up thing about it."

We spent the morning in the rain on the upriver lakes, surprised a cow on the smaller one. Everything was muddy. We were filthy, wet, cold. We returned to camp in the afternoon. Lance roared down out of the sky with the new prop, peanut butter, bread, and ham. He left quickly, before the weather could get much worse. "Is this about as bad as you'll fly in?" I asked.

"Oh, something like that. Where I normally fly, it can get a lot worse. There can be a lot of wind. I mean the visibility kind of sucks now, but I can stay in the air, find my way home. If it got much colder, I'd have to worry about the wings icing, then they stop flying and the plane just falls out of the sky. Man, you guys been doing some serious off-roading with this thing," He said, holding up the old prop and examining the guard. He directed us to clear three big rocks from the landing area and then hopped in his plane and roared into the sky like some 1930's barnstormer.

The boat ran like a race car with the new prop. We took it far upriver in the evening and drifted back down past slate cliffs with pretty creeks gushing from the rain. We climbed some of them and glassed the country. There were wolf tracks on top of our boot tracks from the day before. Shim came and told us that the boat was going flat, taking on water. The drain plug had popped out and one of the valves had come loose. We got it back to camp, where we had to bail and pump up the boat, after dark, in the rain. We were soaked. The whole world seemed slathered in mud.

Shim and I talked about Lewis while he went to take a dump. "The one that got me," Shim said, "was when he was talking about that assisted living place that he owns, and he's like 'Yeah, they're pretty much useless.' Talking about the people who live there, and I'm like, 'Dude, they're still people. What's the matter with you?'"

The next morning we woke in a cloud, the visibility less than a hundred yards, and then it lifted and revealed touches of blue sky. But the blue was quickly enveloped, and the rain came down again. I wanted to get Lew a moose. He never complained about the weather, or anything else about the trip for that matter. But he sighed like a 747, moved through the woods like a team of oxen, lunged in and out of the boat like he was trying to leap across a crevasse, like he'd surely die if he didn't make it across the foot of water separating him from shore. Shim and I held the boat steady, exchanged glances, and stifled laughter every time.

Overweight and under-cardio'd, I thought. I spoke with him about the noise, and he just shrugged. Sometimes I wondered whether he knew he hadn't earned this one. In the boat, to keep it level, Shim and I sat on one side and Lew on the other.

We floated down and checked out a small lake below camp, had a look at the oxbow we'd been watching every day. Continued down to some bluffs near the end of our hunting area. We watched some winding sloughs from the bluffs. Shim saw a cow and a calf. The sixth and seventh moose we'd seen in six days.

I remained cautiously optimistic. I realized that Lew was used to not being liked, that he kind of expected it, but I resolved to like him no matter how much I loathed him. He listened to *The Rise and Fall of the Third Reich* and country music his girlfriend had recorded for him. He stared at the ground.

The river braided into a half dozen shallow channels five miles above camp, and even with the new prop we couldn't get through. A dozen or more bald eagles were hunting the splayed channels every time we went by.

A gang of ravens—cawing, gliding, dipping their wings, and playing chicken—toyed with one another in the air above the bluffs we sat upon. Native elders say that ravens, tricksters of the north, can communicate the whereabouts of moose, but I hadn't had any firsthand experience. I felt like my due at this point would be to have one guide me to an abandoned pile of fat and guts.

I feel that one has to reach an equilibrium with the country before it opens itself to you, divulges its secrets. But sometimes you just get lucky. And the longer you spend in an area, the better the odds of that happening.

We found fresh tracks a hundred feet from the tents when we woke the next morning. I called and scraped the willows there every day. Glassed a grassy slough across the river leading back to a huge lake. I wanted to go hunt there, but it was out of our guide area.

The next day it was raining again. We ran up and down the river scraping, calling, looking at lakes. I let my eyes linger over the raindrops that clung to the spruce trees hanging horizontally above the river. I listened to the slicing of the air as seven teal swooped down to the water from the creamy gray and blue sky.

The river was rising, but sections of it were still difficult to navigate. Shim and I were still hopping out to reef and shove. I broke off the prop guard and reattached it with duct tape. I filed a ding on the prop with my Leatherman. I reminded myself not to allow the pressures of hunting and outboard maintenance to dull my appreciation of the cleaved snow-edged mountains, the river cutting down through the bedded slate, the views of marshes in paisley divisions of yellow, orange, pale green, and black.

The sky turned a rouge color and then black and then filled with stars as we ran the boat back to camp after another long day. The stars proliferated and green and red aurora oozed across the night canvas. Lewis was unimpressed. He'd seen them before. Found more interesting things on the floor of the boat.

At camp Lewis told us he'd killed two elephants. He made barstools and trashcans out of the legs, jackets and gun cases from the hides, the tusks were mounted on his walls like giant harpoons. "The last one was over fifty years old. They only get to fifty-five or sixty. Then they start crapping sticks and stuff, undigested I mean.

"When one goes down, the people from the nearby villages start coming out of the trees with knives. Before long you can barely see the elephant for all the people clustered around it. Knives are flashing in the sun, people are arguing. The entire carcass gets stripped to the bone in a few hours. And I'm like, their hero. It's kind of strange."

I've found that when a client's attitude starts to go south, it helps to get them talking about subjects they're passionate about. With Lew, it was hunting in Africa. He and I had a whiskey and water. Shim had hot chocolate.

I asked Shim if he thought I was going to hell for the premarital sex I'd had. He fumbled around the edges of the topic for a while before saying, "If you don't get right with Jesus, then you will have to face judgment."

"Doesn't that sound a little bit like some medieval comic book to you? I mean the red villain with horns and a tail. A pitchfork?" I said.

He shrugged.

"Premarital sex! What the fuck are you talking about? Hell?!" Lew said to me.

"Hey, don't look at me. I'm not the one saying you're going to be swimming in a lake of fire for eternity 'cause of it."

"Jesus fucking Christ!" Lew laughed. I realized I'd found a new subject about which he was passionate.

"I mean really, most of the sex I had before I got married seemed like it did us both some good. I just don't understand why God hates it so much. Hates me so much for it. I mean really, I'm a pretty nice guy. I love my family, give money to the hungry-looking guy with the sign outside Walmart."

Shim shrugged again. I realized I was being an asshole. Whiskey and stress. Realized if I truly wanted to be the change I wished to see in the world then this was as good a time as any to start. I apologized, let the conversation drift back to baseball.

Daybreak the next morning was a rare event. It was the kind that a human can only expect to witness a few times over the course of a normal lifespan. It began with some swirling combination of orange and violet pushing the blue-gray layer above the eastern horizon. Then the sky turned red. The river rippled scarlet. The mountains wept blood. I said, "God, look at that," as I rowed the boat past the grassy slough.

"Oh my God," Shim said. And he started snapping photos.

Lew turned and looked and then returned his attention to the floor of the boat, said nothing. No reverence. No inkling of the mystery that still might exist in the world for him. We checked on the round grassy lake in the willow, checked the oxbow, kept floating. I saw a cow and a calf. I saw a lone cow. We scraped and called. Nothing.

We climbed the bluffs and watched three ponds and more than two miles of river for three hours. We saw no moose.

In the afternoon we checked out the lakes upriver. Sat on them till dark. Saw a cow and calf on a mountainside, miles away. The twelfth and thirteenth moose in nine days.

Lance came for us the next day. He took Lew first while Shim and I took down the tents and the boat. The sun broke from the clouds within fifteen minutes of Lance's wheels leaving the ground.

Shim and I sat around the fire feeding the last of the garbage into it. With no warning, Lance roared onto the beach a wing's length away. The wingtip almost within reach. Shim and I dove into the brush like we were being bombed. Lance was laughing when he hopped out of the plane. "Sorry," he managed. "I was getting a little bored. You should have seen your faces." He doubled over, slapped his knees. We joined him, our invisible shields cast away, melting in the garbage fire.

We loaded the plane. I hopped in. Lance would return for Shim and the rest of the gear. He banked over the remains of camp as soon as we were in the air. The plane leveled and rose over the dry sloughs that formed concentric circles behind the gravel bar. I gazed down into the spirals, letting my eyes and attention wander. Dissolution.

I saw movement. A large brown body in the golden willow. Another one. Antlers. The bodies touching. Four more bodies farther in the brush. Two big bulls and four cows five hundred yards behind our camp.

I started laughing. Pointed them out for Lance. He turned above them and we watched for the few seconds it took to regain our heading home. "Oh man, that's painful," he said. By the time we rose above the valley walls, we were both laughing.

I wondered whether I would ever do this again. I mean, this part was incredible, whizzing over the wandering ridges and valleys of the Brooks Range, pointing out moose, bear, sheep, wolves, caribou. I'd floated two rivers, spent more than forty days camping and got paid for it.

But some part of me protested, nagged. Was I in some way exploiting the relationship with the natural world I'd spent the last twenty-five years seeking. Was it wrong to end a life for money? For a trophy? For someone I didn't like? For someone who had no reverence for the intimacy of that instant, for the sunrise or the kill?

I let my thoughts scatter like ashes over the south slope of the farthest north cordillera. Fat sporadic raindrops smacked into the windshield of the Maule. Lance brought the plane down out of the clouds, mountain shoulders off our wingtips.

I could sort through it later. I wanted to see my family. Didn't like not seeing Cord for so long. Knew I was missing something every day I was away. The small plane in the storm so far above the Earth was a metaphor for the fragility of our time here. For the endurance of our relationships.

Leaving Winter, 2009

DON'T GET ME WRONG, I like town. I like Thai food, skiing on groomed trails, and espresso. I even like grocery shopping, something I did as infrequently as possible in my bachelor days. I'd stock up on veggies like carrots, cabbage, and potatoes—produce that lasted for weeks in the dank bottom of my dorm-sized fridge. The store just seemed a depressing place, an orgy of consumerism and obesity cast in floodlights and set to Muzak.

But now that I'm a stay-at-home dad during the week, I go shopping with Cord, and I see a different side of it. The guy bumming change outside the liquor store looking like he was eaten by a wolf and then shit off a cliff smiles so suddenly I am startled. He gives Cord a cutesy little finger wave and bends his knees and cocks his scraggly head. He laughs when Cord waves shyly and plunges his face into my leg.

Strangers approach our cart to converse with him. An elderly woman, half pushing and half leaning on her cart, says, "Oh, hello there. Are you helping Daddy do the shopping today?"

"No, I'm just having some cheese puffs," Cord replies. And they'll talk names and ages until the woman turns and tells me he's a fine looking young guy, and I'll say thanks, and we'll have a little connection.

I catch people smiling at us, and I smile back and realize that my son, as only a child can, is exposing the love in people's hearts, drawing them out of their worries and defenses for a few seconds. When the love is exposed, it can't help but get shared, and since learning to shop with Cord, I've started to think this openness is what it's all about.

I buy asparagus and green beans and broccoli, vegetables that are only green for a few days, or hours, beyond the multi-thousand-mile journey from the Lower 48, because we can always go back to the store, Cord and me.

At some point, though, I do begin to doubt the authenticity of our human construction. Our technology and understanding of the world have exploded so vigorously over the last hundred years or so that we're not sure what matters. As the number of wild places decreases and the human population increases, it becomes more and more difficult to remember the mud we crawled out of. And if we don't know where we came from, we can't know where we are. We experience the world without feeling it. Most of the people on the planet are struggling for food and water, while the rest of us post selfies on the Internet. I worry we're losing our way, worry I'm losing my way. I start to feel a constant fine tension, like a ringing in my ears that rises in volume until I want to ram the grocery cart into all the chips and Cocoa Puffs and frozen dinners on display for our shopping pleasure.

I used to just leave, go someplace more elemental. Someplace where the laws are more physical, geological, namely the Alaska backcountry. I wouldn't take a phone or a radio. Sometimes I wouldn't want to come back.

My bachelorhood was built to allow this freedom. The first time I drove a cab, I realized I could work for a few days and scrape together enough cash to go camping for a couple weeks. I didn't even need to call work and tell them I'd be gone. Whenever I got back, they'd be happy to give me a cab for ninety bucks, and I'd get a pizza, pay the rent, then start thinking about leaving again, going somewhere that would allow me another vantage on the flow of matter through space-time.

But now I have a wife and son. I have Cord here with me, right now, asleep upstairs with his mother. They help me see the goodness in human beings; they help tone down that ringing in my ear. Yeah, the need to reorient is still in me, which is why each year I get to spend a couple of weeks on a slow stream looking for moose, a few days beside the violence of the Copper River pulling up salmon, a few weeks guiding up north. I look forward to the day my son can come with me. There's so much I want to show him; there's so much I want to see through his eyes.

I've been living in Fairbanks since 1989, the year Exxon dumped more than eleven million gallons of oil into Prince William Sound. After spending that summer cleaning up beaches and rehabilitating sea otters, I wanted a degree that would be like a machine gun that I could use against the big polluters. But what I discovered was that if I looked south from the University of Alaska Fairbanks, I saw 160 miles of woods, lakes, domes, and rivers rolling like sea swells into the albedo wall of the Alaska Range. The mountains rose two miles from the flat's edge and punctured the cyanic curve of the troposphere.

Those peaks produced an ache in me, a magnetism pulling at the iron in my blood. Glaciers curved around the high summits and deposited billions of tons of broken mountain onto heaps of moraine. Rows of rivers poured north and slid into the westward flow of the Tanana to the Yukon to the Bering Sea. The longer I stared, the more certain I became that the whole thing was moving, that the lithosphere was plasmic and on the go.

Suddenly it was March 2009. My future wife was in Hawaii working for room and board on an organic coffee farm. She was a couple months away from being pregnant. I was forty-two; life-altering events were in play. I knew I wanted to go back to that lonely eastern Alaska Range, ski up the Black Rapids Glacier, through the cold heart of the mountains I'd seen from chemistry lab, and down to Denali Park. From the Richardson Highway to the Parks Highway, 140 miles of glacier travel over three looming passes.

I've never done things because they're dangerous. I don't like to be scared. Some experiences, though, are worth some danger—a balanced equation. But once my son was born, going to places like the Alaska Range—where I could conceivably get crushed by an avalanche or fall two thousand feet into a crevasse—would be difficult to rationalize.

So, eleven months before everything changed, I went back to the Alaska Range. When I think about the trip, I get a chill. I'm not sure if I'll go back again. I'm not sure I'd ever take Cord there. Maybe he won't need to frighten himself so to find his place in this world.

I'd attempted the trip the previous year with my friend Vaughn, but we'd had complications: wind destroyed our first tent, a whiteout bewildered us, and then spring break ended and Vaughn had to get back to nursing school. He would've signed up again, but his dog, Gayloo, was getting old, and he had committed to an attempt of Mount Logan in May, leaving his girlfriend, Erin, to wonder, "What about us?" So Vaughn, Erin, and Gayloo headed for Canyonlands, Utah, instead.

In the meantime, Bob came home from Nepal without the scholarship to glass-blowing school he'd applied for. So he said, "What the hell. I'll ski across the Alaska Range with ya." Our friend Kevin, a local builder, found himself between a kitchen remodel and some finish work and became the third member of the team.

We set the seventh of March as our departure date, but a low-pressure system moving across the north slope sucked air from the Gulf of Alaska through the high passes of the mountains. When the moist air hit the cold Interior, two feet of snow fell, followed by sixty-mile-an-hour winds that blew the snow into drifts and forced the closure of the highway. Then the Siberian and Canadian high-pressure systems joined air masses resulting in a high-pressure ridge that extended halfway around the planet. The daily lows plunged to forty below zero and we decided to wait that shit out.

Thus it became March 17, and the Swiss dog-musher/carpenter Eric drove us and our three hundred pounds of gear out of Fairbanks on a day so clear the mountains loomed above us from 150 miles away. We picked out notches on ridgelines, the north wall of Mount Moffit, the summit nipple of McGinnis Peak.

A few years back two friends had huddled in a snow cave dug into that nipple to wait out a storm after summiting. They were stuck there, freezing to death. They had a transistor radio with them and listened to people they knew on public radio. After four days the front broke, and, starving and frostbitten, they were able to make the treacherous descent.

Eric pulled the big Ford truck onto the shoulder near the ruins of the Black Rapids Roadhouse. Eighty years ago the road was a trail navigated by horse-drawn sleighs in winter and on foot, if at all, in summer. There had been a roadhouse every twenty miles providing food and shelter for the gold miners, trappers, hunters, and adventurers bound for Alaska's interior around the turn of the last century.

In the winter of 1936–37 the Black Rapids Glacier surged more than three miles in three months, acting as if it might cruise across the Delta River and smash the roadhouse. A radio announcer was on-site to describe the anticipated demolition, but the glacier stopped before it reached the river. Geologic evidence suggests it crossed the river at least once in the last few thousand years, temporarily damming it to create a lake.

No wind chilled the sun's radiance as Eric drove away. We skied, sleds trailing behind, across the windblown-clean blue ice of the Delta River and turned up the overflow ice of the creek that flows from the Black Rapids.

The tracks of snowshoe hares pressed into skeins of hoarfrost flowers and blown snow dashed across the creek. The tracks of coyotes and lynx padded alongside. The trail of a meandering moose threaded through those dramas.

The banks of the creek were trimmed in bony cottonwood and black spruce. The forest climbed up the slopes of the mountains we skied toward and ended at scooped cliffs two thousand feet below the snow-sharpened summits. Then the trees stripped away, and we were on a boulder-tossed gravel plain extending north and south, with glacier-cut mountains east and west. Vaughn and I had watched three wolves near here, bounding up and away, aware of us, curious. Their gray coats mottling with the shades of the stone and struggling willow fibered world. I recalled how the creek had melted the snow and ice beneath its thin crust. We'd repeatedly broken through and plunged three feet to the trickling water below. This year the ice was solid, and we skied easily to the moraine, a fifty-square-mile rockpile at the glacier's terminus, gouged by the Black Rapids from the mountains along its twenty-seven-mile path. Great fins of electric blue ice were layered in jumbles of smooth polychromatic rocks.

Caves through the ice traced seasonal riverbeds. Sorted stones teetered atop ice cliffs a hundred feet high.

We skied between seracs into dead ends of ice overhangs and rock piles. We traded skis for crampons and axes. We lowered sleds on the rope. We walked until we started postholing, put skis back on, winding through the woven stone tongues, arguing occasionally about the best route. Everyone was a little grouchy. Having awoken in nice warm beds, we made camp, realizing we were going to have to sleep in this place and eat dinner from a foil bag.

Everyone seemed a little pissed at each other while at the same time respecting each other's inner asshole. Kevin and I had been arguing about the best route, and I was taking it personally. I was the only one of us with experience traveling on glaciers, and I felt like I should be in charge, not arguing over the best route while the limited daylight burned away. It was strange to feel this way in such an awe-inspiring place and realizing this we all sought to bury our apprehensions. It was difficult to keep the ink flowing through the ballpoint into my journal in the deepening cold. The sky was clear as we bedded down in a narrow ravine beside a pile of ice chunks fallen from an ice arch forty feet above.

By morning the mercury in Bob's thermometer was a wee speck at the bottom of the glass tube that ended at thirty degrees below zero. No one was in a hurry to get out of his bag. We waited until nearly noon, when the sun crested an ice wall to the southeast, before breaking camp. We skied up curved ice canyons carved by transient rivers and buried in glacial wreckage.

Much of the Black Rapids Glacier follows the trench formed by the strike slip motion of the Denali Fault. You can see it from space. It runs the length of the Alaska Range and beyond to the Bering Sea on the west and into Canada and Southeast Alaska to the east, more than thirteen hundred miles in all. The Denali Fault is part of a system of faults, including the San Andreas, that define the boundary between the North American and Pacific Tectonic Plates.

The land on the south side of the fault currently moves westward, relative to the north, by about a centimeter a year, or around three hundred miles in the last sixty million years.

The Alaska Range is welded to the more ancient schist and granite of Interior Alaska. Chunks of Interior have been uplifted along with bits of Canadian Rockies ground with shreds of continental margin arcs offset from the Ruby Range Batholith, some 250 miles southeast. Black shale and flysch formed from the muck and sediment left behind by an ancestral Alaska Range tumble in slanting shadows. Rose quartz and limestone and mustard-hued lava tossed onto teetering piles falling ceaselessly into new arrangements.

We skied for a couple hours before we left the rubble of the moraine. A hard snow crust covered the sixteen-hundred-foot-thick glacier. Thirty miles up its smooth boulder-pocked surface we could see the summit ellipse of Mount Aurora and the pass to the Susitna Glacier. A valley to the south opened a thousand feet above the floor, one of many side valleys containing their own arrays of peaks and high basins, discharging moraine that the Black Rapids transported down its margins. These plowed into the piles through which we'd traveled. Sometimes the payloads of the side valleys sprawled all the way across the half-mile-wide glacier.

We spent the afternoon climbing rock slugs. Within them blocks of blue ice the size of tractor trailers were stippled with billions of tiny air bubbles. The translucent blue mirrored the sky and glowed as though plugged in. The bubbles contained samples of the air from this planet thousands of years ago, air with far less carbon dioxide than what we were breathing.

Because we insist on pumping ever more CO_2 into the atmosphere, the planet is getting warmer. These glaciers are melting, releasing their own loads of carbon, accelerating the process. How do I explain to my son that we do this willingly, because we're too stubborn to admit we're making a mistake?

In the cold sun on top, we snacked on home-dried moose and salmon and smoked homegrown marijuana. The temperature rose to eight degrees for a time. An upwelling of dark cumulus—the only cloud in sight—boiled from the black cauldron ridge that joins Mounts Moffit, Shand, and McGinnis. When the ten- to fifteen-mile-per-hour breeze ebbed, it became hot in the white glare. A pair of ravens coasted down from the west and split above us. They rejoined on their way down, their croaks absorbed by the tumbling ice, rock, and snow. There were no snow machine or ski tracks. No sign that another human being had ever been here.

"When we were going along that sidehill forever," Kevin said, "just before we went up onto that first moraine and it started getting really steep and dropped into that cliff-hole thing, and my sled started kind of sliding toward that, I just remember thinking 'Man if I slide down that those guys won't even hear me.' And just realizing how out there we are."

"Yeah, that was kind of freaky. I wonder how deep that thing is, where it goes," I said. "It'd be fun to come back sometime and rap down in there, check it out. I've done that other places, and there are rivers and ice caves and shit under there. Pretty cool."

"Yeah, we should do that. I'd like to bring some real photography equipment and just take pictures of the ice. Not just the crazy shapes but that blue with all the air bubbles. Fill the whole frame with that. It kinda reminds me of glass when it's fluid."

"It kinda reminded me of a multiverse," I said. "Like each of those bubbles was its own universe inside this bigger thing but isolated from each other, not aware of the bigger structure."

That night we dug a snow camp into the glacier, piling it on the uphill side to block the wind as the temp freefell back to the negative thirtysomethings. The ink in the pen froze, and I had to switch to a stub of carpenter's pencil Bob had inadvertently brought in a side pocket.

"Okay, but you gotta carry it the rest of the way," he joked. "That thing was like a rock in my sled."

Looking east I saw the uplifted triangular face of Mount Silvertip and the Delta Mountains cast in the same orange alpenglow that lit the pinnacles of the ridgelines on either side of us. As the sun set, the sky became a wash of color, a creamy rose near the horizon, then zones of crimson, mauve, and cobalt ascended, surrendering to the onrushing night above.

We were up early the next morning. I shoved frozen cooked bacon into my mouth and felt my core warm as my body processed it. We ate butter and dried fruit oatmeal quickly, lest it freeze before we finished.

We spent the day on all fours, crampons on, crawling over moraine, kicking steps, swinging ice axes into wind crust. In the basins between the rocky tentacles, it was hot. Up top, where iced air ran from high valleys, it got cold. We zipped and unzipped vents and removed and replaced layers, hats, gloves.

We decided the rockfalls weren't moraines but remnants of landslides triggered by the Denali Fault Earthquake of November 3, 2002. The quake had three epicenters or subevents that added up to magnitude 7.9. The initial surface rupture began beneath the Susitna Glacier, about twenty-five miles west of where we stood. It transferred to the Denali Fault and tore the faces off the mountains on the south side of the glacier, and then proceeded east, raising geologic havoc for another twenty miles before jumping to a third fault, the Totshunda, and turning southeast to rock the Wrangell volcanoes. It's energy leapt from fault to fault like an errant bolt of electricity rushing to ground.

It had offset the land to the south of the Denali Fault as much as twenty-six feet from the north. The resulting gash was more than two hundred miles long. People felt the quake in Washington State, and it had caused pools to ripple in Louisiana.

I wanted to witness this, to be ground into rockburger, to know that death is nothing to fear but part of a bigger process occurring over billions of years of energy and matter recycling itself. However, my geologist friends tell me I would have been tossed before I was buried. A landslide of this nature, they point out, would be riding atop a cushion of compressed air that would've picked me up and dashed me against a cliff before any debris actually reached me.

I am afraid of dying, and I know I'm not alone. It's hard to imagine our point of view fading to black, things going on without us. But sometimes, usually in the natural world, I can see that we're all the same thing. Life, dust, stars, stone, water, all of it not just along for the ride but the ride itself. It comforts me. Perhaps perception is relative. Maybe it gives us tunnel vision.

The peaks and valleys to the south of the glacier are elegant swooping descents from spiked ridges cascading into ice falls to join other ice rivers on rolling journeys down to the Black

Rapids. The lateral moraines trace the curves, banks, and eddies with patterns of gravity in motion.

In contrast, the mountains on the north side of the valley are much bigger, a rent catastrophe. Five-thousand-foot cliffs with blockish peaks gouged by half cirques and busted arêtes. Ice tongues thicker than football fields scrape chutes clogged with boulders the size of battleships, all of it girdled in corrugated rows of glacial till.

The two sides of the valley are different terranes separated by the Denali Fault. A terrane is a piece of the earth's crust, bounded by faults on all sides, adrift on the mantle. The Alaska Range is basically a logjam of terranes. The land to the north mashed into the Interior fifty million years ago. A group of Cretaceous volcanics arrived next and was crushed by a flood of quartz-rich flysch.

South of the Alaska Range, a large terrane known as the Wrangellia heaves against the flysch. It formed near the equator and sailed the currents of the earth's convective core for three hundred million years. It came spouting magma and debris, spinning, ripping apart, and reforming like planetary goo inside a lava lamp. It impacted Alaska within the last hundred million years.

I've climbed a few mountains around here, mostly the slightly smaller and less intense ones to the east of the Black Rapids, and I've looked southeast to see the baked rock cones of Wrangellia rising more than sixteen thousand feet above sea level, heavy with ice, one still smoking. Huge runs of salmon rush up the torrents that pour from the glaciers covering this remote range. Griz and seals gorge themselves on the flood of life, everything a part of something bigger.

-:::-

The lines of past glacial levels are scoured into the walls of the Black Rapids, recalling times when this place was buried to within a few hundred feet of the highest peaks. The sheared-off summit of Meteor Peak, on the south side of the Black Rapids, takes its name from the cirque at its summit that looks like an impact crater. The glacier was strewn with boulders. Wind-sculpted snow dunes and slacks formed around them.

We camped between Mount Shand and Mount Aurora, expecting to cross the pass to Susitna Glacier the next day. That's where Vaughn and I had once gone whiteout wandering. Kevin said, "It seemed like we were skiing up to Meteor Peak all day, and we never quite got to it. And that long valley with that beautiful ramp peak on that ridge to the south, didn't we ski by that all day? It really drives home how big this country is when you actually travel in it."

"Every time we got on top of one of those rock slides, it kind of blew me away . . . just the square miles of whiteness in every direction. And it seems like we did that quite a few times but, yeah, you're right, every time I looked to the left it seemed like Meteor was still right there," Bob said. "I mean, it's still right there, really, I just gotta turn my head back a little to see it."

We passed the pipe and spiked our tea with shots of Jim Beam, which eased sore muscles, made them feel good. Bob, sitting on his sleeping pad in the snow, doctored blisters on his toes and heels.

"You see that plateau jutting from the south side of the pass, the one that looks like a giant molar all by itself?" I asked. "Doesn't that look like an ocean reef, you know, like once there were fish and kelp and shit living there and now it's like . . . shipwrecked, like Noah's ark or something?"

We dug into our rehydrated food. Lenticulars torn from high peaks lay bloodied and deformed on the ice, like exploded zeppelins crashed to earth and burning.

The next morning, cumulus vapor rode west winds from the Bering Sea up the north side of the range. We smelled the ocean. Occasionally the breeze brought blue holes, and we glimpsed the black fluted fortress of Moffit, Shand, and McGinnis to the north.

The Trident Glacier pours from the north side of those mountains like a flash flood gushing through a canyon, resulting in an impenetrable icefall. I've heard Fairbanks climbers talk about landing a plane in that basin, climbing all three peaks. But from the south side, our side, they looked about as climbable as the volcanoes of Io.

By the time we finished our bacon fat, butter, and oatmeal, the sky was mostly obscured. Occasionally a band of black rock burned through before being reabsorbed. We set the compass at 260 degrees and skied, but it was difficult. Every time I looked up, I started drifting north, awash in the motion of the vapor, unsure if the subtle contours of the snow were bumps or fall lines. I wasn't sure if I was going up or down or sloughing off to one side. It was like being blind and dizzy, and I was desperate to head down, out of this soup.

"Your heading's at 270 and leaning north," Kevin called out.

Whiteouts are plain weird. Seems like there's a default setting in my head, and when vision is removed I start to lean that way. Too bad it's not a little more accurate.

"A little more left," Bob corrected.

I focused on the snow just beyond my ski tips and looked for the vaginal shapes of crevasses hidden in the snow. On the topos, this section is a scarred mess of the blue lines that indicate the cracks in the ice. But they were all bridged by the wind-crusted snow. We untied from our rope to take turns leading and slowly slogged through the mist of the broad-shouldered pass.

Vaughn and I had a similar experience. That day had started clear, but the clouds that had lain like grounded spaceships on the ice coalesced and turned the world opaque. Eventually, we'd run into a crevasse field with the cracks oriented in the same direction we were traveling. I'd led us against the north wall of the valley where the cracks had formed on a tributary glacier, which I realized when I found myself on a snow bridge that ran parallel to our direction of travel. Not a good situation. One wants to approach crevasses perpendicularly so if the leader breaks through the snow bridge, then the person roped behind is able to arrest the fall, rather than break through the same bridge, a plunge that would kill or maim. The crevasses here could be a thousand feet deep. Tons of ice and snow would be dislodged in the accident, crushing the victim.

It was late. We turned perpendicular to the cracks, skied above them, and set up camp. The next morning the sun was out, and we were in a spectacular valley.

Kevin, Bob, and I maintained our 260-degree heading without ever getting too close or too far away from the occasionally discernable black blurs of the north wall. By afternoon it seemed as if the direction of travel was trending down.

We made camp beneath a snow-crusted pile of gray rocks and dug a spot for two tents, a shitter hole, and a cooking and social area. But a thirty-mile-per-hour wind was blowing ice crystals sideways, and we cooked in the tent.

Everyone was mentally fried from staring into the nothingness all day. We had trouble thinking of anything else. Close your eyes and there was the whiteness again. We talked about scrotum massage, camp stoves, Bob's girlfriend moving to Anchorage, and the role of oral sex in relationship harmony.

I said, "Michele and I are talking about having a kid when she gets back. I mean we'd like to travel a little first, but, you know, we're kinda running outta time too."

"Holly and I want to have one," Kevin said. "We're at a pretty good place for that to happen. I mean the house is done. We own it. And I could take this job doing construction inspections on the military bases. It's steady work, good benefits."

"Kinda changes up the old lifestyle, huh?" Bob said.

"Yeah. I guess that's part of the reason, for me, you know," I said.

"I don't," Bob said. "What do you mean?"

"I guess I feel like I'm ready for something different. I mean I think I'll essentially be the same person. I'll probably do a lot of the same things. But I'm ready to change. It doesn't . . . feel natural not to, anymore. What do you think, Kevin?"

"I don't know. I guess I just kind of want a kid. I don't know why exactly. It's hard to explain. I think Holly'd be a great mom, and I guess I feel like I'd be a good dad. Like I'm ready to raise one and teach, and yeah, maybe grow up a little."

"So it's partially a selfish desire?" asked Bob.

"Yeah, partly for sure," I said. "But it's also partly about Michele and the kid. I think it'd be fun. I've been this bro'd up Alaska bachelor guy for twenty-some years, now. I want there to be more love in my life. I've got it to give, Bob!"

"Well, just keep it to yourself on this trip, all right."

"Oh, c'mon bud, roll over and have some love."

"I think I'll just have tea."

When we woke it was clear. To the north was the steep back of Mount Aurora and a nameless twelve-thousand-foot peak, eight hundred feet of fluted snow capping the whale's tail summit, deep blue sky beyond a cliff a mile high. That's where Vaughn and I had awakened when we went off course. He'd said it was as big and impressive as anything he'd seen while climbing in the Himalayas.

To the south a long, ramped valley of canted-plane triangular peaks led up and over the hump of a pass that dropped into the headwaters of Eureka Creek and on to the Delta River, Yukon bound. To the west, the ice crested then fell away to the Maclaren River, which joined the Susitna River above Devils Canyon on the way to Cook Inlet and the Gulf of Alaska.

Icefalls, lit from within, tumbled down the broken finger peaks that divide the East Fork from the main Susitna Glacier. Behind us the Black Rapids flowed to the Delta then north to the Interior. The pass was an intersection of watersheds.

I was ready to go first and stood in the open wind, blowing thirty-five knots. The drawstrings of my jacket stood out straight and flickered against the nylon shell. I let the gale pour through me like exfoliating neutrinos. I felt it scour away the grit and grease of existence until I was empty and clean, until I felt vaporized and ready to be ripped away.

"You ready yet?" I heard Bob shout, grinning. "I mean, I gotta job siding these people's house in like . . . three weeks."

I smiled and we left. It wasn't long till we were looking fifteen miles down the valley of the Susitna Glacier. It turned south down there, but we would turn north, into the eleven-thousand-foot shadow of Mount Balchen, to ascend a pass to the north side of the range.

We veered away from the Black Rapids Glacier, and with a push of the poles, we began the long slide down the Su. Wind had carved the snowpack into psychedelic tongues, layered mounds, and channeled ruts.

On the Susitna side of the pass, the mountains were gray, rusted orange, and white. Interbedded layers of rotten rock were heaved on top of each other in the crosscut path of the receding glacier. Granite crumbled into sand and clay. There were blurs of greenstone high on valley walls and golden flecks of pyrite in sun-warmed metamorphic fragments. We skied down the disfigured hardpack, past valleys filled with amphitheaters of ice thousands of feet high.

Near the bottom of the Susitna, a pile of crushed mountain lay sprawled across the glacier. I recalled how Vaughn and I had attacked it dead center only to be repulsed by wall after wall of jagged landslide. Eventually we'd detoured to the southern side of the glacier and had found a relatively easy way through. This year we made for that point.

On the other side the ice was like the frozen surface of boiling water with bubbles the size of burial mounds. We skied through them to a narrow chute on the north side.

"You know, there's a cool little shortcut to the next glacier at the bottom of this chute," I said. "Vaughn and I found it last year. The snow's pretty deep down there, though. Probably a couple hundred yards of it up to your waist. I think it's where all the blown snow goes."

"I don't know if I'm up for that," Kevin said. Why don't we just go back around that way, over the moraines. There's animal tracks going that way."

"Well, 'cause I know that this way will get us there. I don't know about that way. And I just always figured that, on glaciers and moraines and stuff, it usually works best to go with what you know will work. I mean, you remember what that Black Rapids moraine was like, right?"

"Yeah, I guess. I'm just not really up for any deep snow, right now, though. That other route's looking pretty good. I mean maybe whatever made those tracks knew something we don't."

"I don't know," I said. "I doubt whatever made those tracks is going to the same place we are, but whatever, let's just keep moving. Your way'll be fine."

Bob talked under his breath.

Kevin and I butted heads frequently. He was used to being in charge. He could build houses blindfolded, sketch blueprints to scale on a cocktail napkin at three in the morning. But I'd been in this exact place before and had made a decision that worked. And it was this lack of confidence in me that I found hard to accept. I mean I'm a college dropout, a cab driver. I'm used to having my judgment questioned. I crave the respect of my peers and take it personally when they don't see things my way.

But I decided I was probably just as type A as he was, and we were in this together, and I might as well act like it. He hadn't signed any papers appointing me grand poobah, and it was time to move.

Bob's a contractor also. He's used to telling people what to do. He's probably spent as much of his life camping as I have. But he was resigned to follow my lead in this place he had little experience in. And I'm all right with group decision-making, but there's also a need to move when the weather's amenable to it. And the amount of time Kevin and I spent arguing about things cut into that. I mean one big storm could pin us down for a week and put a serious dent in our supplies.

Kevin's choice of routes wasn't bad. It took a bit longer than I remember the alternative requiring but not bad. Once we were on the other glacier, we skied across it to the mouth of the name-less tributary that led northwest

The shadow of Mount Balchen was as far as Vaughn and I had made it the preceding year. We'd arrived in orange twilight. Mount Balchen rose in the east, the centerpiece of an array of cruelly curved mountains, like sharpened petals of ice and stone. They seemed to be shards left behind by a bigger mountain evis-cerated by ice time, refolded into the matter factory.

The flanks of the peaks were scored by stratigraphic layers uplifted vertical. Over this a million years of glacial scraping left horizontal scars in the dark rock. We'd set up camp and watched the mountains reflect the colors of the fading day until they evened with the night.

Vaughn had talked about skiing down from the pass in the glare of the sun and looking back up and seeing our tracks and those mountains like things disconnected from the Earth and everything rushing down upon us. We'd waited till morning to decide whether to push on or return to the truck, but we both knew the decision had been made for us. Vaughn had too much invested in his nursing degree. His name was written on a schedule at Fairbanks Memorial Hospital, and we knew he'd be there in time if we turned around. But there was no telling if we pushed forward.

Neither of us were far removed from a point in our lives where we would've just said fuck it, felt that freedom like a surge of tide washing over lowland. But responsibility sneaks up on you like years in this world, and we told ourselves we'd decide in the morning so we could pretend we were still the same guys who didn't give a fuck about schedules and social constructions.

But we both knew what we were going to do as we watched the sun burn down the mountain into night, knew we were lucky just to be there.

Kevin, Bob, and I probed a campsite and began to dig. We were standing too close to each other. There was some jostling, and then Kevin hit Bob in the face with his shovel. This made Bob very angry. A number of fuck-yous were exchanged. Kevin accused Bob of poking him with the tent poles whenever we set up camp.

"So you hit me in the head with a fucking shovel?!" Bob replied. And then he hit Kevin in the face with his shovel.

"I can't believe you just did that."

"Why not? You did it to me."

"Not that hard. You're such a fuckin' baby, Bob, I fuckin' swear. I mean if you can't take it—"

"Fuck you, whatever."

"No, fuck you, Bob. I'm not even mad. It's just that you're such a fucking big baby."

Each of them was still holding his shovel in the ready position. Bob was much bigger than Kevin, and I could see Kevin was scared, but he wasn't backing down. The situation was not resolving itself.

I said, "Hey, I'm pretty sure you guys are both mad, but is a shovel fight really the best way to settle it?" We laughed a little, moved a bit farther away from one another, and continued to dig.

Balchen rose above us, its glacial scars like battle wounds from the Ice Wars.

"It felt good to go down," Bob said. "And to keep going down for hours. It was liberating after all the days pulling a sled up the Black Rapids, wearing a pack."

"Yeah, no shit," I said. "I feel like we earned that. But don't worry, there'll be more uphill tomorrow. Just in case you were afraid it'd get too easy."

"Awesome, yeah, I was worried about that. Do you think we'll get over that next pass tomorrow?"

"I hope so. Probably. It'll be a long day, but we should make it. I feel like it's kind of a point of no return. Like after we're over that, it starts to make more sense to push on to the park than to turn back. Like if we get over it, then we're gonna make it."

"Then tomorrow night we'll be by Mount Deborah and Mount Hess, right?" Kevin said.

"I think so. I hope it's clear. I feel like Mount Deborah's why I'm doing this. I mean I've spent so much time staring at it from Fairbanks. Like it's a fucking beacon or some kind of Close Encounters of the Third Kind shit. I don't understand it, but I need to go there."

"I feel the same way," Kevin said. "When I lived in the park, I used to ski or hike up the Yanert just to get a glimpse of it."

"At least we agree on something, huh?" I said.

"Yeah, right, even though neither of us can say exactly what it is." We laughed.

"Well, maybe we'll find out," I said. We sipped our tea.

"Those lynx tracks were pretty awesome, huh?" Kevin said, referring to the set of tracks like pad patterned dinner plates looping from the spruce trees at the bottom of the Susitna into the terminal moraine at the bottom of the glacier we were camped on. "That guy must've been huge."

"What do you think he was doing up here?" Bob asked. "I mean I haven't seen another animal or track of any kind since we got on the Black Rapids."

"I don't know. Maybe there's marmots living in the rocks or something. Last year there were coyote tracks from the Black Rapids all the way to here. They went down into the trees where the lynx came from. Maybe it's some kind of predator pilgrimage or something."

Our eyes followed the valley down to the places where the highest spruce trees cast their stunted shadows in the dying light. We smelled the pitch and talked about how nice it would be to camp down there and have a big fire. Curled brown willow leaves at rest on the snow around us.

The peaks were swallowed by shifting veils of ice motes that gave way to night.

By dawn Balchen shed the weather and reflected a liquid orange sunrise. A pair of ravens coasted down from behind the mountain and turned south a hundred feet above. Their blackness absorbed the sun and glowed iridescent. One uttered a trilling croak that slit the silence and filled it and was sucked away. The receding ravens were the only proof it ever happened. Then they were gone, too.

We roped up and were moving by ten. The sun was high and bright but offered no warmth. The wind blew from the north at forty miles per hour, too loud to talk over. We put our heads down and moved. Black Mountain walls tapered to swift tumbling clouds and stainless sky.

Near the top the glacier opened into a basin of ten square miles. We headed up a steep headwall to the pass, fifteen hundred feet above. Kevin stopped and began to dig an avalanche pit. I told him we should keep moving, that we were pushing darkness and the slope was safe.

"So you can see all the snow layers from up there, huh?" He stood five-feet deep in the pit, not finished.

"No, but we've been on this slope all day and nothing's changed. It's solid wind crust."

"Well I'm not going any farther till I see for myself."

"I think the greater danger here is that we get stuck on top of this thing in the dark."

"Well, fuck it then, we turn around. But I'm not getting caught in an avalanche today."

"It's not gonna slide, man. It's fucking concrete." I sat and pulled wind protection close, ate a bar, took in the view.

"If you guys helped we could get going faster."

I didn't answer. "Fuck you" was all I could think of to say.

Bob was talking under his breath. He looked at me and shrugged. "I think you're right," he said. Then he jumped down in the pit to help Kevin dig. I probably should have got down there, too, but I was ready for a shovel-fight death match in the avalanche pit and felt it best to keep my distance.

Kevin cut the sides of the profile and stomped on it and announced it was solid. We continued. We had to stop and put on crampons and get out ice axes before helping each other over the final pitch. By the time we reached the top, sunset colors were seeping into the southwestern horizon.

Below us to the north, a steep snow gully dropped six hundred feet around rock outcroppings to the surface of the Gillam Glacier. The wind was screaming. The Gillam came down in a flood of slow motion. Unnamed summit daggers and sawtooth ridgelines rose two to four thousand feet from its edges. From them flowed the ice rivers that in their joining became the glacier itself.

We paused, between Interior Alaska and the rest of the world.

I told a story I'd heard from Dave Kramer the night before the 2007 Alaska Mountain Wilderness Classic ski race through the Wrangells. Dave has organized the race for the last twenty years. It doesn't have a specific route. Instead there's a start and a finish, and it's up to the skiers to figure out the rest. The location changes every three years. From 1988 till 1990 the race took place on the Black Rapids to Denali route, but the organizers stopped holding it here because there's no non-glacier alternative, and it's difficult to attract enough competitors with glacial experience to have a race.

"So Dave and three other racers were standing right here like twenty-some years ago. They were looking down through these rocks, just like us, talking about the best way to descend. One of them had his sled strapped onto his back with the bottom facing outward. He caught a crampon in the snow and fell on his back and shot down this slope at Mach 1, upside down and head first.

"The others had to watch him zoom between these stone pinnacles. I guess some of them turned away like 'I don't wanna see him splat.' But the guy made it through. Stopped in the deep snow below, unharmed."

"Let's not do it that way," Bob said.

"Sounds good," I agreed.

We decided I would descend a rope length, and then Bob and Kevin would pull the rope back and use it to lower the sleds. I would catch them and attach them to pickets while they came down. I figured it would take three pitches to get to a place where we could ski to the glacier and put in camp.

Lowering the sleds between the jags of rock turned out to be difficult and time- consuming. Darkness was upon us after the first pitch. The wind remained strong while the temperature fell to ten below. I felt my feet freezing as we worked our way down.

From the deep powder at the bottom of the cliff, I could neither see nor hear my companions feeding the sleds through the rocks. Kevin's came first, and I staked it to a picket and tugged on the line to let them know to take it back. As this happened, the picket popped free and the sled shot down the slope, an orange blur into the thickness, headed for an abysmal crevasse near the bergschrund. I found myself willing the sled with pelvis, abdomen, and arms not to disappear and force us into let's-get-the fuck-outta-here! mode.

At the last second some hidden feature of the moderating slope pushed the sled left and it shot over a snow bridge, fifteen feet from the crack. I noted where it came to rest and looped a sling around a chunk of rock for securing the other sleds. Bob's, then mine, came next. Then Kevin. Kevin took Bob's sled and headed toward his. I belayed Bob. We split my gear and descended.

When we caught up to Kevin, Bob belayed him across the snow bridge to his sled. After we saw Kevin go across with no trouble, Bob followed unroped and was almost across when he punched a hole through a foot of rime and hoar into the darkness below. He shone his headlamp down and watched the beam vanish in the blackness.

"Holy shit!" he said.

"Did you go through?" I asked.

"Fuck yeah! I can't see the bottom of this thing. I'm not sure what I should do."

"Keep going."

And he did. And in the spirit of group stupidity I followed him.

We'd reached a level of exhaustion and cold where our judgment was impaired. My wanting to sit down, eat, warm up, and sleep outweighed the knowledge that if I fell in, I would die or

get so busted up that none of those things would matter anymore. Isn't it interesting how desire can seem more important
than the life that claims to own it?

We dug a lumpy hole and set up our tents in it. When I took
my boots off my socks were frozen to the insoles.

We were slow to break camp the following day and let the morning ease into early afternoon. Eventually we stood on a hump
of lateral moraine looking down onto the eastern arm of the
glacier, which flowed from our right. To our left, out of sight, the
two forks of the Gillam collided obliquely. We discussed whether to ski directly to the glacier or over a rise on our left to reach
it farther down.

I argued we could see the path to the glacier below us, but we
could not see what was on the other side of the rise. If we can see
a way to get from one point to another, then that route is prefer-
able to one that cannot be seen. We agreed and set out.

An east wind came hounding at our backs and pushed us re-
lentlessly down. We rocketed over the twisted snowscape. It was
difficult roped together, and we decided to untie. I punched a
ski pole through the snow to expose a footwide crack filled with
frost. We continued and passed the point where the alternate
route we'd discussed ended in a shattered icefall.

We double poled for miles to the confluence of the glacier.
Dozens of strands of moraine came together and rumbled north,
out the valley, like tectonic freight trains bearing ore from the
earth mines for distribution on the wind and rivers.

Mount Hess rose seven thousand feet into shifting scud, broken into chasms of terrifying height from which boomed the
concussions of unseen ice avalanches. At the base of its north

buttress, the two halves of the glacier came together. A nice lunch spot.

We continued up the west wing of the glacier. It was slightly overcast. We camped on a patch of gray scree. My feet, mildly frostbitten from the previous evening, had developed some blisters. Kevin's were no better, and we spent part of the evening lancing, draining, and sterilizing. Bob's feet were recovering from the early part of the trip.

The clouds ionized and fell away. We were eight thousand feet beneath the summits of Mount Deborah and Hess. There was a time I'd wanted to climb them, but those days were long gone. Now I was content to watch them, like a breaking wave of matter. I realized I wanted something from them: some nirvana or epiphany, some justification for the desire that had brought me here. But they existed for their own reasons. Because of collisions of earth crust set in motion on the far side of the big bang. By the way that the universe was packed together into a pinpoint before the chaos exploded and came unto me, in the trough beneath this rising swell.

Inside the chasm ice avalanches boomed away. Great pythons of moraine wound down and turned out the valley. Night fell and we watched the peaks turn past blue and red stars. Past planets and galaxies. The flood of time to some unknown equilibrium.

We shared a bowl and some whiskey. "Skiing down today I kept having to remind myself that I was on a glacier and not a river," Bob said. "It was almost like floating the way I could just relax and look around at the mountains going by."

"I was thinking of a conveyor belt, myself," Kevin said. "It was pretty fucking awesome, really."

"Yeah, double poling rocks. Almost enough to make you forget about all the shit we've been hauling," I said.

"I'd like to do it the way those guys that win the wilderness classic do some time," Bob said.

We talked about those races. Most of the racers finished in less than five days, skiing sixteen to twenty hours a day. They brought a minimum of food and gear. In contrast we'd been skiing eight to ten hours a day and had brought twelve days' worth of food and gear. We had two tents and a bivy sack. I had a spare pair of beater ski boots in case the first beater pair didn't make it. We had two fifths of whiskey, three stoves, and three gallons of fuel.

The race that Bob and I had done in the Brooks Range was 120 miles, and it took us six days. The winner was from Valdez, a big guy, thirtysomething, who makes his own camping gear. His time was just over three days. His gear fit into a small backpack to which he'd attached P-Tex runners. He could throw it off and drag it like a sled. His food consisted of cooked bacon, peanuts, and a dried mixture of couscous, beef suet, and berries. He took one quart of fuel and skate skied the route without a tent. He slept two to four hours a day.

"I think it'd be cool to just do it like that, just go super light and ski all day and dig a hole in the snow when it's time to camp. Just see how fast I could do it, you know, push it," Bob said.

"Well, there's no way I'd ever bring this much stuff again. And I get it. I mean I'm ready to go home and be warm. It's fuckin' cold. But at the same time, it's cool to have tent space for cooking and hanging out and stuff," Kevin said.

"This whiskey tastes pretty good too," Bob added.

"And I kind of like spending time out here. Bein' able to relax a little. Take in the view. Sleep in when it's cold," I said. "But I could see doing it that way. Not right now, though."

Part of why I do this backcountry stuff is competitive, egotistical. I want to have done the baddest shit, seen the coolest scenes. I don't like that this motivates me, but it does. It helps get me out there. But once I'm there, these competitive urges fall away. Maybe one day the purity of the natural world will rub off on me enough that I'll stop being distracted by things like, "If I just do one more badass thing, then everyone will know what a real badass I am." I feel a little closer each year, wonder if I'll get there before I die.

We broke camp quickly after the morning oats. Kevin led atop a lateral moraine and turned right into a high valley we believed contained the pass to the Yanert. We had a heated discussion about which was the true pass before choosing a big, steep fucker in the middle of a bunch of other big, steep fuckers. We turned to take pictures of Deborah and Hess as the angles between us shifted.

We were on a sliver of a two-hundred-million-year-old magmatic upwelling broken off the floor of a prehistoric ocean, this piece of it cut by extensions of the Denali Fault to the north and south.

The first subevent of the 2002 earthquake was on the Susitna Glacier Fault, on the other side of Mount Deborah. This fault intersects the Denali Fault near the northernmost point of a bend in the Denali Fault's path. From that point, the fault extends southwest toward Denali and southeast back through the Black Rapids glacial trench. The bend is in much the same shape as the southern coast of Alaska between Yakutat and the Alaska Peninsula.

Mounts Deborah, Hess, and Hayes are on the north side of the fault. Denali, the highest mountain in North America, is on the south side of the fault. It's possible that at one time they were part of the same massif. That over the past few million years Denali moved west a hundred miles. Both groups are made of the same light granite that intruded marine sedimentary and metamorphic rocks sixty million years ago. Look at a USGS 1:250,000 scale topo of the Mount McKinley Quadrangle, and you can see how the glaciers that flow off the north side of the mountains make a hard east turn when they cross the fault and their toes get left behind as the mountains that feed them cruise away on the south side.

We changed to crampons and ice axes, put skis and poles on our packs, and decided to drag our sleds. They were too heavy to safely carry, would've been sails in the wind that grew stronger with each step up the six-hundred-foot wall.

We had five pickets, having left one on the last pass. I had a couple ice screws. The snow was waist deep, and we wallowed through it, at times unable to move forward as it collapsed in our path. The wind was angry, and it was too loud to screammunicate. I didn't put any pickets in until we neared the top hundred feet, where the face bulged out to sixty-five degrees and the snow became so hard I could barely sink my front points.

Kevin was moving slowly, and my feet were getting cold, and I didn't trust the pickets, which I couldn't sink all the way. They clattered like wind chimes against my torso. It got steeper, and I realized we were getting in over our heads, but we kept going.

Kevin decided to cut steps, and I yelled that my feet were cold, that my calves were cramping, that we were close and needed to keep moving. But he believed he was going to fall and continued with the steps.

I put in the last picket twenty feet from the point where the slope began to moderate. We slowly made our way, and at the top the slope bulged a little more and I forced the pick of my axe halfway down and put all my weight on it and continued to kick front points into the surface, kept tension on Kevin.

Bob and I were shouting encouragement. "Keep moving! You got it!" And he kept cutting steps with the adze of his axe until our screaming and the wind god's anger were indistinguishable and we came to stand together on the corniced ridge looking down into the next valley. Here the wind was strangely calm.

The cornice was secured to lichen-crusted stone. I rappelled and slid down to the snowpack of the valley funneling to the northwest.

As they lowered the sleds, I was lashed by eighty-mile-an-hour gusts that were saturated with abrasive ice crystals. I sunk the shaft of the axe into the snow and hunkered over it and held on, transfixed, watching the crystals course and scurry a thousand feet down the slope, the surface of the glacier invisible beneath the motion. I watched them turn a bend buttressed by black rock walls that were once more ancient mountains that had eroded into the mudflats of a coast no human ever saw, before being crushed back up into this.

I proposed we down-climb facing the moderate slope, kicking steps, axe shaft buried, sleds trailing below. Kevin wanted to lower the sleds by rope. There were at least three pitches to descend, and the sun was nearly gone, and I was cold and tired and concerned about my feet. I asked him to give my way a try, and if we couldn't do it we'd try it his way.

He said no.

I left him the rope and began descending. Bob came and we made it down in less than an hour, dug a tent site, set up the tent, and warmed it by cooking soup and hot drinks inside. When we went back out, Kevin was sitting in the same place he'd been when we left. We went back in and put on our boots and prepared to go back.

We wondered if he was okay as we began up the slope. Then he pushed his sled over a cliff. We watched the orange plastic spin and flip into dazzling pirouettes and laid-out gainers during its eleven-hundred-vertical-foot dive. We stared for what seemed like minutes, agreeing it was strangely beautiful, and when it came to rest a hundred feet away, we retrieved it and drug it back to the tent.

Kevin started down using the rope. By the time he arrived, the wind was increasing. We'd dug a tent site, and I asked if he wanted a hand with his tent. He said no. I told him we'd get his dinner going, to come over when he was ready, and he said all right.

When I got back into Bob's tent, a furious gust of wind hit it, and we supported the stressed fabric with our hands, hoping to prevent it from shredding. There was some shouting from Kevin as the gust became an unrelenting fury. "Fuck, this wind just totally destroyed my tent!"

"Do you need some help?"

"No, fuck it, I'm just going to bury what's left of it for now. I'll be there in a minute."

When he got inside I handed him a bag of hot food.

There were some angry words. We worked it out over whiskey, weed, and nicotine lozenges.

"Man, that spindrift blowing off Deborah was amazing," Kevin said. "It was like half a mile long or something. I wonder how fast the wind was blowing over there."

"I bet it was blowing sixty here. Probably at least eighty over there," I said.

"Fuck, that was intense," Bob said. "I just put my head down and took the next step, tried not to look up or down. Fuck. Then my crampon fell off and I had to sink my axe all the way in and fix it with those fuckin' pickets dangling around my neck."

"Isn't that a pain in the ass?" I half laughed, too exhausted to really mean it.

"Fuck yeah, then my other crampon fell off. Jesus, if I would've lost one of those . . . I don't know what I could've done."

We watched a video on Kevin's camera that he'd taken at the top.

Bob told a story about biking around Cuba. About paying farmers a few dollars to sleep in their barns and sheds. About how that was several days' pay for many of them.

"Jesus, the wind sounds like drag racing 747s," I said. We held the sides of the only tent against it, wondering if it would collapse and leave us defenseless. The midnight snow cave club.

"Well, I was thinking the wind sounded like giants throwing cars off the ridge," Bob said in a snarky voice, as if we were engaged in a bad metaphor competition.

"That's nothing," Kevin said. "I'm pretty sure it sounds like the inside of a Shop-Vac on steroids." We chuckled as we supported the stressed fabric.

Around 1:00 a.m. we got dressed and returned to the abrasive winds and built the snow walls higher than the dome and put in more guy lines. We were asleep by 2:30.

We woke, beat up and elated. The inside of Bob's tent was crusted with frost. Ice crystals that the winds blew through the vents were everywhere. Kevin had slept in a bivy and told us how the ice dust blew into it and melted. Our gear was strewn about and buried in drifts. But we were buoyed by the fact we'd done it. Had made it over the third and final pass and now stood on the Yanert with only forty-five gradually descending miles to travel before we arrived in Denali National Park, where there would surely be parades and dancing girls to celebrate our journey.

Or had we?

We became wary of the way the glacier bent to the right below us to pour out of the mountains to the north. Shouldn't the valley of the Yanert curve to the left to join with the other fork of the glacier on its way west?

We consulted maps and compass and GPS and were forced to admit that we'd fucked up rather royally. We turned up the wrong valley off the Gillam. No one said anything for a long time.

Eventually, we decided that we were at the headwaters of the west fork of the Little Delta River, which would eventually turn back to the east and return us to where we'd come from. Nobody was happy with this option; we'd worked too hard and it was too far.

We looked back to the looming wall we'd come over and agreed none of us were in a hurry to go back that way. We looked up at the cliffs to the south, knowing that just on the other side was the Yanert, though it may as well have been in North Korea. Morale was low.

We began to break camp. Nobody had any better ideas. After a little while we began to discuss the possibility that it was only our pride that was injured. That we still had had a remarkable trip and needed to stop wallowing in self-pity because there were yet a shitload of miles and mountains between us and home.

We gathered around the maps, spread damp upon the warm snow in the depression where our tent had been. After an hour of haggling and speculation, we decided to ski out of the gorge and down the Little Delta to a pass that led west to the upper Wood River. From there we could ski fifteen miles to another pass that connected to the lower Yanert River and be at the road in a few days. We couldn't tell if the first pass would be possible from the map. If it wasn't, then we'd make a right turn and ski back east along the north face of the range and hopefully reach the Richardson Highway before we ran out of food.

The day seemed a little brighter with a plan. And where we were was an incredible place. All the more so because so few people had ever seen it. There were no fingerprints, no human residues.

We skied past side valleys unloading broken falls of azure ice, as if some sky had fallen there and plastered itself to the umber walls. The glacier descended steeply in broad curves, rolled over ledges, eddied into bowls half a mile wide.

Near the bottom we looked back to the fifteen-hundred-foot granite incisor jutting from the pass that the valley seemed to emerge from. We knew we'd never be there again.

We continued down into the moraine, shedding rope and then skis before arriving at the cerulean iced lake we'd seen from two thousand feet above. Our camp from the night before was three thousand vertical feet above. We were off-glacier for the first time in nine days. We double poled down the creek at the top of the Delta River. It had overflowed so the valley floor shone pale blue among the stone and alder and willow.

Then Bob said, "Hey, look at that cabin. Let's go over there."

The door was nailed shut to keep the bears out, but a claw hammer hung beside it. We clustered inside the eight-by-ten-foot roofed box that might have been dropped from a chopper onto the piled rock and old wood foundation. The wind-crusted tracks of half a dozen wolves came from upriver and circled it and continued down the creek. There was nothing but wind and natural world for many miles.

"I think we should spend the night here," Bob said. "Get a good night's sleep, sort through our gear, head for that pass tomorrow when we're fresh."

"Yeah, I'm up for that," Kevin agreed. "I just kind of shoved my shit into my sled this morning. I wouldn't mind organizing it."

"Sounds good to me," I said. We waxed skis, dried bags and clothes, melted snow, mended tents.

We joked about guiding clients our way and getting sued and imprisoned. We finished the whiskey and the nicotine lozenges while we stood around a fire made from the trip's garbage. Green plastic flames were held sideways by the wind. We decided to name ourselves the Accidental Pioneers and have T-shirts made with a scared and confused dude skiing off a cliff or having a shovel fight.

The cabin was a base camp for fly-in sheep hunters. There was a pile of sheep, moose, and caribou skulls out back. A guy from Fairbanks had applied to the Bureau of Land Management for a tent frame and Super Cub landing strip here in 1950. We wondered if the location might have anything to do with the pass across the creek and if it might indicate whether the pass was possible.

The interior was tight with Blazo cans, action packers, folding chairs and tables, plywood shelves and counters cluttered with nuts and bolts, teas and hot chocolate, old batteries, pliers, wire strippers, bullets, silverware, and enameled plates. We sat on wooden crates that once contained Chevron Aviation Gasoline.

"Man, that was fucked up when we figured out we weren't on the Yanert," Kevin said. "But that was pretty cool how we just dealt with it. It's like we're on a new adventure now, and I'm okay with that. I mean we still have three days' worth of food. We're out of the wind for the night. We're gonna be all right."

"Yeah, what a killer ski down that valley, too. I mean it was kinda tough knowing the Yanert was just over that arête, but I got used to not thinking about it. It's good to be off the glacier too. Nice spot on the cabin, Eagle Eye."

"Yeah, I don't miss digging out a tent site and rigging like a ka-billion fuckin' guy lines up. I feel like I'm almost home you know, how you can stand in one place and turn around 360 degrees and see the big mountains and then these still big but more accessible mountains and then the rolling hills of the Interior, like I could just ski into them and go home. And the trees. You look up there and there's no trees, and here all this willow and down the creek spruce. Just the transition of this place."

We slept on the floor and the one bunk along the back wall not piled high with supplies. The wind blew down from the mountains hard all night, and I was glad the cabin was guy wired into the stone on the upriver side.

The next morning we warmed the cabin with our stoves and put away our gear and had coffee and oatmeal. We nailed the door shut and watched the Alaska Range tumble north into the Middle Tanana Basin, the eighty-five-hundred-square-mile wetland through which its rivers roll. It's been warped downward by the repeated mountain-building events of the last sixty-five million years and filled with layers of conglomeratic sandstone, shale, and coal derived from thirty-million-year-old swamp plants, topped off by several thousand feet of gravel eroded from the Alaska Range. There's an old mountain range buried out there like a sunken Spanish galleon at the bottom of the Atlantic.

Preserved sandbar patterns and material eroded from the ancestral Alaska Range indicate that the rivers once flowed south, through the earlier Alaska Range, to Cook Inlet. As these mountains rose over the last few million years, this path was blocked and drainage was forced back north and west to the Bering Sea.

We skied across the river to the mouth of the creek that flowed from the pass. We skied up the creek, cutting through brown, red, and yellow lava flows.

The skiing was good and after a few hours we reached the bottom of a lonely basin cluttered with fallen boulders and old avalanches. The pass was taut across the top of a high bowl set into the western wall of the basin, fourteen hundred vertical feet above. It looked like we could contour up the southern rim of the bowl and slowly gain elevation below long patches of scree. Kevin didn't want any part of it. Said the avalanche danger was too obvious for him. Said it was probably fine but he wasn't here to be taking chances like that. He elected to travel up the north side of the cirque where he judged the danger less severe. We split up and headed out.

Bob and I climbed with crampons and axes up ribs of dark talus. When we'd get to the top of one, we'd traverse across the face of the slope to the next, which we climbed until it ended. In this manner we made our way to the pass. But it was scary and a bit stupid. The snow was a melted-together slab resting upon barely consolidated hoar frost and loose sugar. As we neared the top, it tilted up to fifty degrees.

We were a couple hundred feet above the pass with one final snow traverse to accomplish before we could descend to the corniced ridge between the two valleys. We felt the frailty of the slope, saw ourselves caught in a high avalanche that swept over the corniced ridge back into the bowl, and imagined the power of that second avalanche as the cornice broke and took the whole valley with it a thousand feet farther down. Our decayed bodies wouldn't be found until summer, unless some animals ate them first.

What will it feel like when the slope breaks? When will I know that I'm going to die? Will there be a moment to recognize my departure from this world? To say good-bye? Would it matter? What will come next? Shut Up! Take the next step. Plant the axe shaft or the pick when the snow gets too hard. Let the feet roll until all the crampon points are in contact with the snow. Cut steps when it gets too hard. Move gently. Breathe. Control the panic. Next step. When we're standing on the ridge, I can give myself grief about diving into unknown conditions, but for now just take the next step.

And soon we were on the ridge, giddy with relief. We smoked and took pictures and high-fived because we were alive and looking down a much more moderate slope to the Wood River and we were going to make it!

We waited an hour for Kevin and began to form contingency plans. Should we go look for him? Should we ski like hell for the road and send a plane? Had he returned to the cabin? The wind was angry, and our calls were swept away with the rainbowed spindrift.

But eventually he made it, and we high-fived some more and dropped into the upper Wood, down through narrow lava canyons and back into willow, where we heard the soft nasal clucks of horny rock ptarmigan. They burst from the snow in groups of five or six when we got close. A dozen sheep stood on a high black wall. The trails they used were etched into the mountains by their passing. We skied over the humped piles of old avalanches and a large antlerless moose ran from us near a narrow snow-covered lake. A red fox stood his ground until we were almost upon him, and then he turned and blended with the alder.

As we neared the bottom, the snow began to deteriorate. It became a mixture of breakaway crust, wet cement, and loose sugar. We were exhausted, and the skiing was sucking out our mojo, but we continued into the dusk and camped in a clutch of willow and cottonwood in the middle of the river. We shoveled the wet snow four feet down to solid ice and set up camp within sight of the first spruce trees we would pass in two weeks.

Our excitement at getting over the pass was tempered by the difficult snow conditions. We wondered if it would remain this way for the rest of the trip as the daily highs were reaching above freezing and the smell of earth and water and moss and trees was tactile on the air for the first time in months. We talked about how the snow surface would be frozen in the morning and how we should get an early start traveling on it. Stars burned through the mist rising off the cooling snow, and we prayed for cold.

Kevin was up as twilight was touching the valley and stars were still in the sky. "Hey, Rob, I'm leaving. I just can't wait anymore. Here's the map. I'm just going to ski for sixteen hours or something. Try and get out."

We broke down the tent and I got the stove going while Kevin went ahead, putting in trail. An hour-and-a-half later Bob and I were putting on ski boots. They'd gotten wet the previous day, and I'd forgotten to sleep with them. They were frozen solid. The outer halves of both my big toes and both my little toes were black and blistered. My right heel was a black blister on top of another black blister. A tear forced its way from each of my squeezed shut eyes as I forced my feet into the boots. It took about five minutes per foot.

We skied out of the white world of the Wood. The mountains leaned down steep faces and scree slopes to the rounded hills of the Interior. The tops were lost in clouds, shifting mists, and fickle masses of airborne ice dust.

The breakaway crust was patterned with the tracks of lynx, fox, and wolf and punched through by moose. The snow conditions were good in the morning, but temperatures rose above freezing by noon and things deteriorated.

In the early afternoon we passed a fly-in wilderness lodge. No one was there. A snow-machine trail we'd been following ended. Past the lodge the valley that led to the final pass opened across the river. Bob stopped and had a mug of hot chocolate waiting for me when I caught him. We crossed and headed up the trail, marked by blazes in the spruce, which had grown orange over the decades with oozing pitch. A pair of ospreys, like a wedge of dark matter, circled in the gray and blue sky, just back from Mexico, hungry.

It was after twilight when I came above the last of the willow and then the alder into the rolling whiteness of the pass. The contours of the snow were imperceptible in the diffuse light, and a hard wind blew down the valley. I skied for miles into the darkness as the pass became Dean Creek and wove to the Yanert. Rock ptarmigan exploded around me, and at times there were hundreds of them in the air. I hadn't seen Bob for hours, but I knew he was ahead of me somewhere, with a fire, probably.

But I wouldn't catch him that day. Eventually I dug a shallow grave behind a granite boulder the size of a Pizza Hut and lined it with the fly of Bob's tent and got into my sleeping bag within it. For dinner I had moose jerky and raisins and snow.

Breakfast was raisins, Advil, and snow. I ran into Bob fifteen minutes after I'd set off. I drank a quart of water without taking my mouth from the bottle and had some tea and oatmeal and headed out while he broke camp.

He caught up and left me behind within a half hour. Another two hours and I arrived at the confluence with the Yanert, swollen with cobalt *aufeis*. A brisk wind swept snow over the surface and water gushed from a four-inch outlet hole. I sat on my sled and ate everything I had left. I was shoving the last handful of muesli into my face when a snow machine came from upriver.

The rider's name was Dennis. He was a retired heavy equipment operator from Healy, twenty miles north on the Parks Highway. He'd come upriver as snow machine support for a young couple from Healy, Hal and Mia, who'd run a team of ten dogs up. Kevin had contacted them at their camp the previous night and asked if they could carry his sled to the road. Kevin had camped below them on the river and skated out in the morning. Dennis was out for a morning ride when he ran into me.

He offered me and my stuff a ride. "I mean I don't want to end your adventure too soon or anything." He was grinning.

"Oh, I guess I'm ready."

We loaded my gear onto his sled and headed downriver a mile to Hal and Mia's camp and loaded up Kevin's gear. We waited while they hooked up their dogs. Hal drove the team while Mia drove a snow machine. They told me they had a house in Goldstream Valley but had moved back to Healy, where Mia's from, when she got a job driving a truck at the Usibelli Coal Mine.

Dennis and I were talking about the tracks we'd been seeing when we overtook Bob and loaded his gear onto Mia's machine. He jumped on behind her and we were off again. Whenever we'd catch up to Hal, we'd pull over and let him go for a while. I asked Dennis how his retirement was treating him.

"Oh, I love it, Rob, I love it. Wednesday's when they pick up the garbage so that's the only time I even know what day it is. I go snowshoeing, look for animals, read. It's great."

We made it to McKinley Village in less than an hour and met up with Kevin, who'd just arrived. Dennis offered us a ride to the Totem, a local watering hole. When we got there, he wished us luck and went home.

We ordered bacon double cheeseburgers with french fries and milkshakes served by a pleasant woman in her forties who called us *hon* and *dear*. She brought us coffee and hot pie with ice cream. We moved to the bar and washed it down with whiskey cokes and cigarettes while we waited for Eric to come get us.

We sat on tall stools at a small round table. From the big screen we learned that a mentally ill man with guns had killed eight people at a nursing home, that shutting down Guantanamo would be more difficult than originally thought, and that North Carolina, Villanova, Michigan State, and UConn would be in the Final Four that weekend.

A group of kids came in and shot some pool at the room's only table. But the bartender checked their IDs and told them they couldn't be in the room until they turned twenty-one.

I watched through the window as they walked away in the wind. Watched the atoms of snow caught in the cold air rushing north. Felt the gravity pulling us along.

Yoga Breathing in the Midnight Sun, 2012

I HAVE A CALL at Lin's Massage. I'm on the highway. It's summertime, 11:15 p.m. The sun is an elongated red blur pressed against the northern horizon. The windows are down. Though it was pushing ninety today, the air is cool, raising goose bumps on my forearms. The smell of blooming willow and dry spruce gushes through the car. I feel birch pollen in the tender passageways that connect my nose and throat. I smell smoke from a wildfire the size of Delaware smoldering beyond the Yukon River.

I take the first exit I come to, Bison Road. People from the west end have difficulty saying it without grimacing. It's the land of poisoned well water, exploding meth trailers, homemade religion. I take a left and head down a two-lane past partially disassembled cars abandoned in ditches, past trailers that look like they've been torn open with a Sawzall, mold-blotched insulation oozing out and effervescing into the still air. Lin's is behind a tall fence made from the strips of wood ripped from logs being milled into rough cut. There's still bark on one side and the ends stick up at different lengths, curl like unkempt toenails.

Inside the compound are four Atco trailers welded together at right angles. Blown foam insulation that was once yellow is now a dark orange and bubbles from the joints like scabs.

I park in the courtyard formed by the semicircle of Atcos, hop out, head for the office. A blue and red neon sign in a window says OPEN. It's the only indication this place is a business. Miss Lin's assistant, Sue, steps out of a door next to the window and crosses her skinny arms over her skinny chest. She smiles a predatory smile. At first she appears youthful, desirous. But looking closer I see that the smooth skin of her face is a puttied façade, the carefree black hair a slightly off-center wig, the jocular thrust of her hips a nod to the arthritis creeping into her back. "What, you no bring nobody for me today?" she says scoldingly, just enough of a smile to let me know she's teasing.

"Uh, no, they told me you had someone for me today."

"Oh, yeah. She in there." She extends a bony arm like a dying branch to a door in the adjoining Atco. "She quitting on me. Girls no want to work. Can't find girl who want to work. They think they live in Hollywood movie. You get her out of here for me, okay? I got no time for movie star. I need girl who want to work, make the money, you know."

"Okay," I say as I walk to the indicated door. The oblique slant of the sun's last light casts a rusty stain on the gravel yard and the faded white trailers. There's no one else here.

It used to be different. When Miss Lin first opened and went head to head with Carmine over at the Oriental Massage, she'd had up to a half dozen girls. Many of them were quite attractive. Between the soldiers and the oil field workers, there were always customers around.

She used to give us money for bringing her new customers. We were like a big happy fucked-up family. She toppled Carmine's empire. He went to prison for money laundering, and she had all the business. But nothing lasts forever. The military banned its personnel from the premises, the state shut her down, and a fire destroyed the original building. Sue left town.

But she came back. A new Miss Lin's rose from the ashes, a treacherous bird with most of its feathers stripped away, an eye poked out, scabs on its talons. Now I'm here to take away this latest dove, and Sue will be left to take care of the customers herself, until she can arrange for a new girl to be sent from someplace that's losing the game of unregulated global capitalism, leaving its citizens to see working in a whorehouse off Bison Road as a good opportunity.

I knock on the door. Someone pulls it open, jerks on it to force it over the uneven lumps of the floor. She's a tiny woman, appears fragile. I wonder how she can take the hammering of 250-pound weight-lifting beef-eating GIs. She smiles, averts her eyes, crooked teeth, light brown skin. "How you today?" she asks.

"Good. You?"

"Good, yeah." She nods sideways at a mountain of crap piled next to the door. I look back to the Hyundai I've been driving lately. I love a Crown Vic but with gas over four bucks a gallon, I can no longer justify the extra $200 a month that the hungry motor requires. But what a trunk! I could've put all this woman's possessions and the Hyundai in the trunk of a Crown Vic. I haul garbage bags full of clothes, mountains of pillows. What the hell could anyone do with all these pillows? I wonder. There's a folding massage table, a mat that fits onto it, boxes of oils, perfumes, incense, unguents, air fresheners. Boxes of cosmetics, curling irons, blow dryers, hair care products.

Sue wanders into the room and inspects the proceedings. She yells at the woman in rapid-fire Mandarin. She points to a pizza box rattling with discarded crusts and fingernail clippings. She points to some dust on the floor, a smudge on the window. The woman nods and attends to each detail. Sue heaps her scorn as I pile up cheap possessions until the car is resting on its axles and Sue's fury is spent. I squeeze into the front. The young woman gets in after me holding a small plastic kennel containing a shy toy poodle. She balances the kennel in her lap. We roll out of the lot and scrape bottom on the hump of the culvert.

"I'm Leicha," she says, head down, hand extended. I take her hand, feel the delicate bones within it, like a small defenseless creature that could be crushed by accident.

"Hi, Leicha. I'm Rob. Where you headed?"

"You know hotel? Not too cheap but not expensive one too. I have dog so hotel has to let dog stay too. Maybe close to airport would be good."

"How 'bout the Super 8. It's not the closest, but it's on your way, medium priced. I'm not sure about the dog but probably as good a chance as anyplace."

"Okay, okay, Supah 8 then. And you help me with my stuff?"

"Sure, I can help. You've got a lot of stuff."

"Ohhh, I know. Sorry. It for my work."

"You do massage?"

"Yeah, I good at massage. I like it. Why, you want massage?"

"No, no, I'm good. Thanks, though."

"Yeah, I like to do real massage. I want to get certified massage therapist. Nobody want that kind of massage, though. Nobody that comes to Miss Lin's, anyway. But that's okay, I make good money here. Now I go see my friend in San Francisco. I have money for massage school. Sue no like it but I not like Miss Lin's. I mean she help me with this job, but this is *my* chance, you know. My visa only good a short time. I work for her two month already. That's enough."

"Yeah, I could see that getting old."

"Yeah, like the men that come to Miss Lin's. Old and drunk," she cackles, leans forward, claps her hands. "I come from Thailand. From Issan, you never hear of it, right?"

"Sure, northeast, by Laos."

"Ooohh, how you know about Issan?"

"I lived in Thailand for a while, about a year and a half."

"Ahhhh, *puhd Thai dai mai?*"

"*Puhd Thai dai, nit noy.*"

"*Oi, mai nit noy. Puhd dii.*"

"Yeah, I don't really remember all that much. I loved it over there, though. I'd go back just to eat."

"I miss the food too. But is very poor where I'm from. I making two, three dollars a day. I can speak Chinese, Japanese, English, Thai. This is my chance, and I'm taking it."

We're pulling in under the awning of the motel. "Let me check in, okay, then I pay you, okay?"

"Yeah, that's fine. I'll start unloading."

"Thank you."

"No problem." I get about two-thirds of her stuff in the lobby. The hotel has agreed to the dog for a price. Leicha pulls from her purse a wad of twenties that must be six inches thick. The intent young Indian desk clerk looks at it with wide eyes. She looks as though she's about to hold her nose, makes no attempt to touch the money Leicha holds out to her.

"Ummm, we don't take cash," she says. "We got robbed too many times."

"Awww, c'mon, this woman needs a place to stay. And I really don't want to reload all this stuff. Can't you just take her money?" But the woman shakes her head.

I put the room on my credit card. Leicha reimburses me in cash. She tips me twenty on the cab fare. She hugs me. I return to the cab. I'm glad to help, but I'll spend the next month worrying that my credit information is being shopped around the Internet the way Leicha was offered to Fairbanks.

Josh is dispatching. He's the grandson of Don, patron saint and founder of United Cab. Don showed up here twenty-five years ago with a suitcase containing $80,000 in cash, which he earned working on off-shore drilling rigs in the Gulf of Mexico. He helped a friend manage Fairbanks Taxi for several years before starting this company.

He snuck it into existence, secretly buying the land, painting the cars, erecting the radio tower and dispatch offices while still managing the affairs at Fairbanks Taxi. When the time came, he took the best drivers from Fairbanks and hit the road with a fleet of new cabs he'd purchased at auctions through a guy named Guido in Las Vegas. Don was illiterate. He battled addictions to meth and opioids. He was a dedicated gambler, ran book for the company. He was also a millionaire when he died earlier this year. The business remains in the family. His last accomplishment was to get to know his daughter and show her the business and give it to her.

But Josh is the one who understands how it works. He's dispatched, driven, worked in the shop and the front office. His first child, a son, was born just after Don passed away.

"Red South," I tell him.

"Mornin', bro," he says. "You're one South. Lookin' at one South, three City, two North, and four West." It takes him 1.3 seconds to say this. I roll next door and sit at the Goldstream Theatre. The last shows are letting out, people trickling into the twilight. I watch their faces as they notice (or fail to notice) the metallic lavender sunset oozing across the northern horizon.

My favorite part of summertime night cab driving is the sunsets. Or I should say the sunset/sunrises, since the one begins before the other has ended. They last for hours, beginning around eleven and lingering past four in the morning. It's kind of a private show since most of the big village is either drunk or sleeping during this time.

The same thing happens in reverse in the winter. Around eleven in the morning the earth rotates past the point where the gaseous fireball peeks over the southern horizon and slides above the teeth of the Alaska Range. The air is filled with microscopic particles of ice that alter the light, stretch and twist it like a clown performing with balloons, cast it through ephemeral prisms that separate it into different color spectrums.

There are three Inupiaq kids walking to the cab. The guy in the lead opens the door, pushes a shower of straight black hair away from his eyes. He's wearing a new sweatshirt emblazoned with the University of Alaska Fairbanks logo and polar bear mascot. "Can you take us to UAF?" he asks shyly.

"Yeah, man, hop in," I say.

He and the two girls get in the back. "Moore Hall," he says.

They're attending summer school. They're from Point Hope, a small whaling community on the Arctic Ocean. Where they're from, polar bears are not mascots, they're intense predators that sometimes hunt people. They come into the village and feed on the carcasses of the whales the people harvest. This behavior is only increasing as climate change melts the ice they depend on to hunt the seals that are their primary source of nutrition. Conflicts are becoming more common.

Where they're from the sun never sets in the summer and never rises in the winter. I think of the odyssey their DNA has endured to become corporeal in this lifetime and find it improbable. Yet they whisper happily in the back, smelling of buttered popcorn and new clothes. Occasionally a giggle escapes one of the girls. I get them to the dorm and take their money and wish them well. I call Josh and tell him I'm ready for another one and he puts me two U.

But then Marius, from Bulgaria, goes West and a couple minutes later Josh sends me to the Pumphouse, a restaurant with a big deck hanging over the Chena River. Eighty years ago the building was used to pump water out of the river and over Chena Ridge in thick pipes. As the water rushed down the other side of the ridge, the diameter of the conveyance pipe narrowed until it was a fat hose. The water blasted out of the hose with enough force to erode entire hillsides of dirt and gravel into giant sluice boxes that filtered out tiny particles of gold. These days it's a popular tourist restaurant filled with stuffed bears, moose antlers, and sepia-toned photographs of men in suits digging through the muck in pursuit of the yellow metal.

My people are standing in front of the corrugated gray metal building when I pull up. A couple in their fifties, pudgy and tan. He's wearing a polo shirt and a red windbreaker. She's got on a new sweatshirt emblazoned with a drawing of howling wolves against the backdrop of Mount McKinley, "Denali" written in perfect cursive underneath.

We exchange greetings and they tell me to take them downtown, to the Westmark Hotel. I pull onto Chena Pump Road and lower the pedal, hear the squirrels under the hood begin to spin their wheel faster, the car responding in due time. "So do you live here year-round?" the guy asks me.

"Yeah, twenty-five years now."

"Really, you're the first person we've met that actually lives here. What do you do here? Isn't it like cold and dark all the time?" she says.

It's ironic that the people hired by the big tourist operations to guide these folks around the state are usually Outsiders armed with a script about the natural wonders and pristine beauty of the place. For many, this cab ride back to their hotel after the busses have returned to the barn will be their only contact with a person who actually lives here. It's perhaps even stranger that so few of the visitors even notice this dynamic.

Most of the people who live here couldn't afford to work for the low wages the corporate vacation outfits are willing to pay. The relationship between the big operators and the people who live here is an uneasy one. Every year they insulate themselves further, build their own restaurants and hotels, hire their own people, send their money Outside. I've always felt compelled to tell these people there are things that happen up here that are not connected with the livestock tourism industry.

"Well it's cold and dark a lot of the time, but the sun does come up every day of the year. The shortest day's a little under three hours, but twilight lasts an hour and a half or so on either end of that.

"What do you do? Can you even go outside when it's sixty below zero?" he says.

"Well, it's usually not sixty below. And no, it's not much fun to go outside when it is. But there's plenty of days when it's above zero. And there's this whole huge matrix of trails that only exists in the winter, so if you like to ski or mush or ride snow machines, winter's the time to do it. I ski until about thirty below.

"And it's beautiful out when it's cold. And it's a good excuse to relax, catch up on the reading, stoke the woodstove. Eat moose and salmon."

"You hunt the moose?" she says.

"Yeah, between the moose and the salmon we harvest about 75 percent of the meat we eat. And we usually have potatoes, carrots, beets, cabbage, turnips from the garden till January or so. I mean I guess that's part of wanting to be here, you know, living a little closer to your means."

Okay, I'm working my tip now. By the time we get to the Westmark, these people think I'm Grizzly Adams. They have a hotel employee take their picture with me. They'll go back to California or Texas or Wisconsin and tell their friends about the wild and wooly wilderness cabbie. Their friends will see them in a new light. Their friends will travel to Alaska and call a cab from the Pumphouse and get an obese guy with anger management issues that smells like he hasn't wiped his ass for a week. It's a numbers game, remember?

They tip me ten bucks. I thank them.

The sunset/sunrise is trending orange as the home star reaches for its nadir. It reflects off the north slope of the Alaska Range. The light is granular. It has texture. It sounds like the ocean. I call in and Josh sends me to the Texaco on Airport Way. I don't see anyone standing outside. I circle the building, slow down to peer in the windows of the mini-mart. It's after midnight. The store is closed. I'm wondering why someone would have a cab sent to a closed business. Maybe it's an employee. The left rear door opens, and someone hops in behind me. Dammit, I hate it when people sit back there. It's not an employee. It's a scrawny white guy with long, greasy ginger hair, a pointy face, bad teeth. He looks twenty going on fifty. "Farmers Loop," he says.

"Where on Farmers Loop?" I say.

"Skyline. I'll show you," he says with a hint of menace.

"How 'bout you tell me now so I can let my dispatcher know."

"I don't know the name of the road. It's about a mile up there," he's annoyed.

I'm on edge. I don't know why I don't say fuck that, man. Show me some fuckin' money, first. Don't sit behind me like that. But I don't. It's like something is joining us, and I'm in it now, and the only way out is to run the trip. I call it in and point the car east, then north. It's like I don't want to offend the guy or show any fear.

"So how you doin' today?" I ask. If I can engage him in conversation I can get a better idea where this is going.

"Shitty," he says.

"Sorry. Nice sunset, anyway, huh?" He doesn't answer. I think of Cord. I wonder if I ever do get killed whether there'll be a moment before I'm gone when I'll realize that I will never see him again and realize he's going to grow up without me. I feel an immense sadness, bigger than all Alaska, followed by a giant surge of adrenaline. I have a death grip on the wheel. I could rip it out of the dash if I wanted to. I reach into my pocket and slide out a folding knife, open it, and place the blade beneath my thigh so the handle is quickly accessible. I lower my chin to my chest so it will be difficult for the guy to slip something over my throat. I realize I'm ready to kill this motherfucker. I realize if he has a gun, none of my preparations will matter. I note he's not wearing his seat belt, and if I crash the car into a ditch at fifty, that might take him out. I'm ready for war and violence. It always surprises me how easily this transformation occurs. How easy it is to descend to the subterranean river of blood flowing just beneath the veneer of social convention.

I try to slow down time by being aware of every detail. The more I notice will force time to expand to accommodate all that's taking place within it. Changing it by elongating the space it must cover. I recall how physicists say things like "the flow of time is different depending on where in the universe one resides." That, maybe, what we think of as time is really no more than a local metric measuring a thing whose true nature remains elusive.

I think about how, in *Slaughterhouse Five*, Billy Pilgrim—because he's become unstuck in time—knows when and where he'll be killed, yet he's powerless to do anything different. Is this how that feels, I wonder.

We turn down a narrow, unmarked gravel road off Skyline Drive. I have one hand on the wheel and the other on my microphone. The guy says, "Right here'll be good," at the entrance to a driveway curving down on the left.

"Nineteen'll be good."

He hands me a twenty. Says, "Keep it," and hops out, walks down the driveway. Just like that it's over, everything's okay again.

I exhale, turn the car around, and head back to town. Call in. Josh puts me two North and a bit deep. I'm doing the yoga breathing Michele taught me. I think about the kid having a mother, somewhere, maybe worried about him. Maybe down at the end of that driveway. I'm thinking that maybe his frustration came from recognizing my reaction. That maybe it forced him to confront his powerlessness in this world.

I think about rich people making millions betting on mortgages (that they approved) to fail and calling it work while getting pissed about food stamps and unemployment benefits. This is counterproductive. Things are what they are. I breathe the violence away. Breathe till there's only the faintest residue of cortisol swelling my throat. Think about seeing my family in a few hours. Think about finding some other thing to do.

As I reenter the lit lanes of town, Josh is holding in the city so I shoot across the expressway bridge and call red City.

"Let's see 55, red City . . ." I can picture him running his thick hand through his thinning brown hair, pushing back his Green Bay Packers hat, scratching where the headband digs into his scalp. Josh loves the Packers. A few years ago he bought into the organization, theirs being the only NFL franchise that is owned by its fans. "Let's see, uh, go get the Golden Towers for Henry. I know he'll be there."

The Golden Towers is an assisted living facility. Henry is a miserable old bastard. I've picked him up dozens of times. He goes to Denny's. It's always $5.60 on the meter, and he always gives me $5, says $5.60's too much, he's on a fixed income, my meter must be wrong, I must be trying to rip him off. What kind of a shithead must I be to be ripping off an old man? But I've talked to other drivers. It's $5.60 on their meters too. And some of them insist on that 60 cents. I've always just said whatever. But whatever.

I pull up to the entrance. He's standing there with a cane and an oxygen machine, the clear thin tubes running into his long beak. I hop out and unhook the oxygen tube from the machine. He gets in the front seat and I put his oxygen in the back, and hook the tube.

I get in next to him. "Where to?"

"Denny's. Same place I go every fuckin' night. I gotta stop eatin' their fuckin' gravy, though. It's been givin' me the shits."

"Sorry."

"No, you're not. You don't give a shit about the gravy fuckin' with my shits. You're probably still shittin' hard logs that shoot outta there and hardly leave a stain on the paper. You fuckin' kids don't know how good you got it. I fuckin' love gravy, god-dammit!"

"All right, sorry."

"Quit fuckin' sayin' that! I don't want your fuckin' sorries. I want some gravy and a normal shit. You don't even know what it's like, so just shut the fuck up."

I don't say anything. He's worse than usual. I'm thinking how I'll be fifty soon, and while I won't claim to be in posses-sion of the wisdom of my golden years yet, I do kind of resent him calling me a kid. But that's only because he's using it as a synonym for stupid a-hole. I like being part kid. I try to nurture my inner child, and I don't feel too woo-woo about saying that. And if being a kid is the alternative to being him, then I prefer it. I'm calming down. I'm breathing through it. I'm wondering why he's like this. I mean I know lots of old people, and none of them are like this guy. What happened to him? And then it hits me. Maybe this is what happens when the love's all gone but you got old anyway. I'm not sure why I think this, but I know it's true. I think that all I can do is try to be more pleasant when my time comes. To go there with love in my heart. "I kind of understand," I say. "I mean, I like gravy."

He grunts, stares ahead. He's pulled out an electronic cig and is supplementing the oxygen with nicotine vapor.

We pull into Denny's. "$5.60," I say.

"What?!" he says. "It's always only $5. What kind of a shit head goes around ripping off old men?"

"It's been over two years since it was $5. Most days I'll play along, but not today. You gotta be nicer if you wanna pay $5."

He pulls a flimsy wad of ones and fives from his pants pocket, gives me a $5 bill, hands shaking. "I said I'd give you $5, you rip-off motherfucker, and that's all you're getting."

His face is inches from mine, spittle is flying off his lips, spraying my face. My hand is in motion before I realize what I'm doing. I'm scared for a billi-second that I'm going to hit him. But instead I grab the thick wire-rimmed glasses off his nose, transfer them to my left hand, and hold them by the door, out of his reach. I do this without contacting a molecule on the pale parchment of his skin. "What the fuck?! Give me my fuckin' glasses back." He paws the air sightlessly.

"You owe me 60 cents. Pay me or I'll throw 'em across the parking lot, leave you on the curb with your oxygen unplugged. How you like that?"

"I'll call the police."

"Go ahead. But you should know I'll have to charge you time while we wait for them. And they will back me up. Make you pay me. There's a statute on the books that makes theft of services a crime. And that is what you're doing by not paying me what you owe me. Now give me my fucking 60 cents, and I'll get your fucking O-2 out and plug it in, and if you're nice to me, next time you can just pay me $5. How about that?"

"This is fucking bullshit," he says. He hands me a single. "I want my 40 cents back," he says.

I give it to him—a quarter, dime, and nickel. I return his glasses. He gets out. I get his oxygen and plug it back in. He shuffles to the door.

I call Josh. He puts me four South. I notice it's beginning to get lighter out. The Earth turning back toward the life-giving nuclear inferno. It's just a hint at first. You'd have to have survived a winter up here to even notice it at this point. I look at the clock, 12:51. I think about how Henry almost seemed to be grinning there at the end. Grinning at me like "This is livin', ain't it, kid?"

"What the fuck?" I say. A begrudged chuckle escapes my lips. I decide to go West. From this point I could also go City or North with equal ease, but there are three City and two North and the last car that said red West, about three minutes ago, got a trip at the Boatel. The bar that used to be a boat and hotel until it burned down a few decades ago.

I turn left on Airport, and as I'm approaching Peger Road I'm accelerating, hitting fifty-five in a forty-five, half expecting to hear some other driver beat me to it. I call in and tell Josh I'm red West. He sends me to 1921 Sunset, a card house, Texas hold'em mostly. I say, "Check." Three seconds later 79 goes red West. She gets a one position. I'm at the house on Roosevelt in four minutes.

There's a young guy outside smoking a cigarette. As he walks to the car, he points to the cigarette, raises his eyebrows. I give him a thumbs-up. He's tall, has to fold himself into the Hyundai.

He's maybe twenty-five, has a soft dreamy face, mop of brown hair. "Yo," he says with classic surfer dude pronunciation.

"How's it goin?" I say.

"Awesome, bro. Take me home, Madcap Road."

"All right."

"Man, it's so weird. Like, I just broke up with my girlfriend. Well, I mean she's still at my place 'cause she doesn't have another place, yet. So, I'm gonna go stay with this other girl. I move on, you know."

I wait for a few seconds. "Man, that's not that weird," I say.

"Oh, yeah. What's weird is that while I was standing there waiting for you, I got a text from this girl I used to go out with. She's like a lawyer in San Francisco now. But she sends me this picture, and she's wearing this negligee, here check this out." He holds his phone in front of my face. I jerk my head left to see around it. I glance at the phone, but my near vision has gotten blurry, I need reading glasses to see anything right in front of my face. The woman on the phone is an elliptical blur. "Wow, she's hot," I say.

"Right?"

I swipe his hand away from my face. "You kids are all alike!" I say in old man Henry's voice.

"Huh?" he says.

"All you care about is fucking and texting and . . . and . . . and poker games!" I change back to my own voice. "Just kidding," I say. "It's been kind of a weird couple hours. Speaking of weird, what's so weird about a picture of a woman in negligee?"

"Oh, yeah. Umm, well, the last time I broke up with a chick, like three months ago or something, I got a text from a hot old girlfriend in a bikini, you know, weird, huh?"

I think about it for a few seconds. "If it happens again, it's a little weird, yeah. As it is, barely a coincidence. I mean how many texts from girls in their underwear do you get?"

"Yeah, a few, I guess." He chuckles.

"So, how was the game?"

"Oh good, good. I was working tonight. I'm the dealer. That's my job. I deal two or three games a week, play two or three games a week. I'm kinda all about just doin' what I want, keepin' a positive vibe. Doing what feels right, you know?"

I think about it. "Yeah, sounds good . . . Unless, you know, what feels right is kidnapping little girls."

"What?!"

"I didn't mean you, you seem like a decent guy. But you know, there's a lot of people in the world who want fucked up shit. 'Cause of their DNA or how they were raised or whatever. And they can't live like that or they'll go to jail. I guess some of them do live like that. Some of them even get away with it. But a lot of them just live with it and never get to live like . . . 'whatever feels right in the moment,' you know."

"So what're you saying? Like I should get a day job or go back to school. Be more responsible."

"No, I just think it's good to keep in mind, you know. Don't take it for granted."

"Okay, I hear you. I get it. It's how you look at it, right?"

"Pretty much."

"It's that blue duplex, with the silver Honda in the driveway."

"Eleven bucks'll be good."

"All right. Here's fifteen. Thanks."

"Take care, man."

"Later." The door bangs shut.

I call Josh. "Whatdya want 55?"

"I wanna be red U . . . I think."

"Ha, you're one U. I got three West, two South, two City, four North."

I stay U, park at the twenty-four-hour gas station mini-mart. It's 1:30 a.m. The bars close in half an hour. The bottoms of the brushed cirrus in the north are glowing fuchsia. The sun is close. The Earth is poised for its arrival. Birds sing their frenetic love songs from the brush that grows from every crack in this sprawl. The cab radio dies. No one needs a ride anywhere. It happens.

I read a fifty-page short story about basketball and coming to some kind of peace with the mess of our lives and deaths. At least that's what I think it's about. I read the whole thing without looking up. When I do, I see that the sun has risen, looking like a gored hole in the guts of the universe. A tear rolls down one of my cheeks. It's time to say thanks and good night.

One Water, 2008 & 2009

A FRIEND USED TO float this river two or three times a year, until he was killed in a car accident on his way to the put-in. At least it happened there, I guess, the anticipation of wildness in his nerves.

Eric had let the river become a part of him. Let it flow in his veins. He was a beautiful young man. Had this smile that seemed to make you part of something good and true. In his memory, I'm going to call this river the Skoog.

It was the end of May, seven years after Eric's death, when I floated the river for the first time. The sound of snowmelt pouring from mountains roared through every pore as if it could wash us clean, save us from our tragic lives. As if its pure surge of renewal might be possible for me, and for him as well. I'd spent several days sitting at home listening to this. I knew the Skoog would be running high and realized that it was time to go there.

I strapped an old Old Town onto the rusty blue Toyota, loaded some supplies, and hit the road.

By late afternoon I stand in a dusty pullout by a gravel road. The day is hazy with a warm sun, and the river sparkling in its touch. I can see I'll spend some time dragging the boat through shallows, but this is a kind of blessing, barring the motorized riff-raff.

I leave a note on the inside of the windshield so that it can be read from the outside: *To whom it may concern: On the river till the 20th. Please don't tow or destroy my vehicle. Thank you. Have a good day.*

So many vehicles thus left behind. This is wild Alaska, for me. Just abandon a car and walk any direction the road doesn't go. Become something vestigial, something essential, something utterly insignificant. Become the taiga, the Arctic tundra, the aurora borealis. Go there willing to die for the experience. Return with the shards of creation breaking through your bones.

For me the Skoog is not a river, not a place. For me it's a living thing with the same genetic code as the farthest flung galaxies. For me it's the world and every journey through it a lifetime one must surrender to when the boat is pushed from the bank and the network of roads recedes to yesterday.

This river guts old mountains, slowly returning them to the sea. It's always low here at the put-in, and I pull the canoe over humped beds of small dark gravel. The current cuts through several meters of silt to the schist bedrock. The silt, a water-logged black goo rising to a layer of dry ochre, gives way to an eight-inch layer of dark active soil in which the forest is rooted.

Glaciers scoured the silt from the north flanks of the rising Alaska Range over the last two million years. It was deposited by moving masses of air that rushed off the ice and may yet wander, ghostlike, across the Earth. As the dust, or loess, settled, plants and animals lived on and were buried in it. Entire species and ecosystems migrated into the storm and never reemerged, their remains entombed in frozen mountain dust.

Over time the Skoog cut down into the sealed soil layers, exposing banks to oxygen and sunlight. They began to thaw and, at last, to decompose. The smell is rich. Prehistoric decay and wild rose, a hint of methane and spruce.

If you place a few shovelfuls of the muck in a strainer and pour water over it to rinse away the loess, you might be left with the leaves of ferns extinct since warmer times or the bones of shrews thousands of years dead or the teeth of tigers no one ever knew to be.

What will happen to all the labile carbon currently in the form of dead but not decomposed organisms that are stored in these frozen soils should global temperatures rise beyond a point where permafrost exists? It's been calculated that 28 percent of the world's soil carbon inventory resides in the circumpolar boreal forest. If the ground isn't frozen, then all this will decompose.

Methane and CO_2 are primary by-products of this decay. These two compounds are suspected to be responsible for 80 percent of the atmospheric absorption of long-wave solar radiation that's driving climate change. Could the thawing of the north push global warming into a growth curve? Yes.

Birch and cottonwood lean at precarious angles over the black-tinted water. With spring come tiny leaves that, from a distance, look like migrations of emerald birds. By June the fully flocked branches glow green in the sun's rays. From the middle of September, the leaves are reduced to golden-rouged husks spiraling down in wind-worn waves, blanketing the surface of the river.

Eventually the water's passage will eat away the soil from around the roots of the trees yawning from the cut banks. In the upper sections fallen trees often block the river, forcing me to empty the canoe and carry it around the beached sylvan whale carcasses.

I usually don't travel far the first day. I find a gravel bar strewn with driftwood after a few hours, but there's no need to pull off at all. The sun only scoops below the northern horizon for a couple hours, leaving the land in fuzzy red twilight, before reemerging a few degrees east, soaked in the blood of a new day.

But, I think, best to pull over, have a drink and a smoke, build a driftwood bonfire, and watch the sun-scorched river endlessly flow. This is a ride best appreciated on a time scale that can only be grasped in epochs. And besides, soon enough there will be no more wood-strewn gravel bars. Enjoy. Breathe.

After the first few hours on the Skoog the following day, the banks of the river reach higher to support the spruce, birch, willow, and poplar forest. The flow nestles down inside the rising walls of water-chiseled loess. Woven mats of undercut forest floor, roots, and moss hang from the tops of eroding meanders.

The layer of dark soil beneath the vegetation mat represents the last thirty thousand years or so of windblown deposition, a peak of glacial advance. It's within this layer that the mummified remains of wooly mammoths, and giant ground sloths await a warmer day when bones, tusks, and tissue might be recycled into the realm of life. Below this is a layer of roots and tree debris that are the remains of an interstadial time, when things warmed a bit thirty-five to forty thousand years ago and the glaciers momentarily retreated, a period perhaps similar to now.

The water becomes deep and black, conceals the scoured trunks of toppled trees. I'll be cruising, amazed at the speeds I'm achieving after the dragging and portaging of the previous day, and then there's a sliding sound and the boat slows and rises from bow to stern. Sometimes I have to get out, stand on the submerged timber, and lift the canoe free. Other times I can push with the paddle and fly away.

The sky is a shifting strip between taiga canopies rising from the river on wings of mud. Blue-fringed, silver-tipped cumulus singe the air gray and spit mist. The illusion of sun-seared atmosphere returns. I close my eyes and see gold, red, and purple banding the horizon, building the dome of winter night, the truth that breathes this dream of summer.

The Skoog has received several tributaries at this point. Plunging my paddle into the water to my elbow, I can't touch the bottom, but I could throw a stone across it underhanded. I come around a bend, and thirty feet off the bow two trumpeter swans are dimpled into the surface tension of the flow. Their necks trace ivory parabolas from the islands of their bodies to their black bills and eyes. They turn to each other and converse in reedy exclamations about my intrusion. I sense I've provoked a squabble as their conversation becomes urgent.

"Come on, let's go!" the larger male seems to be saying.

"I'm not ready yet," the female replies.

"Come on! I mean it! We gotta go!"

"Go ahead then. I'm not sure it's even necessary."

"Are you crazy!? That's a human right there. We're lucky we're not dead already."

"Whatever you say, Mr. Moves-a-lot. I suppose I'm ready now."

They run down the river on black feet, beating down the air with seven and a half feet of wingspan. The tips strike the surface with audible pops as they whip the water into spray. The wings gain purchase on the air, black legs lift into white bellies.

It doesn't seem like the river is big enough for this. Within the sculpted loess channel, we're intimate and then they're gone, circling above the trees, blue lakes multiplying in the green and gold ropes of forest below.

In the 1930s overhunting and habitat depletion in the Pacific Northwest brought these creatures to the edge of extinction. They were reintroduced using eggs from Alaska trumpeter swans that knew better than to come around people. As the swans' traditional estuaries were turned into harbors, they adapted to eating crops. They survive because we let them.

Today about 80 percent, around thirteen thousand, of the world's trumpeter swans breed in the marshes, lakes, and ponds of Interior and Southcentral Alaska. They come back to the country from the Pacific Northwest in April to hatch and raise their young. They'll be among the last of the migrants to leave in autumn.

Despite a 1991 ban on lead shots for hunting waterfowl, thousands of swans in the southern British Columbia–Northern Puget Sound region have died of lead poisoning since 1999. They eat remnant pellets from muddy lake bottoms. Biologists have resorted to scaring swans away from some of the most contaminated lakes using noisemakers and flares. Some wonder, after two decades of the ban on lead shot (which remains available commercially), whether there might be more recent sources of contamination.

I pull out and make tea over a fire on a slip of gravel bar. It begins to rain and then hail. I pull on raingear, hood up, and hunch over the fire, so the ice won't go into the flames. High cirrus were moving east, up the Yukon, when I began the trip. This morning purple-black cumulo-octopi crowded the sky. I drink the tea and let the storm pour off me.

Around another bend an otter slides down the bank into the river beside me. His tapered weasel head bobs above the surface for a while, regarding me curiously, without fear, within the reach of a paddle, before he slips silently beneath the black water, rejoining itself in his absence.

Foot-long belted kingfishers flit from one side of the river to the other, regaling me from the boughs of birch and spruce with squirrel-like scolding. They're powder blue with white bellies and blue-gray belts around their chest, the female's accented by auburn highlights. Their night-blue crests rise in agitation when I'm too close, making their heads seem bigger. In the late fall they'll move far enough south, on the other side of the Alaska Range, to ensure a food supply.

I pass a twisted fan of roots protruding a dozen feet above the cold water. I pass a fat, scoured, gray trunk pointing down the river like a gnarled finger toward a fantastic destiny and pass the thin, blue edge of an ice lens, big as a parking lot, buried in the loess.

When I pull off to camp, my rubber boots sink in black mud to the top of the calf. I try to free my leg and pull my foot out of the boot, leaving it stuck in the slippery mud. The trick is to wriggle and twist the boot slowly. First one way, then the other, repeating the process until you reach a point where you only sink a few inches. The prints of a moose are pressed into it near the top of the bank and then, in a heels-splayed track, slide to the river.

My camp is up a steep slope in the spruce and birch. It takes three trips to haul gear: a cooler of food; a duffel with more food plus stove, fuel, axe, cookware, and rifle; a dry bag with a sleeping bag, tent, clothes, shoes; an ammo can full of books, journals, pens, compass, batteries; a folding chair; and a camping pad. I fill a five-gallon bucket with mud and haul it up, dump it onto the duff, do it again. When the mud has been flattened into a disc, I break some dry, dead branches from the lower trunks of spruce trees and peel away a few scraps of bark from the trunk of a birch. I hold the bundle and trip a lighter beneath it. Within seconds flames reach a few feet above my hands. I place the fire on the mud so it doesn't spread to the forest floor and quickly toss in some sticks from the dry moss. Then I find a standing dead tree and chop it down.

Tonight I'll have some brown rice and lay a couple grayling from the river onto the coals at the fire's edge. I toss a couple red carrots in with the rice.

I lie back in the late spring forest, in horsetails verdant and nubile. I could make a horsetail angel if I wanted to. Through the summer their wiry green leaves stretch up and out until individuals join hands and obscure the ground. By the dying season the weight of the mat becomes too great, and it falls, brittle and brown, back to the earth in a fragile web.

The green buds of prickly rose grow fat. Soon, magenta petals will unfold from the sepaline womb to reveal the golden stamens. The shrubs grow in patches, up to eight feet tall, twisting around each other and competing for sun. The clusters of pink erupting through square miles of boreal forest seem impossible considering this was all frozen solid and under snow a couple months ago. I wear leather gloves so I can move through them without getting handfuls of thorns.

The rose doesn't bloom long. Usually wind and rain have knocked away petals by early July. By the middle of August, the flowers have metamorphosed into rose hips, reddish football-shaped berries of mellow sweet paste and seeds. Suck the goo and swallow it, spit out the seeds. Rose hips are high in vitamin C.

Songbirds dash through the forest like pulses of electricity in a neuro-boreal network. Two white-crowned sparrows with black-and-white striped heads scramble in the branches of a spruce before darting in opposite directions. Fucking, fighting, feeding, whatever it takes to create new sparrows to ride the air masses to the coast of Old Mexico. The male lands on a low branch of another spruce and calls a long rising-high note before dropping through a quick series of tones to end in a drawn-out low.

I wonder if any creatures live closer to oblivion than migratory birds? Their existence depends upon a chain of habitats sprawling from Alaska to South America, a chain increasingly patch-worked with clear-cuts, oil spills, rising sea levels, another new subdivision, another new irrigation project. These birds and their migrations, evolving through tens of thousands of years, are probably seeing the texture of the globe change faster than at any other time in the history of winged diaspora. Will they adapt fast enough to keep up with the pace at which we're consuming the regions that sustain them? Again, nobody knows.

The white tail feathers of dark-eyed juncos flash within willows as a small group darts to earth and scratches through the red stem moss for seeds. The males whistle a tentative high-pitched trill occasionally followed by a few *cheeps* for emphasis.

And there, on a spruce branch, a little black-and-white-streaked bird with a black cap and yellow legs, the one making that soft high-pitched trickling song that dips just so at the end. That's a blackpoll warbler, winter resident of Venezuela. When he returns there, he'll first fly across the breadth of Canada to the Atlantic Ocean and pause to replenish his fat reserves. When he's increased his body mass by about 50 percent, he, along with thousands of his kind, will climb to a height of five thousand feet and head out over the Atlantic. He'll trace a long arc descending to the south even as he and his flock are pushed off the East Coast by northwest winds that won't begin to fade until the Tropic of Cancer. By this time the group will be approaching a point where some might begin to think, *Maybe we oughta just go to Africa this year. I mean I've never been there, but I hear it's nice and it's not that much farther, really.* But then subtropical trade winds out of the northeast will influence their ruminations. *Ah, what the hell, let's just go to South America, I mean we know it, we like it there. If they haven't cut it all down, should be nice.* And they'll curve back toward the Americas.

When they touch down they'll have been in flight, nonstop, for eighty hours, having traveled more than two thousand miles, flapping their tiny wings twenty times a second, at a cruising speed of twenty miles per hour.

Crew members of freighters have reported hundreds of dead blackpolls on their decks following storms. How many more are swallowed by the ocean? What an odyssey for a bird weighing less than half an ounce to undergo annually in order to survive. But the availability of insects, seeds, and berries is nonexistent in Alaska in the winter, and in the places between here and there, the ecological niches are full.

Migration is a last resort refined over thousands of years to deliver a species to the ecosystems on Earth where they can survive. At least until our tilted planet returns to the span of its orbit where the north is never out of the reach of the sun.

The wind hurrying through the tail feathers of a diving snipe makes a resonant *hoohoohoo*, saturating the forest as it falls to earth. Before crawling into my bag, I chamber a round in the .06 and lay it beside me. I leave the zipper partially undone should I need to reach for it in the night. The bird sounds weave around each other until they become a unified song, a celebration of the sun-powered land bursting into leaves, love, and food.

I rise and break camp and relax with strong coffee. A downy woodpecker pounds a wildfire-charred spruce with urgent frequency, calling out his territory. He's a year-round inhabitant of the Interior, six and a half inches long with black-and-white checked wings, black-and-white head stripes, and a bright red mark at the back of his skull. He lands on a dead birch and begins to excavate the punky wood, looking for bugs.

It's the middle of the afternoon before I'm on the river. In the summer it doesn't matter, I could paddle as long or as little as I want. It's hot and sunny, and the sky is an immaculate blue conception. I take off my shirt and feel the sun and cool breeze on my skin.

Around a bend, four white-fronted geese move on orange feet from a silt bar into the water. They take to flight on four and a half feet of wing when I move the paddle to straighten the boat. They're mottled gray and brown with orange bills. Well before this country is sealed in its winter carapace, they'll be on their way to the West Coast and Mexico. Their honking spins into audio pirouettes as they rise and continue north.

I'm being observed by a red-and-blue cross fox seated on a dirt promontory. I turn around in still water and paddle toward him. He lazily scratches a red ear and his blue face and ignores me until I'm thirty feet away, then he moves behind some tall brown grass. I can see his eyes when he moves them to the slits between the blades, considering. When the canoe is almost touching the bank, he pads into the brush.

The banks of the river are tan and rocky. Gravel bars extend from them to form beaches and islands. When the river bends northeast, I catch glimpses of a smooth dome of shimmering deciduous green. To the west, a north-south ridge. I'm down in the trough of the river now, and that's all there is to the view.

Another turn brings a big cow moose and her one fuzzy off-spring. The mother, worn out and ragged from the long winter and wild birth, stands in contrast to the fresh-scrubbed scruffiness and eager flexing of little ribs, fifty or sixty pounds of help-lessness.

Mom's teaching her calf the correct method of crossing a river. The calf has made it to a small gravel bar, but the next crossing is swifter and deeper. The nervous calf is a week or two old. It sits down in the river as if its quivering legs aren't yet strong enough to hold it up. The mother crosses and moves out of sight behind a line of willow. The calf paces back and forth, wading several feet into the river before reluctantly retreating and trying again. I walk down the bank until I see the mother again. She notices me and stomps farther into the brush and stamps the ground impatiently.

The calf is fraught with anxiety. It steps in and out of the river, paces the gravel bar, begins to bleat little piping noises that sound much like the *wah!* favored by human infants. She commits just below the gravel bar in front of some wood sticking out of the river. I see the current welling against the tiny body. She scoots to the other side and shakes awkwardly before joining mom in the brush.

I get back in the canoe and resume paddling, but when I come around the bend, I see that mom has recrossed the river and has climbed a dirt bank on the far side. She is mad. She stomps her hooves, exhales twenty gallons of compressed air in a deep bass *UUUUGGGGHHH!* that creates its own wind. Her stomping shakes the loess. She does it again and plunges down the bank. I'm scared, grab the .06. She charges back up the bank, excavating giant chunks of it with each step, grunting at the freaked-out calf. She charges back down again, barking and growling, and charges back up. Finally, the calf recrosses, struggles up the bank, and they slide silently into the willows. My heart is fucking pounding.

And I realize this is what I love. The river delivers me to the elemental, into the lives of the creatures who live here. Me and the moose gotta deal with each other. We matter to one another.

I'm arriving in the middle third of the river. Farthest from the road at the put-in and the road at the take-out. It's concentrated nature, distilled Interior essence.

I see a white owl, motionless in a birch tree. Even his talons are concealed by white feathers. It seems like good camouflage, but two copper-breasted robins dive and screech at him. They must have eggs nearby.

Snowy owls don't follow a traditional migration but fan out from the high Arctic during the dark time, when the lemmings that comprise most of their diet descend to the subnivean.

A golden eagle leaps from the topmost branch of a dead spruce stretching over the river. It flaps powerfully away, the limb still swaying after he's gone from sight. The golden is one of the first migrants to return to Alaska, arriving toward the end of March, having spent the winter in the mountains of the American West and beyond, in the deserts of Mexico.

I pull out and struggle up the bank, crawl into the green leaves of high-bush cranberry abloom with white flowers that will become red berries hanging in bunches. The berries are sweet, tangy, and tart, They're curiously hydrating when you've run out of water and it's still an hour to camp. Various parts of the plant have been used to relieve pain, sore throats, kidney problems, and backaches. The berries can be boiled and made into jams, juices, and liqueurs. They're high in vitamin C. But my favorite thing about the plant is how it smells in the fall, when its leaves are a deep blood red and the whole forest is simmering in its musty ferment.

I walk back from the river to find a reflective blue pond filled with Canada geese. The air is in motion with their voices. The iridescent green heads and large bills of northern shovelers sit amid the geese. I wonder how long they've been traveling together. The shovelers began their journey north from the American Southwest. They could have hooked up with the geese in California, where they caught a low-pressure system pulling them into the Gulf of Alaska. I want to join them, eat some pond weeds, hear some migration stories.

Back on the river I pass a big cow moose sprawled on a mud bank with two calves nursing between her splayed legs. She looks rugged with patches of hair missing. The way her legs are tossed I wonder if something is wrong. They stick in opposite directions, as if, in a cartoon, a car has been dropped atop her. But she stands up just fine when she sees me, her legs extending under her like bolts of lightning. It's a little unnerving to be close enough to a moose to hold a conversation of unstrained volume, unsure whether she will take the trouble to cross the river, rear above me, and rain down combinations of lethal hoof jabs.

In this case they move up the bank into the forest, the calves casting anxious glances my way. I feel sorry for disturbing their sun-washed afternoon. They deserve their days at the beach.

I see four more cows with calves in the next two hours. The last is the smallest. She doesn't look like she could be more than a yearling herself. She's very dark, almost black, and her calf walks underneath her as they climb the bank.

I've eaten relatives of these moose, taken their protein and made it mine. It's a strange thing to think about, like we're related somehow. I want to know them. They are the country—the willow, birch, and pond weed as well as the mud from which those grow.

I chase two buffleheads and a green-winged teal down the river for hours. Whenever I get to within forty feet, they flap downstream and land around the next bend. The teal's head is a deep burgundy with green eye bars reaching back to the nape of the neck, shimmering in afternoon sun. Clouds of mosquitoes hang in the shadow above the river, filtering the sun that moves through the canopy of breeze-tousled spruce, birch, and cottonwood. When the sun hits the buffleheads, the black swooshes around the white head splotches turn an iridescent purple. The teal flashes green speculums as they rise on small blurred wings over the spruce. I wonder if they know one another from migration ponds between here and Washington State. If they recognize each other. If they're friends.

I pass a tributary gathered from the north side of the dome. The day and I drift along. For the next couple hours, I float past forest raked by fire. Most of the birch have had their trunks scorched black, their roots smoldered away. They topple chaotically into each other, the understory reduced to ash and scorched dirt. Yet roses, willows, fireweed, and grass are clambering into the void, paving the way for the next generation of deciduous forest that will predominate in another twenty years. These birch, aspen, and willow will be shaded out by slower growing white spruce in a hundred years, if they don't catch on fire again first. After another century it'll be all spruce, all the time.

Birch, aspen, and willow shed their leaves every year. Much of this leaf litter is decomposed by soil fungi and bacteria, recycled into inorganic nutrients, but a lot of it sits there and accumulates.

When the succession of spruce takes over, there is far less leaf litter because needles are only shed every seven years. Mosses begin to colonize the newly exposed forest floor, eventually establishing themselves in thick layers.

In late fall and early winter, snow falls, melts into the moss, and freezes. This frozen, saturated moss provides poor insulation to the soil underneath and allows the blunt sledgehammer of winter to sink deep. But this is arid country. It only receives about 10 inches of water-equivalent precipitation annually, about 8 inches more than Death Valley, California, and 140 inches less than Ketchikan, Alaska. So in the summer the moss gets very dry and provides excellent insulation for the cold below.

A few hundred years of this and substantial permafrost has developed. The successional tide begins to turn to black spruce, which have no problem with poorly drained acidic soils, and in fact require them for seed germination. Black spruce are gnarly, stunted, twisted motherfuckers; perhaps, pound for pound, the toughest trees alive. They can grow in soil ten inches deep. They ride at the vanguard of the coniferous movement to retake the North Slope.

The black spruce era can endure up to eight hundred years. It's not a pretty sight: ragged individual trees sparsely covering a mineral bog of moss, grass, and oil-sheened water, leaning at divergent angles in response to the annual thawing and freezing of ice wedges and lenses in the loess. They've had branches scoured off by wind, splintered by rutting bull moose, broken by the weight of snow. They cling to life by a half dozen boughs half full of needles. It's the kind of country you look at and think, "Hmmm, don't really want to walk through that."

Someday there'll be a lightning strike, and fire will burn the moss away. The permafrost will melt without the insulation. Maybe the site drains, gets buried by a mudslide, or drowned in the sediment of a shifting river, and then roses, willow, fireweed, and grass struggle into the void.

I'm moved by how plainly the land offers its stories upon the canvas of the Interior, stretched between the Alaska and Brooks Ranges, 127,000 square miles.

Moose tracks pock every beach. The tracks of half a dozen wolves on one. The tracks of a medium-sized black bear on another. Brown-spotted sandpipers dart up and down the river. They stand in dark water with their butts bobbing rhythmically on their long skinny legs. They seem too fragile and sticklike to fly to South America every year. But that doesn't stop them.

I pass a great horned owl sitting on a gray piece of wood jutting from the mud bank. Big yellow eyes on me like he's checking out the insides of my pores. His tufts fold down. He launches himself six feet above me and turns into the trees. The perfect silence of this motion provides no alarm to the rodents he preys upon. But there's more to it. Relying on his ears to guide him, he often doesn't see his quarry until it's almost in his talons. So the silence also allows him to listen as he descends. A resonant *Hoo-huh-Hoohooohooo* issues from the shadows.

Around another bend a large piece of the Earth leaps from the bank above me. For an instant I realize that an undercut chunk of river wall has succumbed to gravity and is crashing down. It happens all the time. I just never thought the timing would be so precise as to bury me. I cover up expecting impact, but the chunk sprouts wings and becomes a bald eagle pumping, turning, gliding to land on a bleached root downstream.

It's late when I camp. I content myself with rehydrated food from a foil pouch, a few shots of bourbon, a few tokes from the peace pipe. I drift away in a bed of low-bush cranberry, deflated fruits still clinging to maroon and green leaves.

Before I'm gone I hear wolves. Disparate voices, four or five joining, rising to a gibbous moon hung in the twilit sky. Silence.

A morning breeze blows softly off the river as sunshine pours through the blue lens of atmosphere to the green sway of earth and becomes leaves in gentle motion. Allow this morning limbo to stretch as long as it will, because soon the photosynthetic urgency of the plants, whose lives are never far from winter, is contagious.

I slide down the bank to fill the pots. At the water line my boots get slyly sucked into the mud so that when my brain sends the signal for *turn around and walk* down my spine, my legs cannot respond. But the rest of my body is in motion, and I topple to my knees, spill the water, stand up, refill the pots. I begin to wriggle the right foot slowly free, telling myself to get used to it. I mean, if you don't like bottomless organic muck, what are you doin' on a river in Interior Alaska, right?

At the put-in, the soil was only a few feet deep, and the river cut down through it to bedrock. Here, at the bottom of the valley, the depth of this mountain dust has grown to over two hundred feet. The channel is now a fifty-foot-deep gash meandering through. The loess-laden winds of the Pleistocene filled in the land from the bottom up, scaling the bedrock at the rate of an inch every fifteen centuries for two million years. The accumulation thinned as the land gained elevation, until only the top of the ridge and the broad-shouldered dome remained salient.

The dome is granite, formed when magma intruded the schist bedrock and crystallized into an igneous plug 110 million years ago. The magma came from miles below the surface when much older crust was melted and pushed out. At the contact zone the schist was cooked, shattered, and partially melted by the heat of the intrusion. As it cooled, it was shot through with veins of quartz containing gold. The same stuff that convinced white people to stampede the Klondike, invade Alaska, stake claims, and establish settlements.

The schist is a metamorphic rock formed from sedimentary rocks of the Precambrian, that nebulous 90 percent of geologic time that began five billion years ago when the earth formed and lasted through the genesis of continental crust, oceans, atmosphere, and multicellular organisms to end 570 million years ago. Not much is known about the Precambrian.

The protolith of the schist was crushed, plasticized, and deformed as it was transported north along the fault zone between the North American and Pacific Plates. It slammed into the sheared continental fragments already gathered at the end of the tectonic road—Alaska, the accumulating spindrift of a dynamic planet.

As these microterranes came together, more mountains rose up and eroded away, slivers of ocean reef and river residue were torn from one and welded to others.

It's still going on. The Alaska Range is almost finished crumpling, but the Chugach Mountains have just begun to rise. Southern California's only twenty million years away, which seems about right.

The distant cackle of sandhill cranes, like something out of the Mesozoic, stirs me from my reverie. They have four and a half feet of trachea looped inside their chest, which they can contort into the oddest frequencies. They can hear and identify one another from miles away.

I'm excited to make it to a lake I like, so I break camp and have the canoe loaded by ten in the morning. The Skoog flows uninterrupted. Logs and bunches of sticks jut from the water with drift-debris ensnarled.

There are lots of beavers, who seem to grow from the mud walls until, fully realized, they slide to the dark water. Swimming belly down, face above the surface, they ferry sticks for dam repair or food for the young, the newborn beavers on the banks with their families.

Beaver breeding occurs in January and February within a lodge constructed from mud and sticks within a pond created by incessant dam building. When the country's frozen, the lodges are impenetrable to most predators. Families of up to ten animals wait it out in rooms five feet across and three feet high, feeding from a pile of sticks stockpiled during warmer months.

Often, before I actually see them, I hear the *tuk tuk tuk* sound of their teeth scraping the lining of birch saplings, peeling back the bark with their claws.

The Skoog is a listening float. Down in the earth trough, with the brush woven together atop the banks, eyes follow ears to oscillations in the atmosphere. Nothing lives without a wake.

I look up to a displacement of air to see fourteen tundra swans twenty feet above the trees. The sky is busy with northbound ducks, geese, and cranes. The din of their calls fills the valley.

In places the mud banks are a jumble of ancient trees, as if a logjam had formed there long ago and become so choked with silt that the river had to carve a new channel around it, abandoning the old way to the muck and substrata. And then one day, a few thousand years later, the river shifted back and reexposed it. You could take one of these mummified logs, dry it out, and it'd burn as well as the day it was buried.

Sometimes the beavers hiss sharp exhalations through closed teeth. Most of them slap the surface of the water with their flat tails before diving out of sight. I find that if I'm able to clear my mind of malice and look into their eyes calmly, sometimes they don't slap but slide smoothly away.

It's late when I camp at a favorite spot. I walk from the river through a forest of 120-foot-tall white spruce to the lake beyond. In the small inlet next to camp there are a dozen mallards. I raise the .22 and place the sights on the head of a male in the cattails, but I get distracted by the way his green head shimmers in the sun and golden stalks. I count them and find an equal number of males and females, decide not to break up any families today. Not wanting to startle them, I crawl back a ways before I stand and walk back to the mud for my gear.

When the gear is on top of the bluff, I bring a few more buckets of mud and add them to the fire barrier. After dinner I sit by the river and have a drink before bed.

I remember a nice bull moose we got here a few years back. Unfortunately I took him in the lake and was in that frigid water for two hours pulling him to this camp where my partners and I were able to work on him, pulling off quarters, ribs, and guts until he was light enough to drag onto land.

My amigos, Will and Steve, were kind enough to have a blaze going for me when I got back in the middle of a rainy September night. I kept that fire going for six days, smoking moose meat, while they looked for another bull downriver. Before they left, Will and I took a walk around the southern end of the lake to a small pond circled by birch trees. The forest was in the throes of the dying season, the understory a smoldering pile of coals from which the flames of deciduous gold flared into the smoke of flat cumulus skating sparsely across the sky. We walked across a raft of moss floating on the edge of the lake, transforming it back to terra firma. Each step pushed the moss down, and then it rebounded and rippled, as if we trod upon a two-acre waterbed.

We walked on, stripped naked to cross a chest-deep slough, holding clothes, guns, and boots overhead while our toes sank in mud. On the other side Will crawled on palms and shins in the wet moss, his nose twitching as he plunged it into the ground, inhaling the country. "Here, Rob, here!" He gestured urgently pointing to a spot where the moss had been broken and scraped away before shoving his face back into it. "Fuck, man, I knew I smelled something. This is some seriously in-the-rut bull piss, check it out!" I stuck my head down and smelled the musky vinegar urine.

"Goddamn, I'm glad that didn't come out of me."

"No shit, huh, but it'd be a hell of an advantage to be able to produce that, chum up the area."

The urine is saturated with pheromones. Bulls like to splash it with their antlers until they reek of the stuff, advertising their virility to any cow within two hundred yards. By this time they're salivating uncontrollably. The spit is also rich in pheromones and eventually soaks the front end of the moose down to his hooves. Each track is a statement of his sexual prowess.

Steve called us on the radio. "You guys should get back here and check this out. There's a big bull on the other side of the lake."

He was at least sixty inches across his antlers. On the far side of the lake with a harem of four cows, he was busy sniffing and licking. Cow pee is loaded with pheromones as well. Through the scope, we could see the bull's upper lip curl back to allow the vomerones emanating from the cows' vulvas to be detected by a pair of mucosal tissue-lined glands at the rear of the bull's palate. The cows were bawling their heads off, begging for it, but they stopped short of doing it.

We tried to call him in. Will scraped the brush with a scapula. Steve let out a series of tortured bull grunts and challenges. I threw in a cow call, a real moose fiesta. The big guy across the lake turned and faced us, his antlers like sheets of plywood reflecting the sun. He shook them angrily. He rolled them slowly from one side to the other to display their size, as if to say "You motha fuckas wanna piece uh this!?" And then he ignored us, went back to his cows. Like he was saying, "Hey moose, you wanna mess wit me, you gonna have to come over here. If you think I'm gonna go over there, when I got four prime bitches here, then you're out your damn mind!" We watched until dark.

The next day Will and Steve left and I sat in a lawn chair by the river, stoking the fire, taking walks to the lake, writing in a journal. At one point a three-year-old bull wandered out of the shedding birch and willow on the opposite bank. He was shy, didn't want to leave the brush. I crooned some cow calls, and he walked out to the edge of the river and looked about, like he couldn't believe his good fortune, like he was looking for the big bull rushing over to stomp his ass, like he was wondering, "What the fuck is happening to me!? I know that's not a real cow, but I am powerless not to come check it out!" Ahhh, to be young and drunk on toxic love chemicals.

The day after that, still in the lawn chair, I saw a black wolf working his way toward me through the yellowed grass on the other bank. I sat and watched for an hour before it slipped into the golden brush a final time. An hour later, same thing happened, only this wolf was bigger, close to 150 pounds.

When I returned to the Skoog the following spring I found that a ground fire had spread from my campfire, scorched a few hundred square feet of the forest. Blackened fingers of burned moss and ash followed the roots of some of the spruce, devoured an old trapper's shack, the tin roofing sitting atop tan ash within a pit that had provided half the structure's height. The two spruce trees that had grown from the roof were reduced to lumps of charcoal.

When I found the forest fire I had caused, I had a companion with me, a black lab mix named Sippi after the river that ran beside the animal shelter he was rescued from. Sippi belonged to a woman I used to go out with. She'd wanted me to bring him so he could be wild and free for a while. Agreeing to this was a good move.

The day after I arrived I was sitting in a dumpster-score lawn chair, writing in a journal about the peace of the river and all that. Something snapped downriver, behind me. Sippi was up before the twig had finished cracking and was charging past me, teeth bared, barking like a demon. I turned around to find that a 180-pound black bear had sauntered into camp and was forty feet and closing from my turned back. Sippi was nearly to the bear and, at a quarter its weight, appeared ready to fight to the death. Just before they came together, the bear turned right and shot sixty feet up a spruce tree faster than I could've sprinted the same distance on flat ground. She didn't so much climb the tree as attack it, broken branches and bark bits flying as if from a cyclone.

But still on the ground, fifty feet downstream, on the far side of the incinerated cabin was another bear, same size. The bears were both exhaling angry exclamation points and gnashing their teeth. I realized I didn't know where the .06 was. Looking frantically around, I grabbed the first threatening thing I could find, the shovel, cocked it back like the Babe, ready to knock the nearest bear head across the lake. I yelled at the bears and backed slowly toward the tent where the rifle was propped against a tree.

We spent an hour together, me and Sipp and the two bears. I used the time to consider my options. The safest seemed to be to shoot the bear in the tree. Then it was likely that her sibling would be scared off and the situation would be over. I also considered packing up and leaving. But what, I wondered, would happen if the bear came down the tree in the two hours it would take to accomplish this. I mean a bear clinging to a tree is a much surer shot than a bear crashing down its trunk or charging toward me at twenty-five miles per hour. I was scared, endorphins coursing through my system like needles full of speed-balls. I could see these critters eating me and my dog out here where our cracked bones would never be found.

I decided I could take care of the meat, could hang and smoke it from the same pole we'd used for the moose the previous fall. It was early summer and warmer but it was three days to the take-out, and I felt confident I could get it out.

I walked around the tree until I had a reasonably clear shot at the chest cavity. Everyone was very excited. Sippi was bark-ing himself hoarse, and the bears were woofing and breaking branches. Fuck! I did not want to kill that animal. She was beau-tiful up there. I recall the loose fit of her skin on her taut body, like sweats on a perfectly honed athlete. The tips of the guard hairs shimmered in the sun. The stubby tan snout the only con-trast to the vacuum of her blackness. She seemed as confused as threatening. They'd probably been awake just over a month and being younger bears were probably hungry as hell, which is what had led them into this. The animal was trying to squeeze itself within the boughs of the tree.

I raised the rifle and found her in the scope. Damn, I wasn't into this. But I fired anyway. Hit her in the lungs. She clung to the trunk, scrambling frantically. I went to pull back the bolt but it was jammed! I looked for the .22 and found it leaning against the tree by the tent. I made it back as the bear fell from the tree and hit the forest floor. I fired three rounds into her brain and she was still.

The sibling, instead of fleeing, had climbed her own tree and resumed making threatening noises. I yelled at her to get away. Fired a few more shots from the .22, threw some sticks and cans from the burned cabin, but she didn't leave.

I retrieved some knives and a bone saw and began to work on the dead bear while yelling at the other, who finally descended and ran into the downriver woods from which she'd come.

Before I hung the meat, I stoked the fire and cooked back-strap. I resolved that, for the duration of the trip, Sipp would be the best-fed dog in Alaska. We sat in the moss and ate bear. Probably the most intense bonding experience I've shared with a dog.

Afterward I tied two clove hitches around the trees we'd hung the moose from in the fall and inserted a birch pole through loops I tied with the excess rope. I hung the first hindquarter and was preparing the second when I heard a familiar grunting, exhaling, gnashing of teeth, and clawing of bark.

The sibling had returned and climbed a fat spruce by the river. I yelled at her to leave while I worked on a front quarter. When she finally did, I fired the rifle into the woods after her. Again the gun jammed. I cursed myself for not cleaning it before I left. I had had no intention of killing anything larger than a fish or duck on this journey. The rifle was along to provide token bear security, but even a token bear, I thought, requires a functional gun.

I haven't always felt this way. I've been in the presence of bears without any means of defense many times, an experience as real and exhilarating as little else. But I've read too many stories, have come to see it like a numbers game with a number corresponding to me out there somewhere.

I was able to unjam the gun by emptying the mag and mess-ing with the bolt release and safety levers. I rubbed the bolt down with lube but realized I was working with a single shot. Realized I should probably kill the sibling when she returned. She would sneak back. She was my size. She was going to be drawn through hunger to the hundred or so pounds of meat hanging from the crosspiece.

I consulted Sippi. He looked at me blankly, as if to say, "What are you asking me for? You already know what I think. You should've capped 'em both as soon as I risked my life to stop them attacking you from behind. Are you waiting for him to come back in the night when you won't even be able to aim your boom-stick? Why are we not eating more bear meat is what I want to know. Humans!" He snorted and returned his attention to the forest.

Thus dressed down I resolved to finish it when the bear returned and resumed butchering.

But when the sibling came back an hour later I chased it off. The next time it came from upriver. I felt as if I were being stalked. The bear was able to disappear by dropping into the willow and wild rose. I chased it off. The next time she came from downriver. I didn't hear her till she was twenty feet up the old spruce. I was rarely aware of her until she was close enough to charge across camp from the trees beyond. I ignored her and made dinner, ate. When I was done, she came down from the tree. I put her in my sights and held, but I couldn't quite pull the trigger. She sprinted away. I wondered if I'd regret that.

I kept hearing noises from the woods downriver, not big bear noises, more of a scratching on bark. I went to investigate and found two twenty-pound cubs clinging to the bases of two spruce trees. I became very alert for any noise from the mother, who must be nearby. The little guys' fur was all spiky and sparse. They had a bewildered air about them. They looked so vulnerable and innocent, as if they could've been wearing diapers. I wanted to cuddle them but recognized this as an unhealthy impulse.

"Are these two from the female I killed?" I wondered. I didn't think so. I had scanned the woods pretty thoroughly in the hour before I pulled the trigger and hadn't seen any sign of them. And she hadn't been nursing.

Black bears usually don't mature sexually until they're three to six years old. I speculated that the dead bear had been a three-year-old. That she and her litter mate had spent a second winter in a den with their mother, as black bears in northern Alaska sometimes do. By last June or July my bears had already been weaned. Because she wasn't nursing, the mother went into estrus again. She bred with a big rough male who left as soon as he was done and cared nothing about the hardships and uncertainty his offspring would have to face. If he was around now, he'd probably kill the cubs to induce the female back into estrus. How's that for foreplay?

Wild sex with a rogue bear prompted the mom's ovary to release two ova that were fertilized. But the fertilized eggs weren't implanted into the uterine wall for another four and a half months, when she was going to den. These cubs were born in the den another three and a half months after that, in February, making them three to four months old. They'd probably been out walking around a few weeks at that point. And mom would be close.

I looked into the darkening forest for a long time. Then I saw her, lumps of ears on a black head peering from behind a birch tree. She was big and a hundred yards away in open broken woods. I was glad not to be responsible for orphaning the cubs, still clinging awkwardly to the base of the tree. But that also meant there were four hungry bears around my camp. There had been five.

Where else were they gonna go? My camp was located where the lake and the river bend closest to one other. There are game trails along the shores on either side, the strip between the river and lake no wider than a highway.

I cut open the dead bear's stomach. It was packed with the leaves of low-bush cranberries, a few fruits here and there. There was zero fat anywhere on her body or in her guts. She was ready for something a little more substantial. They might have come here to search for duck eggs around the grassy margins of the lake and then I'd paddled into the picture.

I returned to camp and sat by the fire and tried to relax. It was late. The coffee was cold. The whiskey almost gone. I wanted a cigarette worse than at any time on the trip. Ransacked the chocolate stash. Thought about how I couldn't have a smoke for a thousand dollars, four days without one at that point.

At sunset golden cattails and bluestem flowed in the breeze around the lake. The sky tinted rouge. There were a pair of American widgeons and a pair of greater scaups in the inlet. A beaver was doing somersault rolls. Two bull moose were on the far shore. It was hard to tell at six hundred yards with the scope on thirty-six power, but I thought one of them might have been the big one we'd been unable to call in the previous fall. They were hanging out, ripping up cattails, grass, and pondweed in the fading sun.

In the light of the middle of the night, the noise of birdsongs became a symphony of sandhills, Canada geese, trumpeters, robins, the booming bass of a great gray owl, the clucking of wood frogs, the whoosh of the wings of new arrivals touching down in the inlet.

I'd heard no new noises from the woods for some time and decided to risk a little sleep. I locked and loaded both guns and put them in the tent. I let Sipp sleep in the tent to get him out of the bugs. I stoked the fire into an inferno to give a bear something to think about and finished the whiskey.

I hadn't slept more than a couple hours when I woke at sunrise to take a leak. I went to the lake to have a look and found four young moose on the far side of the inlet eating mare's tail. Three of them would be legal in the fall. There's a good chance one of them was the one I would eventually catch. After half an hour they became aware of me and slowly moved into the water, across the lake, like synchronized swimmers.

I went back to bed. Woke a little later with Sipp crazy to get out of the tent. As soon as it was unzipped he charged into the upriver brush. I saw nothing, and he came back and laid beside me while I pissed, the .06 leaned against a spruce.

I looked back and there was the young bear, ten feet—or less than one second—away. She was standing up, my height, her arms held before her at chest level with the wrists limp, paws hanging. She looked guileless, harmless, lost. I raised the rifle but couldn't do it. I lowered the gun and moved it to the side and fired to scare her off.

But something went wrong. It was too early. I wasn't awake. My brain was not completely rebooted to reflect the realities of space and time. I remember for just a moment the bear seemed shocked with me, as if I'd broken a trust. When she ran off she was limping. FUCK! I had missed missing the shot.

I'd hit her left rear leg. It was broken. I followed her a hundred yards into the woods and found her lain over a decomposing birch gasping for air. When she tried to get up I apologized and shot her.

I skinned, gutted, and quartered her, and then I walked back to camp and had breakfast. I packed the meat back and hung it next to her sister. I carried the skin of the first bear over to the skin of her sister and laid them out the way my friend Jacob had showed me, with the fur side down and spread so that the pale white hide was open to the sky, setting free the animal's spirit.

It sucked. But we did get all the meat out, Sipp and I, and gave a lot of it away. A lot of people ate those bears.

-:::-

At daybreak I lie in the shade by the river. Blue chiming bell flowers like tiny pyrotechnic sparks cascade to the ground around me. I listen to the whimsical notes of auburn robins, the whistling of yellow warblers, the twittering of maroon cloaked redpolls slowing to end in plaintive questions.

While the robins and warblers could spend the cold months anywhere from the western United States to Bolivia, the redpolls will wait it out right here. By winter they'll have increased their feather mass by 50 percent. They'll spend the limited daylight eating birch and other seeds. But they won't digest all the seeds. Some will be packed away in pockets of their diverticulated esophagi. These seeds will be digested throughout the long night while the group huddles in the nest, the metabolic heat within the extra feather mass within the group, the only reason they're not a bunch of half ounce meat-cicles in the morning.

Black-capped chickadees employ a different strategy. During five or six hours of light, they'll increase fat stores by 10 percent. When they return to roost in the hollows they've excavated in punky birch, fluffing out their feathers to increase their insulative value, they will lower their body temperatures about ten degrees, further reducing the amount of heat lost to the surrounding air.

I drag the canoe up the riverbank and across the open ground to the lake. I slide it over green and honey-colored grass onto the blue surface that reflects scudding cumulous, orange sun, ghost husk of moon.

The boat cuts silently across the water, past banks of straw-hued tussock and sedge. In the southeast corner, two moose stand on opposite sides of a birch-shrouded lagoon. One of them is big, the beams of his antlers stick out a foot from either side of

his head with the palms, spikes, and tines still a fist-like cluster
gloved in velvet. He looks like a stag moose stepped out of the
Pleistocene. He's aware of me before I am of him, and he turns
and trots into the stunted spruce. The other moose is a small
cow that stops eating long enough to check me out before returning to the swamp grass.

There are millions of green pinky-length lake chub, the only
Alaska minnow species, moving as one just beneath the surface,
their course changing at the subtlest persuasion like phospho-
rescent quicksilver.

A red-necked grebe dives in the reeds at the edge of the water, stays down so long I start to forget about him. I wonder if
he's feasting on the lake chub. He resurfaces. It's a male, a real
punk-rocker of a waterfowl. A stark white wave across his head
lends the darker feathers above the appearance of a mohawk in
contrast to the bone skull color below. His long neck is the shade
of oxidized iron, pegged off at a yellow-and-black marlin spike of
a bill. He keeps a floating nest of plants anchored to the bottom
with enough slack so it doesn't get submerged during high water.

A boreal owl cuts through the air and settles on top of a dead
spruce. A pair of trumpeter swans is never closer than a hundred
yards; though I could see them from a thousand. I'm grateful
not to startle them. Seems like you could drive a car a mile with
the energy they use taking off. Rusty blackbirds perch in dwarf
birch. They dart and snag bugs and sing a high-pitched helter-
skelter piping, like a cassette rewound while the play button's
down.

I paddle through clasping leaf pondweed that's grown up
to the surface only to trail off in the direction of the prevailing
wind and current. I pick up a strand and notice the translucence
of the leaves, the complete lack of rigidity of the stems that have

been supported by the water for their entire lives. A half an hour in the sun and it's dried so completely it crumbles when touched.

The flat four-square-mile expanse of the lake, shaped like a drop of blue paint splatted on a glass table, offers fantastic freedom of movement relative to the seething thicket around it. What is water was once forest, but the insulating ground layer was removed and the permafrost underneath melted.

A good hot fire is the most likely cause. But a single moose could have started the ball rolling a thousand years ago by walking through a muskeg. The hoofprints it pressed into the taigic skin allowed cold to escape and heat to seep in, melt the ice, and expand.

From a plane the lake looks like a series of moose trail systems coming together, thawing, expanding its boundaries. But as this is going on, the lake is being filled with windblown dirt and the detritus of surrounding vegetation, nurturing pondweeds and other aquatics, which in turn contribute to a rising peat layer that eventually reclaims the lake margins in a succession of moss, willow, alder, larch, and black spruce. The lake is not changing in size so much as shifting its shape.

Back in the lawn chair, I ponder: Each of us, each plant, bird, stone, mammal is just a tiny piece of one thing. But what is that? What's our function? Where are we? I don't know, and I don't expect to in this lifetime. Maybe in the instant of death, but for now, not. And neither does anyone else, which is actually pretty liberating. Just do the best you can. Be true to yourself. Unless you're an axe murderer or something.

A yellow-breasted warbler shoots past my shoulder so close I jump. The peeps of least and spotted sandpipers rise from the channel. A tiny beaver swims up the river with momma close behind.

I take the axe upriver, cut three spruce, and drag them back to camp. I think about accidentally calling in bulls by chopping wood.

My friend Jacob and I took a young bull here once. We were up all night getting him to camp, hanging him, and cutting wood for smoking. We'd scarcely been asleep an hour when I was awakened by the shaking of the earth. My first thought was bear, and I was out of the tent with the .06. Nothing. I figured it must have been an earthquake and laughed at myself for confusing the two. I apologized to Jacob for taking him away from needed sleep.

Jacob didn't respond right away, instead listening to a distant buzz. "That's a twin, huh? Probably a Navajo PA13." He said, looking at me and smiling slyly. "Dude, I've been listening to airplanes for my whole life. That's probably that Warbelows flight to Fort Yukon."

"I'll have to take your word for it." I said.

"Sounds like that left engine's missing on that number three cylinder."

"Uh-huh." I smile. He grew up in roadless Alaska, hunting seal and moose, playing the plane game before he could talk.

There was loud breaking and a rush of splashing in the inlet. We ran over in time to see a four-year-old bull turned broadside to us, defiant, chest deep in the blue water. He faced us and lowered his head to display four feet of white antler in the shape of a calcium sunrise. We stood together a few minutes before the moose splashed out the other side and continued his day. We found his tracks and followed them back through the woodcutting area, where he'd stomped on the wood chips up to our tent, one hoofprint two feet away from where my head had lain a few minutes earlier.

-:⁘:-

Hundreds of white dogwood flowers sprout from the moss. Stickish shrubs of Labrador tea offer violet flowers to pollen-hazed stabs of sun. I gather some of the thin leathery leaves and some new growth spruce tips and brew a cup of tea that expands through my chest like vitamin C solvent.

A tundra swan, big as a tuba, flaps just above the reach of the trees. A gang of gray jays descends upon camp, hustles about for scraps. Black scoters squabble in the inlet. They're only here a few weeks to hatch eggs before returning to the open ocean, where they spend the vast majority of their lives. The last sound I hear is the cry of a common loon, like bagpipes mourning slain ancestors.

I wake to distinctly spaced raindrop pings on the tent fly, lie there, fall back to sleep. When I rise the sun is almost due east, a late morning. I start a fire and haul some water.

A hawk owl lands atop a broken birch twenty yards into the forest. I watch through the scope as he preens his wings. Looks from side to side. Checks me out, yellow eyes unblinking, arched black marks where eyebrows would be. A red squirrel scolds a robin and the owl regards them. He's about sixteen inches long, dark with thin black and tan chest striations.

I stoke the fire and boil river water two quarts at a time, pouring it into a five- gallon jug. It's three days to the take-out, and I'm boiling what I'll drink now. There's a brief rush of south wind and the sound of a birch falling, the tree the owl had been perched in. I look in time to see him slicing across the river, out of sight. I put two handfuls of coffee in one and a half quarts of boiled water and set it aside.

I check out a rustling in the willow between camp and the inlet to find a baby porcupine the size of two cupped hands clinging to a thin branch. Its quills are just spiky hairs. The mother is nowhere to be seen. The baby is awkwardly folding full-sized willow leaves into its mouth. I remember a fat porcupine breathing strangely under the curled lip of veg-mat hung over the riverbank.

Porcupines only have one baby a year. It requires 210 days in utero. Moms usually nurse their young for three to four months. I wonder if this guy's mom is dead. Or off feeding. Or standing nearby hoping I'll leave, which I do, returning to the lawn chair to pour the coffee from the settled grounds. Thinking about sitting here with Jacob sipping whiskey, smoking moose, tripping on the aurora.

"Textbook, Rob, that was textbook. That's what I'm gonna tell people about it when they ask."

"Yeah that was pretty good, huh?"

"Yeah."

We'd put a canoe on the lake, found a bull moose in the back lagoon, took him from the bow. Two hours later he was dressed and loaded. An hour after that he was hanging in camp getting smoke. Another hour and we'd eaten backstrap with some swamp greens Jacob found by the inlet.

He started laughing.

"What?"

"I'm still wearing my office pants, from work on Monday."

I laughed. "Well they're black. Maybe the blood won't show."

He shrugs. "There's like sixty-five people that work in that building, and I'm the only Yupik."

"Oh yeah? That's kind of ironic, huh."

"Yeah. So it's okay to have blood on my clothes. They understand."

"You the token savage?"

"Yeah." Jacob works for the feds. He's a backcountry toxic waste detective with an office, equipment, and a budget. He writes management plans for chunks of land the size of states, coordinates emergency response to seasonal flooding on the Yukon River.

"But we're amateurs, Rob, you and me," he says. "My uncle was the real deal. I remember hunting with him before I was old enough to have a gun, when they brought me along to sharpen the knives. We'd travel up the river for days and then he'd just say 'Stop,' like in the middle of nowhere, and go into the woods by himself and get a huge moose. He just knew where they were. I never knew how he did it. They don't make 'em like him anymore."

We talk about women and animals. Listen to the dark forest.

"That's a good omen, Rob, that was a good omen."

"What's that?"

"That he died facing the east. That's how Yupik people leave the animal. Open to the sky and facing east."

"At the rising sun?"

"Yeah, sometimes."

The forest seems to be buzzing, and I'm not sure when it started. Dragonflies are emerging, unfurling and drying their wings, taking to the air. I see northern bluets and American emeralds. A four-spotted skimmer plunges into a cloud of mosquitoes, slows from thirty-five miles an hour to nothin' on an atom, hovers, flies backward, accelerates to full speed on a new tangent in the time it takes me to spit out the coffee grounds.

They had to survive a grueling competition to get here. Since the nymphs emerged from the eggs mom laid in the lake one to six years ago, they've triumphed in repeated cannibalistic battles and chowed insects, fish fry, and tadpoles while avoiding becoming the stomach contents of grebes, kittiwakes, kingfishers, and pike. They've spent five months a year frozen in ice that never got too cold or lasted too long and have undergone a dozen molts to finally step from the water and receive their wings.

The next day I haul camp down the bluff, take the requisite number of falls, and utter a corresponding number of *motherfuckers* until the canoe is loaded and my knees, ass, and hands are covered with dirt. Then I return to the lake, to a downed birch which makes a fine bench. I finish the coffee and run the scope around the shore.

A northern harrier glides low and slow above the reeds and sedge on the far side. He pulls his wings back and up and almost stops in the invisible fingers of air and drops into the golden glow of swamp grass. He reemerges flapping, climbs to the height of a dwarf tree, and spills out over the water, crossing the lake with subtle movements of broad wings. He comes right to me and begins to hunt the mare's tail on the far side of the inlet. Again he slows, stalls, and falls from the air that he seemed a part of and into the fuzz of grass and then rises with a vole in his left talon, heads for the trees.

It feels good to slide the canoe back in the river. I swish my right boot around in the water to wash away the mud and then place it in the boat, push off with the left but go nowhere, the left is still six inches deep in the mud. I wriggle it free, swish it around, and push off with the paddle.

·:·

The day Jacob and I took the young moose from here was a good day. We stopped at a smaller lake an hour downriver. We were in a hurry to get home and take care of the meat, but at such times you have to ask yourself "Will I ever be here again?" and act accordingly. So we'd pulled over and climbed the steep filthy banks, grabbing rose bushes to arrest falls. We crept through the debris of a burned birch forest. A sensuous task of slithering over, under, and through the fallen trunks that were wrapped in grass, rose, and willow, crawling like bugs through the matted fur of some gargantuan beast.

The small lake breathed mist. Overcast skies left behind by the morning colored the day drab, left it still. Like things had changed little in ten thousand years.

We saw the first set of antlers when we were twenty feet from the edge of the trees. They rose above the edge of grass in an elegant curve. We sank into the ground and crept closer. As we approached, we heard the urgent moans of a cow hidden in the forest. From the edge we could see two big bulls facing each other in the tall grass a hundred yards away. The larger bull's antlers were more than sixty inches across; a dewlap hanging a foot down from his throat. The smaller one, easily a fifty-incher, had his broad ass to us and seemed to be challenging the larger animal.

The clash of antlers slamming together was loud.

The hindquarters of the smaller bull buckled and were pushed down. It took about two minutes. The bigger bull stood over the smaller one a few minutes before walking a few steps away and lying down, the twin curves of their antlers the only things above the grass tips.

We decided to have a little fun.

Jacob stayed while I snuck to the canoe and grabbed the .06 and scapula. I returned and scraped some small cottonwood trees, whipped snakes of willow, bunches of wild rose. I picked up a birch stick and swung it into the trunk of a cottonwood, the loud *CRACK!* splitting the placid air. Jacob grunted.

The smaller bull was up and working his way toward us through the fringe of forest at the edge of the clearing. He stayed inside the cover of the aspen and willow as the breaking of trees and brush grew louder. He stepped out and stuck his head into some wild rose and shredded it, came for us with broken rose snared in his antlers.

"That big one sent out his enforcer to check us out, huh?" Jacob said.

"He's sure not leaving that cow, is he?" I scraped the scapula through the brush again, broke some more stuff.

"Dude, I don't think you need to do anymore. He's coming," Jacob said, starting to back away.

As if on cue, the approach of the moose got a lot louder. We were hearing the gulping cluck he produced at the back of the throat. And suddenly there he was, fifteen hundred pounds of pissed off moose muscle, flexing and throbbing, fifteen yards away, between two slender birch trees. I swear to god his features were twisted into an expression of malicious disapproval. I dropped the scapula and held the rifle with shaking hands. Jacob and I backed away.

"Hey, moose!" I yelled. "Hey, we're people here! No need to stomp us. Why don't you go back to your buddies. We're just people here."

The bull eyed us angrily. He stomped the ground with a front hoof and released an enormous quantity of air from his lungs in a disgusted manner.

Boom! I fired the rifle into the ground. "Hey, come on now moose," I yelled. "Move along."

This seemed to jog him out of his intoxication. He trotted twenty yards back in the direction he'd come from before turning broadside between us and the cow. As if to say, "All right, don't come any closer and I'll let you live."

I retrieved the scapula and was very careful not to let it scrape against anything as we hustled back to the boats. "Man, he came at us like we owed him money," Jacob said.

About an hour later we were floating, I was a little ahead of Jacob. It was one of those classic autumn high-pressure days with pinches of altocumuli squeezed from the taut window of sky. The air was so clean and cool I'd catch myself trying to grab a piece, put it in my mouth.

The river was narrow and low, an obstacle course of fallen trees lodged in gooey mud. A hunk of blackness came down the bank on my left to a narrow strip of beach. I didn't immediately register that it was moving until it passed me, and then I realized this was a large black bear, maybe 350 pounds, and that it was less than twenty feet away, moving in the same direction, though much faster. The bear more scared of me than I was of . . . okay, maybe it was a draw.

I pulled the .06 from the case, laid it across my lap, and began back paddling into an eddy like a madman. When the bear was ten yards in front of me, it turned and lunged into the river until, buoyed up, he began to swim with just his black head and tan nose above the flow. When he reached the other side, he charged up the loess bluff, gouging out chunks of muck. Slipping and sliding, he reached the overhung bluff and dug his claws into the grassy ground above and pulled himself up. His rear paws left the ground and kicked in the air like a junior high kid trying to squeeze out one final pull-up in PE class. And then he was gone. Breeze and sky.

Another hour and we were in a long straightaway with steep banks topped by ten-foot-tall willows. A young cow idled on the downriver right, and I stopped paddling, let the boat drift to her. She was unaware of me, staring across the river at an older cow that stared back but also looked downriver and at me. A fat willow smacked an antler.

Below the older cow a very large bull moose emerged with a dirty white rack that looked like a medieval torture wall. He moved ponderously up the river toward us, bending over the willows in his path, releasing a grunt, *UGHHn!*, every time he took a step. Sounded like blue balls, like the slightest testicular contact with anything produced dull resonant agony.

The bull came to a stop forty feet below us and turned to the river. All we could see was his head rising from the brush. The older cow ran away. The bull focused on the younger one across the river, nervously looking our way every few minutes. He was grunting and crooning his heart out. The cow could not tear herself away, though she seemed very anxious. The air was fat with sexual tension, pheromones as palpable as a meat market at last call.

Eventually he couldn't hold back any longer and started down the bluff. A deep grunt escaped his mouth with each step. I understood them to mean "Fuggit, shoot me if you must, but I just gotta go and get me some of that prime moose meat on the other side. Goddamn, that's gonna be the death of me yet."

He didn't hesitate, walked right in, swam the middle, and walked out the other side. He paused to shake twenty gallons of water from his coat in a dazzling cloud of sun-fired spray. The mist formed diaphanous rainbows in the crystal cool air. He made for the point recently vacated by the younger cow. When he got to the top of the bank he casually stepped up the undercut overhang. Then he disappeared, leaving only desperate grunts and breaking trees to mark his passage.

A peregrine falcon shrieks, coasts in slow circles on backswept wings, lands on a spruce peak above the river. Stratocumulus rolls up the Yukon, descends in dark veils to the flats. A pair of olive-green Arctic warblers flits around in the willow. The male sings a high chirping song. Unlike other warblers that return to Alaska, these small songbirds will fly southwest to Asia at the approach of autumn. By winter they'll be in a rainforest in the Philippines.

A flurry of gray-and-white feathers is surrounded by lynx tracks. A mink scrambles through jumbled logs and brush, leaping over, diving under, wriggling between.

Something bumps my paddle. Probably a northern pike, curious whether the red blade might be food. And why not? From the pike's perspective, just about everything else in this river—other pike, ducklings, muskrats, water shrews, and all of the remaining fish species—are food. The presence of the pike is probably why there are no salmon here. Their mottled olive-brown skin is a perfect camouflage in the mud and vegetation, the gaping mouth lined with rows of ripping teeth with smaller teeth covering the tongue and roof. Twenty-year-old fish weighing twenty-five to thirty pounds aren't uncommon.

Around here a few falls ago I saw a young cow with her rump facing me. She was looking my way over her left shoulder, her sex pointed at me like a gun. I pulled my paddle from the water and scraped the moose rack in front of me. The cow turned 360 degrees, a dainty cabriole, and resumed eyeing me provocatively. I scraped again and her gaze didn't waver. There was forest-breaking thunder from the trees beyond. The cow turned, and a large pissed-off bull exploded from the woods behind her. His antlers were lowered so that the brow tines were aimed up her reproductive region. That cow took off like she was shot from a cannon, and they both went hard up the river for as long as I could hear them.

I climb eighty feet up an old spruce canted over the water, intertwine my limbs with the tree, and hang out for an hour watching the lakes reach back to the ridgelines. A light wind moves the treetop gently back and forth, like it had nothing in the world better to do. I scan the far reaches of the wetlands but don't see any animals. It's too hot in the afternoon sun. By the time I've descended, there are broken twigs and pieces of bark in my hair and down my shirt and pants, pitch gobbed on my hands and arms.

I peel away clothes as I return to the canoe, mud squishing up between my toes, and walk into the brown water and let it take me. Let the country, the valley, the world have me. But the water is fucking cold, so I don't let it have me for long before I'm on the bank pulling on polypro like it was an Olympic event. I like this point, when the country's smeared all over me, when I couldn't smell like anything else if I wanted to.

The day is lit by a slanted evening sun. I camp an hour later. I wish someone was there to help as I haul stuff up the banks, chop a tent site from the wild rose and high-bush cranberry, set up the tent, chop the firewood, start a fire, haul food and water, make dinner, eat.

Sometimes I get frustrated, like I'll be old, ugly, impotent, and alone too soon if I don't hurry. I tell myself it's happening.

Keep moving. Keep taking trips. Keep writing. Keep building the house. Do something good for humanity from time to time. But keep moving and be aware of each step to be truly alive and free. And everything else will fall into place. And if I'm wrong, at least I'll have lived fully. And that's all I can ask for.

And keep not smoking. Nine days now without one. I congratulate myself, but soon I'll be back in the world of temptation. How hard would it be to quit shooting heroin if every Quickie Mart sold it for five bucks a pack?

Across the river a great horned owl watches me. He sits as motionless as a chunk of wood on a thin birch branch. The air fills with rapid *cheeping*, sharp-cutting tree swallows. They attack the birch where the owl is sitting. They're joined by a pair of robins. They give the owl tremendous hell. Chase it across the river and into a pond beyond. I follow and find the pond full of scoters and Canadians. They begin a low continuous din of honking and quacking. I back away, hoping they don't fly.

On the low bluff in the morning sun, my back against a birch tree, the edge of the bank is just beyond my outstretched legs. Below, the brown Skoog flows soundlessly, a powerful sun burns down but there's a cool breeze and the shade of a hundred-year-old spruce. The ground is covered with dry cones and needles and the husks of dozens of dead birch, the wood disintegrating into cells and dirt and air while the waxy white bark remains.

From over the trees a pair of trumpeter swans descends and tilts their wings up and back. They drop into the banks, pumping down the air. They cease flapping as they slow to landing speed, twenty feet in front of me, air hissing through outstretched pinions, the entire wing apparatus humming with a fine tension. A final back arc of the wings, and they touch the Skoog and float, as if that final wing stretch was only the first motion of folding them against their bodies, long necks curving into position.

Painted lady butterflies flash yellow, orange, black. A red-tailed hawk returns to a nest in a broken spruce tree with a limp red squirrel.

Soon enough I'm paddling. Bubbles released from the mud rise to the surface and pop. This has been going on the whole trip. The bubbles contain methane produced by the anaerobic decomposition of ancient plants and animals trapped within the thawed muck of the riverbed.

My neighbor, Kurt the organic farmer, likes to go onto the frozen ponds around Goldstream Valley before they get covered with snow. He finds big bubbles of swamp gas locked in the ice, drives a log spike into a bubble and holds a butane torch in the escaping gas as it flares four feet high. Kurt smirks and giggles within his snot-cicled beard.

I stop at a blue lake nested in spruce hills. There's an old tree stand looking over the water. I look for the bear that left the fresh piles of bony shit on the trail along the river.

Back in the flow, a belted kingfisher does a loop the loop and captures something in its beak. He looks at me, flexes his mohawk, and disappears into the mud. When I drift by I see the tiny hole opening into a four-foot-long passageway that leads to his excavated nest chamber.

Hoary woodpeckers dart through burned-up spruce. They pound hollow logs producing rapid bursts of resonant percussion. I wonder if they're aware of the collective rhythms they're creating, if they're trying to make music. They're loud, too, little jackhammers with steel-cabled necks.

Another turn and I come against a logjam wedged in a meander. It's a catastrophe, sprawling a quarter mile down the river.

Broken trees jut out of interlocked trunks, the water pouring though making the sound of rapids. I pull the canoe onto an extra gooey mudbar, unload it, and carry everything to the other end, where I reload on another awkward mud slope. It takes six trips and three hours before I'm back on the river. Exhale.

One time Jacob and I hit four smaller jams in addition to this big kahuna. The beaver population had exploded that year, and the river was thick with their cast-offs. We leaned from the bows of the canoes to pull the jumbled sticks from the cold water, climbed over logs to pull boats under others, cut submerged trees with a small chainsaw that threw a water rooster tail twenty feet in the air.

"We should come down here in the spring and shoot like two hundred beavers, fill up the canoes," Jacob said while we worked.

"What're we gonna do with two hundred beavers?"

"Eat 'em and make mittens, man. I got a big family."

"How 'bout for the outhouse seat?"

"Yeah."

I'm grateful for the logjams. As with the shallows on the upriver end, it serves as a guardian of this remnant swath of wildness. Ain't nobody gonna be haulin' their jet boat over that.

I surprise a pair of greater white-fronted geese on the bank, and they go instantly ape shit, honking and flapping, and then I see why. They're pushing five tiny pale yellow goslings down to the water, the female urgently shooing them with sweeping motions of her left wing. Two of them stumble and tumble down into the water.

I'm thinking, "Oh no, man, this is all my fault." But they pop back up and begin swimming around in circles, disoriented, like it's their first time. I paddle to the far side and try to sneak by nonchalantly. The parents and the other three goslings reach the river, and the parents head down swiftly, but the little ones can't keep up, pop beneath the dark surface, reemerge spinning confused patterns until they all see the parents at the same time. They run to them, their tiny feet pattering the surface, their unformed wings futilely flapping. The male herds the five of them together while the female leads me down the river, feigning a wing injury, honking, "Take me, take me, just don't eat my babies!" Always a catch.

I think about Sippi. How he loved to dive after the beavers. How it kind of freaked me out like, *Uh, hey Sipp, you know they're as big as you are and you're in their element, and uh, maybe you should be careful.* Could never decide if Sipp was messing with the beavers or vice versa.

I drew the line, though, when it came to otters. Once an otter poked its head out of the water a few feet away from Sipp, all playful like "Hey, I'm a river otter, what are you?" And Sipp went after it despite my command to the contrary. The otter slipped away. But it resurfaced and Sipp went after it again, and I called him off again, but it didn't return. I decided I couldn't say anything after letting him go after the beavers. Hard to explain to a dog that otters are the sensitive spirit of fun and playfulness while beavers could stand to lighten up a little.

Sippi got over it, though. He was having a ball running alongside the canoe, crashing through the brush and dust and flotsam, crossing the river whenever he pleased, diving for beaver. Suddenly he stopped cold. When I came around the corner I saw a giant cow moose lying on the bank just below Sipp. It seemed to take her a long time to unwind those endless legs and stand up, look down on us. Straw-colored hackles stood up between her shoulders. Her ears folded back. She began to make long exha-

lations that ended in ominous grunts. I made some cow noises.
She slid into the birch.

The riverbanks are ebbing into flats. Thousands of dragonflies
and dashing swallows fill the air, feasting on mosquitoes. The river bends into and away from a series of tall bluffs. The top of the
last and highest is pocked with hundreds of burrows occupied by
brown bank swallows that have returned from South America to
this bend in the Skoog for generations. When I pass below, skeins
of them fly out and circle above, scolding and diving.

I pass a pair of bohemian waxwings in a willow tree. Their
bodies glimmer and shimmer blue and gray, reflect the orange,
red, and yellow of the tail and face. They change color as they
shift in the light, serious little songbirds, punkish and confident.
Waxwings don't have a set migration. They're vagabond oppor-
tunists living niche to niche between here and the Lower 48. It's
always a bit of a surprise to see them because you never know
where they'll be. Yesterday eating seeds in a mountain pass, today bugs in the flats.

I camp on a lake below the last bluff. It's filled with ducks,
grebes, geese, swans. There's a clearing with a well-used fire area
and a stack of dry spruce and willow against a tree. It's probably been an Athabaskan hunting camp for a thousand years.
The sun sets in the northwest and illuminates high strands of
combed cirrus, silver blue bellies of upwelling cumulus. The in-
sect-dappled lake surface reflects sky and white-trunked birch
canopy. Orange and yellow pond lilies bloom in the shaded
backwater nearest camp. A cow and calf are across the lake. The
calf stands up in the brown border grass from time to time and
then lays back down. Mom eats and eats and eats and eats. She

switches from pond grass to willow to birch saplings, pauses to look in all directions. I have my dinner in the grass, watch them while I eat. The mom runs to the calf and grunts. The calf is up quickly, and they bolt west up a small slough.

Ten minutes later two large black bears walk toward the spot where the moose were. I'm downwind of them, a hundred yards away. They sniff the grass and air. I fire the rifle twice into the mud and the bears look at me, register no alarm, return to their pursuit. It adds a bit of zing to the evening. Before I go to bed I build a driftwood bonfire on the mud near my tent and lock and load both guns.

A raven gives a croak quickly answered by its cohort perched in the birch. I give a trilling caw and both take off squawking their disapproval of my butchered ravenese. A beaver swims circles around two Canadians in the river. The sun goes down in a collage of black lavender and burnt orange.

At daybreak there's a bull where the cow, calf, and bears were.

I take my time eating, drinking coffee, and watching the bull. Soon enough I'm smoking that bowl, the last thing before getting in the canoe. It's hot and just past noon when I push off. The color of the water becomes bluer as sediment settles from slackening current, as the river sprawls into flats. The sky is blue from horizon to horizon and the sun is close. I take my cap and soak it and put it back on. Let it drain down.

I climb a two-hundred-foot hill on the north side of the river and stare over the lakes, blue jewels glistening in the sun and greening grass. I count five cows and four calves. A bit later I pass a large lake where the trumpeter swans gather in the fall. Jacob and I stopped here once, and he counted over four hundred with more descending. "It's all about seeing them in groups," he was saying. "Like there's twenty of them there and another fifteen in that back corner. You just count the groups."

Jacob, stuffing his boots with dry grass to absorb the moisture, cutting up sourdock to add to our freeze-dried dinners, filling his canoe with river sage 'cause he likes the smell.

A bald eagle leaps from a cluster of gulls and beats muscular wings. A foot-long whitefish is in his talons. The group of gulls is up in a curled wave of pursuit. A second eagle cuts in from downriver and turns upside down. The first eagle releases the fish and the partner grabs it and coasts to the ground. The first eagle circles down, providing cover. The gulls remain aloft while the eagles pull the guts from the still-quivering fish.

It's shortly after this that I hear, for the first time in a couple weeks, the sound of a car hurtling through the distance.

Return, 2013

CORD WAS FOUR THE first time he floated the Skoog. During the first couple hours on the river he was more concerned with unbuckling his life vest than anything else. But gradually he began to notice the forest sliding by like a never-ending superhero show on his beloved Netflix. "When are we gonna see any bears?" he asks.

"I don't know. We might not see any. We have to be looking and listening all the time. I mean the bears are kinda scared of us, so they're looking and listening and smelling for us too. And if they see us first, we might not see them."

"They might run away before we even know they're there," Michele says.

It's early June. Michele has just finished school for the summer. It's her first trip down this river as well. It's good to see her smile after the grind of finals and the musical-chair melee of being an educator during a time of budget cuts. The Republican enthusiasm for balancing the budget on the backs of someone else's education is running high.

She has set up an area for our son in the middle of the canoe with toy dinosaurs and Batman and Pooh Bear. "Well if we see any grizzly bears, I'm gonna punch them right in the face and roar at them to get them to not hurt us. So don't shoot them, okay Dad?"

"Sounds good, bud. I don't want to shoot them anyway. I like to just look at them. I only brought the gun in case they try to get us."

"And if they do try to do that I'll take care of it, Okay, Dad."

"Okay, bud, we'll see."

We pull over on a sandy beach strewn with driftwood. Michele and I get a fire going while Cord races and roars like Hulk through the willows that grow taller than he is. After dinner he digs through the sand in search of dinosaur bones. He's already filthy. I'm very proud.

The next day we float in the rain for hours. We don our raingear and let it come, soaking through the coated vinyl. Sandpipers peep and scurry along the banks. Cord doesn't complain, but when I see him shivering, I feel as though I've done a terrible thing. But I also realize that I want this for him. I want him to be exposed to the weather. To know the rain that pours from the sky as the rivers and oceans, as the piss of dinosaurs, and the blood pumping through his rapid little heart. To sense its creation in the genesis of stars and our own transience so tied to its flow through the cosmos. We pull over on a narrow strip of beach.

"But Dad," he says, "can't we pull over on a warm island?"

"I think this is as close as we're gonna get right now, amigo," I tell him. "But let's get the tent set up and get a fire going and maybe this one'll work, okay?"

"Can I bring my dinos in the tent?"

"Heck, yeah."

"All right, this is gonna be awesome."

"Yeah, bud, I think so too."

Michele sets the tent up while I gather driftwood for a fire. A kestrel alights in a cottonwood across the river, observes our preparations. I hear Michele reading about the time Pooh and Christopher Robin and the gang played pooh sticks with Eeyore's old house, then worked together to build Eeyore a new house.

We saw four moose before we pulled over. The first was nearly all white, with her calf on a gravel bar. The second pair was in the river. I saw them first and watched them see us, mom's ears focusing like antennae. They stopped midstream and turned toward us. Michele and I back paddled. The five of us in this limbo, this suspension for drawn moments before they moved out of the water, ambled downriver, and turned the corner. The rain rolled off our hats and we let the river carry us down.

This is what I want to give him, an awareness of the river, the forest. I want him to drink and breathe it. To surrender to it. But mainly I want him to have fun, to want to do this again. I look in the tent and watch him sleeping within the warm curve of my wife. Elmo is curled in his arms in his sleeping bag.

The next morning a large chunk of the mud bank across the river falls. Waves wash across the channel and roll up onto our beach. Michele and Cord are still in the tent; fire of birch bark, willow, and driftwood; coffee soaking in the hot water; sunshine breaking through the willow and wild rose bursting into flowers.

"I love the way this place smells," Michele had said. "Like I could smell that big cottonwood we just passed way before I could see it. And I can start to smell the roses opening and the willows and cranberries."

"That's awesome," I said. "Tell me when you smell the cottonwood again. I wanna know what that smells like."

This was just before I let the boat get pinned against a large spruce that had fallen across the river. I tried to hit a narrow opening in the middle, where the trunk sagged beneath the surface, but some weird current turned me away from it. I got out and stood on the tree and tried to pull the boat through, but it kept turning. So we paddled back upriver and beached it, and Michele chopped through the tip of the tree with a hatchet and pulled the canoe through.

My boy's fragile breathing and his head that I can hold in my palm contrast with the immutable power of the river that could suck the canoe right under that log. This dynamic led me to more cautious decision-making. If I'd been alone, I would've tried again to shoot that gap midriver. But instead I saw Cord getting pulled under, getting his vest pulled off. It's still a constant battle of wills to keep all the buckles buckled. And, nowadays I opt for caution, breathe through the cortisol release.

Five swans high above murmur their clarinet conversations and cut in front of the sun. Ptarmigans drum their wings in the brush. Wind whistles through the tail feathers of snipe falling from the sky.

Soon enough Cord is up in a fury of noise and motion. Soon enough we're on the river. Cord is loud when he's awake. I have to force myself not to be bothered by this muffling of my nature buzz. I want to tell him to talk more quietly, to not shout "Land Ho!" at the top of his lungs every time we see a new gravel bar, or squeal ecstatically every time a beaver slaps his tail on the water and dives. But mostly I want him to be, to not be too burdened with rules. And it gives him such joy to turn around and see that I approve of him, that I love him, that I don't want to temper his beingness with rules. After all, part of the joy of this place is the rulelessness. So we make a deal for silence at some later unspecified time. "Land Ho!"

We come around a corner and a mother moose is focused intently upon us, ready to fight to the death. Her month-old scruffy brown calf, clueless and wide-eyed, is beside her. We back paddle and wait as they trot into the birch and willow.

It's late afternoon when we arrive at the lake. The woods are full of songbird music. I start a fire from a pile of dry wood left against a spruce, whose branches kept the rain and snow away. Bob left the wood here. I'd shown him this spot on the map the previous fall. He and his girlfriend had come here and gotten a big bull. He's blowing glass in North Carolina these days. But he'll be back. We're going to frame a shop for him when he returns in December. We'll go for some skis around the valley, he'll take a turn pulling Cord. Then he'll go to Asia or South America or Papua, New Guinea, till the sun returns. Cord will start his own ski lessons before he's back.

Kevin and his family moved back East. He and his wife, Holly, had a baby girl, Linda, a few months after Cord was born. A baby boy, Charlie, a couple years after that. Michele has known Kevin and Holly for many years. We ended up sharing a few meals and holidays together over the years between the Black Rapids and their relocation. We did the dishes, drank beer, watched our kids play together. We never discussed those two weeks on the ice. I guess we didn't like each other that much while it was happening. And it never seemed like a good time to broach that on the Thanksgivings, Christmases, and kids' birthdays that followed. Until, eventually, neither of us cared anymore. He's still building, and they're closer to grandparents, which I'm coming to discover is pretty damn helpful.

There are three moose at the south end of the lake. A blonde cow, a brown cow, and a very large dark walnut bull. His antlers are already well beyond fifty inches wide. We watch him through the binos for a long time. I wonder if he'll be here in the fall.

Last October, on my way back from guiding, I called Jacob and asked if he wanted to go down the river again. It had been three years. He said, "Fuck yeah!" And so it will be.

I told Neal I needed to be in the woods for my own reasons. That for me hunting was about spiritual renewal as well as filling the freezer. That I couldn't really do both and see to the client's needs as well. He said I could work for him again. But looking across that blue mirror of lake reflecting the sky and green fringe of trees, I'm pretty sure I'm done with it.

Neal was cool with it. I mean he didn't understand my reasoning. For him, death is exhilarating. And it's business. And there's no contradiction with his values. But he can appreciate that it's not for everyone. He got married. He's living his dream, and I wish him well. We'll have a drink together the next time he rolls through town.

Two large swans coast down from the sky and skid across the lake surface to float beside the moose. The moose don't look up from their feeding. A common goldeneye with its red head and white neck dips about the inlet.

We pass several groups of Canadians and their bright yellow goslings on the river. The adults put themselves between us and the goslings. They're aggressive, bending their necks and hissing their honks at us like a threat. The dazed little ones popping beneath the black water. River drama. The adults lead us on faux injury pursuits.

"You can go back now. Go back to your kids," Michele says to the pair, concerned and laughing at herself at once. Soon they take off and circle high above us as they return to their brood.

But at some point they'd let one get away. We find him, so tiny and confused, spinning alone in a back eddy. His parents fly urgently up and down the river calling and cajoling but they do not see the gosling. We talk about rescuing it, about bringing it home with us and naming it Grace and letting it live out its days waddling around our yard. But in the end we float by, hoping for the best.

It reminds me of the time Will and I were sea kayaking in Kachemak Bay and the weather kicked up into waves and froth, and we found a baby sea otter abandoned amid the rocks we had to paddle through to get to land. We picked it up and held it, and it cuddled into our warmth and cooed, and we wondered if we should carry it home with us. But in the end we returned it to the water from which it had risen and to which it would one day return.

Will and his partner, Sara, and their daughter, Macy, live up the road in a cabin they built themselves. They have a dog team and a garden and a smokehouse. It's been almost thirty years since we were busboys together at a ski resort in southwest Colorado. Thirty years since we threw our gear in the back of a stranger's pick-up and headed for Alaska.

And sometimes I wonder if we exist in all the moments of our lives simultaneously, and we're still those wide-eyed, barely-old-enough-to-drink guys on the adventure of a lifetime. I like to think it's true. I like to think that somewhere Sippi, who died of cancer, is still crashing down the riverbanks, bobbing for beavers. And Eric is the one sitting on the fallen birch watching the big moose at the far end of the lake, turning to smile at me, still golden and alive. I swear I can feel them rubbing against me sometimes.

Cord is running naked through the wild rose. He is covered in mosquito bites and scratches and smears of mud. "Do you see any bears yet, Dad?"

"Not yet, buddy. But we'll keep looking, okay?"

"And I'll protect us, Dad, I'll protect us."

"I know you will, bud, I know you will."

References

Alaska Department of Fish and Games Wildlife Notebook Series. Juneau:
Alaska Department of Fish and Game, 1994. Print.

Armstrong, Robert H. *Alaska's Birds.* Portland, OR: Alaska Northwest
Books, Graphic Arts Center Publishing Co., 2004. Print.

Bates, Robert L., and Julia A. Jackson, eds. *Dictionary of Geological Terms,*
3rd edition. New York: Anchor Books, 1984. Print.

Chapin, F. Stuart, III, Mark W. Oswood, Keith van Cleve, Leslie A. Viereck,
David Verbyla, eds. *Alaska's Changing Boreal Forest.* New York: Oxford
University Press, 2006. Print.

Cole, Dermot. *Fairbanks: A Goldrush Town That Beat the Odds.* Fairbanks:
University of Alaska Press, 1999. Print.

Connor, O'Haire. *Roadside Geology of Alaska.* Missoula: Mountain Press
Publishing Co., 1988. Print.

Franzman, Albert W., and Charles C. Schwartz, eds. *Ecology and Management of the North American Moose,* 2nd edition. Boulder: University
Press of Colorado, 2007. Print.

Green, Jim. *Alaska Cloud and Weather Field Guide.* Haines, AK: Williwaw
Publishing Co., 2004. Print.

Johnson, Derek, Linda J. Kershaw, Andy MacKinnon, and Jim Pojar. *Plants
of the Western Boreal Forest and Aspen Parkland.* Edmonton, AB: Lone
Pine Publishing, 1995. Print.

Kaufman, John. *Alaska's Brooks Range: The Ultimate Mountains.* Seattle: The Mountaineers Books, 1992. Print.

Kavanagh, James. *Alaska Butterflies and Moths.* Dunedin, FL: Waterford Press, Inc, 2008. Print.

Langdon, Steve J. *The Native People of Alaska.* Anchorage: Greatland Graphics, 2002. Print.

Mammals of Alaska. Anchorage: The Alaska Geographic Society, 1996. Print.

Miller, Debbie. "An Arctic Dream." *Alaska Geographic* 20.3 (1993): 10–33. Print.

Mull, Gil. "Mystic Mountains." *Alaska Geographic* 23.3 (1996): 4–37. Print.

Napoleon, Harold. *Yuuyaraq: The Way of the Human Being.* Fairbanks: Alaska Native Knowledge Network, 1996. Print.

Peter, Katherine. *Living in the Chandalar Country.* Fairbanks: Alaska Native Language Center, 2001. Print.

Peyton, Leonard J. *Bird Songs of Alaska.* Ithaca, NY: Cornell Laboratory of Ornithology, 1999. CD.

Plafker, George. *The Geology of Alaska: Book and Plates.* Edited by Henry C. Berg. Boulder, CO: Geological Society of North America, 1994. Print.

Pratt, Verna E. *Field Guide to Alaskan Wildflowers.* Anchorage: Alaskakrafts, 1990. Print.

Schofield, Janice J. *Discovering Wild Plants: Alaska, Western Canada, the Northwest.* Anchorage: Alaska Northwest Books, 1989. Print.

Smith, Ronald L. *Interior and Northern Alaska.* Bothell, WA: Book Publishers Network, 2008. Print.

Stall, Chris. *Animal Tracks of Alaska.* Seattle: The Mountaineers Books, 1993. Print.

Stone, Wallace. "A Geological Framework of Alaska." *Episodes* 10.4 (1987): 283–88. Print.

Tekiela, Stan. *Birds of Alaska Field Guide.* Cambridge, MN: Adventure Publications, 2005. Print.

Thorson, Robert M., Jean S. Aigner, Mary Lee Guthrie, R. Dale Guthrie, William Samuel Schneider, Richard K. Nelson. *Interior Alaska*. Anchorage: The Alaska Geographic Society, 1986. Print.

Weidensaul, Scott. *Living on the Wind*. New York: North Point Press, 2000. Print.

Wilson, Frederic H., and Florence R. Weber. "Prehistoric Alaska." *Alaska Geographic* 21.4 (1994): n.p. Print.

Young, Steven B. *To the Arctic: An Introduction to the Far Northern World*. New York: John Wiley and Sons, 1994. Print.

Author Bio

Rob McCue has lived in Alaska for thirty years. He has worked as a commercial fisherman, cab driver, construction worker, and backcountry guide. He has spent several years camping in the Alaskan wilderness. He enjoys hanging out in the woods, letting his mind wander and being with his family. He currently lives with his wife and son outside of Fairbanks.